SCHOOL DEVELOPMENT SERIES
General Editors: David Hopkins and David Reynolds

QUALITY SCHOOLING

GW00546541

QUALITY SCHOOLING
A Pragmatic Approach to Some Current Problems, Topics and Issues

David N. Aspin

and

Judith D. Chapman

with

Vernon R. Wilkinson

CASSELL

Cassell
Villiers House   387 Park Avenue South
41/47 Strand   New York
London WC2N 5JE   NY 10016–8810

First published 1994

British Library Cataloguing-in-Publication Data
A catalogue record for this book is available from the British Library

ISBN 0–304–32751–4 (hardback)
      0–304–32753–0 (paperback)

Phototypeset by Intype, London
Printed and bound in Great Britain by Redwood Books, Trowbridge, Wiltshire

DEDICATION

This book is dedicated to the memory of:

James Aspin
1907–1975

and

Albert Chapman
1910–1993

Contents

Series Editors' Foreword

This is a timely, creative and policy-relevant account of key issues to be considered in any discussion of 'Quality' in education. Often this concept is 'taken for granted' and the means to achieve quality goals are assumed to be unproblematic, but as this book shows, there is an urgent need to explore the ramifications of adopting a 'quality' perspective.

Drawing on a large scale empirical study conducted with principals, parents, teachers, school administrators and representatives of educational 'interest' groups, David Aspin, Judith Chapman and Vernon Wilkinson very usefully explore such issues as the definition of quality, the changing administrative framework of schooling, the pressures on school managers, the complexities of the new patterns of relationships between schools and the other educational 'levels', and the potential impact of policy changes upon the quality of pupils' learning experiences. In an educational world which abounds in simple recipes for the attaining of apparently straightforward goals, this book reminds us that there are multiple possibilities and multiple complexities.

The authors take us further, though, than mere complexity with their own commitments to a post empiricist methodology, to education as a public good and to notions of the importance of mutual, reciprocal and supportive relationships between individuals in a society and between the educational actors in the educational settings that create individuals. All individuals involved in school effectiveness and school improvement should consider with care what this book has to say, and the implications of its findings for both the framing of research questions and the practical tasks of improving school quality.

David Hopkins
David Reynolds

July 1994

Acknowledgements

This book would not have been produced without the co-operation and support of a range of people and institutions:

- Members of the education profession and broader educational community in Australia who generously shared their views on 'Quality Schooling';
- Members of the Secretariat of OECD – Professor Malcolm Skilbeck; Mr Pierre Laderriere, Mr Costas Soumelis, Dr Alan Wagner – who contributed to the conceptualization of the work;
- Colleagues at Monash University associated with the School Decision Making and Management Centre, in particular Dr Lawrence Angus and Dr Brian Spicer, who participated in the conduct of interviews, and Dr Joan Addinsal, Ms Charin Naksook, Ms Olive Hamilton, Dr Don Sinclair and Ms Ros Winter, who contributed to the conduct of the literature review;
- Ms Julie Gray and Ms Sandra Bosman, who provided invaluable secretarial assistance in the early stages of the work, and Ms Jenny Foo and Ms Robyn Wilson, who meticulously prepared the final manuscript.

To each of the above we are sincerely grateful.

Sections of the work have been developed from our contributions to OECD activities on: 'The Effectiveness of School and of Educational Resource Management' and 'The Curriculum Redefined: Schooling for the Twenty-First Century'.

Introduction

This book appears at an especially important time for its theme. 'Quality' is one of the key terms in current educational debates: 'quality schooling', 'quality management', 'quality teaching and learning', and 'quality assurance' are all themes that exercise the attention and draw the criticism of policy-makers, administrators and practitioners widely across the international arena. No one is against 'quality': everyone wants to be assured that they will obtain it. But what *is* it, and how would we know when we have found it or failed it? Once having identified it, or secured some broad agreement on what it consists in, how are we then to conceptualize it for delivery in our educational institutions? How are we to assess it? What measures need to be introduced to promote it – and in ways that do not threaten or compromise other good things in our education and social systems? It is to the tentative answering of some of these questions that this book is addressed.

In this book we endeavour to integrate much of our previous work in this domain, drawing on the theoretical and research literature in areas such as educational policy and the management and organization of educational systems, institutions and schools; educational change; school effectiveness and school improvement; changing conceptions of knowledge and research; and new versions of curricula. This material is integrated with a new and substantial piece of empirical/analytical work, which examines conceptions of educational quality, the role of the school in recent proposals for enhancing quality, and the broad development of centralized educational policy, designed to bring about quality in schools and school systems.

Although the major data source for the book is the close analysis of Australian educational policy and school reform, it addresses a theme of international theoretical and practical importance. The research was informed by international considerations of issues pertaining to quality education and the effectiveness of schooling. In designing the study we drew upon work undertaken by the authors on behalf of OECD and devised a framework for the consideration of these issues in the Australian context. An interview schedule reflecting major areas of enquiry was developed, and interview responses were analysed using the Ethnograph package.

Data were collected in each of the Australian states and territories. The perspectives available to the researchers emanated from principals, teachers, parents and students in schools; senior personnel (such as directors-general of education and chairpersons of national and state commissions); middle-level management in educational systems (including directors of divisions, regional officers and inspectors); presidents and officers of organizations such as teacher associations, parent associations, principal associations, religious orders; support personnel (such as curriculum and professional development officers, teacher trainers and lecturers in faculties of education); and members of the wider community including representatives from business.

The theoretical perspective from which the book is written is not one that has been widely used in past reflections on and analyses of school quality. We are operating from a post-empiricist view of educational theory and research, in which we eschew positivist paradigms which hold fast to the tenability of theses resting upon alleged hard 'empirical' data, 'facts' that are purported to be free of value or theoretical prejudice, and 'findings' that are claimed to be neutral, impersonal and totally objective.

We reject such approaches and prefer to adopt one of a pragmatic kind, which draws upon the writing of thinkers like Dewey, Quine, Popper and Lakatos, and tackles real problems, topics and difficulties that we believe constitute the staple of an agenda devoted to the examination and elucidation of 'quality' issues. We concentrate upon the examination, comparison and criticism of various theoretical perspectives, taking our analysis to be one involving critical theory competition and correction, as a part of a process of bringing to bear the various judgments we believe it is possible to make about the nature, values and goals of quality institutions, teaching and schooling.

We do this by taking a 'problem-based' approach in which we try to identify and isolate those problems that are amenable to treatment and capable of resolution. We do not look for the arrival of any educational millennium, and we are aware that our own conclusions may well turn out to be just one further set of hypotheses that stand as candidates for criticism and possible refutation. We are also aware, in our approach to the tentative conceptualization and application of theories to real problems, that we do not come to such an enterprise free of 'prejudices' and theories of our own.

What we seek to provide for our readers is access to a range of problems, issues and trends, that will enhance the understanding of policy-makers, administrators, teachers and parents as they address the theme of 'Quality Schooling' in their schools and in school systems around the world.

Chapter 1

The Concept of Quality and the Provision of Quality Schooling: International Concern

TALK ABOUT QUALITY

Issues of 'Quality' in education have been a matter of interest and concern for some time in different institutions, systems and countries. Saying something clear and comprehensive about that elusive concept has, however, proved far more difficult.

The reason for this is not far to seek. Like 'time', with which St Augustine had so much difficulty, we may also feel that, whenever we encounter 'quality', we have no problem recognizing it; but if anyone asks us to define or describe it, suddenly we are in trouble. 'Quality' and 'time' are protean terms: they defy precise specification and are recalcitrant to our most persistent attempts to analyse them. This is because, like 'art', 'religion' and 'democracy', 'quality' (and 'time') are examples of what W. B. Gallie (1964) called 'essentially contested concepts': the only thing one can be certain about, in our vain search for what some might hope to discover as the 'real' or the 'essential' meaning of such terms, is that people will be fundamentally *un*certain about them and will profoundly disagree in their discussion and use of them. To think that one *can* find an 'essential', 'basic' or uncontestable account of the meaning of such terms is to embark upon a search for that mythical beast, the chimera.

The best we can do in our attempt to get a clear grip on the meaning of such terms is to follow Wittgenstein's advice and 'look at their *use*' (1958). And when we do actually observe the occasions of talk about 'quality', we realize that such talk is like a rope in which many fibres, of widely varied colours, textures and lengths, criss-cross and intertwine. In discussions and debates about 'quality', what matters and what helps us begin dimly to discern some sort of 'truth' is the irregular flow and the shifting interplay of such factors as: the intellectual backgrounds and traditions, the disciplinary upbringings and the individual and collective intentions of participants in debates about 'quality'; the contexts in which such debates take place; the outcomes aimed at and the purposes held in mind; the considerations that make certain criteria important and certain moves decisive. These will give us far more of the flavour, direction and sense of the particular ways in which 'quality' has significance in such discussions.

Robert Pirsig (1974) knew this intuitively: the lyrical account of 'quality' in the latter pages of his *Zen and the Art of Motorcycle Maintenance* tells us far more about the meanings, implications and motives behind the application of such terms to machines, institutions and human beings, and to truths about them expressed by users of the term 'quality', than any number of sophisticated – but ultimately pointless – definitions and conceptual analyses.

It is for this reason that recent demands for 'quality' and 'quality assurance' in school systems, schools and higher education institutions around the world have been so bedevilled by opacity, confusion and inconclusiveness: not only were the things that investigations of such institutions and systems were seeking often inimical to such demands, the very terms themselves were open to the widest variety of interpretations precisely because of their protean character. That did not, of course, discourage such investigators and legislators from persisting with their enquiries: after all, they believed, 'quality' was the one magical ingredient that would bestow upon their institutions the magic touch of public credibility, respect and admiration. And from that acceptance, they believed, would follow the increased resources they maintained were indispensable to their continued successful operation and increasing growth.

Different countries around the world have, therefore, in their various ways, been attempting to address the concept of 'quality', and determine the ways and means by which it may be created, fostered and increased in schools and other types of educational institutions. 'Mission statements', for what is internally and externally regarded as a corporate enterprise, have come to occupy a prominent place in the discourse by which institutions promote themselves to their 'clients' and seek to involve their 'stakeholders'. 'Accountability' has become a major watchword in institutional funding and management. 'Performance indicators' have been recommended, and, in some cases, come to be developed and applied to every aspect and phase of an institution's activities. Such publicly observable features of institutional 'success' as growth in access, equity and participation rates have come to be relied upon as having primacy over other, much less tangible but nonetheless indispensable, characteristics of an institution's nature, purpose and ethos.

These preoccupations are increasingly dominant in talk about and questions addressed to the activities and purposes of education institutions in the present day. It would now be widely agreed that public perception of many education institutions finds them wanting. Adverse comment arises, not only as a result of parents' anxieties about their children's futures, but also as a result of the criticism of educational institutions' 'performance' (or alleged lack of it) directed at them by politicians and economists who hold particular conceptions and theories about the standards against which a country's education system, economic welfare, and future prosperity can be measured and properly planned. It is our endeavour, in this book, to subject such anxieties, theories and ideologies to critical scrutiny. We shall be arguing that many of the apprehensions about the quality of schools, and the aspersions cast on quality, arise from mistaken, misconceived and often mischievous notions regarding the nature, aims and values of a country's education system. Along with this often goes a forgetfulness or deliberate unwillingness to appreciate that many of a country's economic difficulties arise from and are bound up in international economic developments, tendencies and complexities over which single countries have relatively little control, and for the solution of which large-scale, internationally co-ordinated policies and initiatives are required.

We wish to argue, instead, that school and school systems must not be held totally responsible for dysfunctional economic, social and political phenomena, the origin and continuance of which lie largely outside their control. Certainly, 'quality schooling' must address economic purposes and prepare the next generation for contributing to its economic welfare, but the dimensions of quality schooling must, we argue, be far broader than this. In the conception of quality schooling we put forward in the concluding chapters of this book, we have endeavoured to ensure that the full range of community views about what constitutes quality are included. We try to identify those problems, to do with securing quality, that are accessible to school and system administrators, and to establish that the criteria against which the quality of schooling might be assessed are realistic, fair and sufficiently comprehensive to cover all the concerns of education which members and sections of the community most widely share.

POLITICAL, ETHICAL AND ECONOMIC CONCERNS

The question of how quality education is to be secured, and in what most cost-efficient manner, is an issue of major concern in countries around the world.

Government policy and administrative responses to this question indicate the extent to which a central issue in quality schooling is a political/ethical one. Decisions upon this matter have to do with, and concentrate upon, the commitments people have to some fundamental set of beliefs regarding the nature of human beings and the ways in which they can best arrange and institutionalize their relationships for the various purposes – individual, social and communal – they have in mind and desire to achieve.

Proponents of quality schooling in countries such as Denmark, France and Norway have traditionally supported the principle that access to intellectual challenge, a high-quality and empowering curriculum in a caring and personally concerned educational environment, is among the most important foundations of a more just and equitable society – one in which equity and equality of educational opportunity become achievable goals.

The 'conservative' philosophy, however, adopted by such countries as England and Wales, is more minimalist as regards equity and social justice. In the form in which it has been applied to education, it originates from, rests on and embodies the view that education as an agency can do little to redress the major inequalities existing in society. These are held to reside in and be caused much more by factors of individual make-up and personal motivation than those arising from structural features of society. This latter, conservatives maintain, is a reification that has no ontological existence: 'there is not such thing as society', so one of its doughtiest protagonists asserts. From such a perspective, the administrative response to the promotion of quality schooling should, it is felt, be of a more minimalist and individual kind, leaving much more responsibility for improvement to individual autonomy and personal motivation.

It must be pointed out, however, that there is no simple and direct relationship between ideology, goals, and administrative structures and processes. The impact of economic forces and the influences of international corporatist and managerialist trends have resulted in the need for a whole complex and heterogeneous series of responses to the issue of improving the quality of schools.

3

A distinctive feature of recent educational reforms in New Zealand, for example, has been the attempt to combine structural changes of a minimalist kind with the maintenance of equity goals. This is particularly evident in New Zealand's efforts to provide increased resource support for schools with large numbers of pupils from low-income families, and in endeavours to promote gender and racial equality in all aspects of schooling. Thus, whilst the reform efforts in New Zealand, originally driven by a Labour Government, appear to exhibit considerable similarities to the Conservative Government's reforms in England and Wales, significant differences in priorities and structural arrangements can be discerned in response to the high priority given by the New Zealand Government to matters of equity and social justice.

In France and most Scandinavian countries, the provision of a structurally uniform and homogeneously organized system of schooling has been seen, traditionally, as a means of providing quality and equal access to all. Although more recently there has been greater decentralization of decision-making in such countries, the differentiation and diversity which have been regarded as desirable means of ensuring the availability of *choice* at the local level, as evident in England and Wales and in New Zealand, have not been a part of their reform efforts.

In countries such as England, Wales and New Zealand, by contrast, wider choice has been regarded as a crucial means of helping to improve quality and raise standards. One further way in which quality is believed to be improved is via the emphasis on introducing competition into the provision of education, at no extra financial cost to the 'consumer'. In England and Wales, one way of facilitating choice is claimed to have been provided by means of a policy of open enrolment; another has been via the mechanism of 'grant-maintained schools', whereby schools are able to 'opt out' of local financial provision and receive total funding directly from the UK Department for Education and Science, thus achieving independence from the local education authority. This has created a choice of three types of schools available to the educational 'consumer': schools that wish to stay within the local authority; those receiving direct grants; and those in the private sector with 'assisted places'. Publication of examination results, information days at schools and extensive public relations campaigns organized by individual schools are among the means by which parents are provided with the information that will, it is believed, enable them to discriminate among schools and exercise the choice available to them under these arrangements.

Of course the notion of 'choice' is only meaningful if people have the capacity and the freedom to choose. If that capacity or freedom is severely constrained, then, so far as freedom of choice is concerned, a substantial part of the population becomes disenfranchised. Among the questions to be addressed in considerations of quality, therefore, are: How can governments subsidize educational choice at the same time as providing equal opportunity? How are all parents able to exercise their right to choose? – if indeed they have the freedom and the appropriate powers and resources to make such a choice.

The provision of grant-maintained status to facilitate choice in England and Wales highlights other features of the policy of governments such as those of New Zealand, England and Wales. Underlying reforms in those countries is the commitment to a particular philosophy: the notion of the *sale* of educational services as a commodity in the market place, and a concomitant emphasis upon and search for a larger degree of private involvement in educational provision. A grant-maintained school, for instance, no longer has access to free services provided by the local educational authority. Instead, the providers of educational services to schools, whether they be traditional providers such as LEAs or universities, or new contributors to the educational service, must compete on the open market. This is one manifestation of a far more fundamental change: *a change in the very concept of public service itself.*

THE NEW CONCEPT OF PUBLIC SERVICE

It is clear that over the past decade, the social, political and ethical foundations upon which systems of public education were developed have been subjected to radical scrutiny in many places. In countries such as Australia, Norway, Denmark, Finland and France, public education systems were traditionally based on the assumption that the public interest was best served when public goods such as education were provided by agencies under public control exercised through the various 'welfare' institutions of the state. The new view, now being embraced in England and Wales and accepted by the New Zealand authorities, rests upon the notion that education is to be conceived of less as a public good or a form of welfare agency and much more as a *commodity*, the selection of which is a matter of private choice and hence dependent upon personal provision and the norms of the market place.

This solution to the provision of public education is supposed to give 'consumers' (that is, parents and members of the broader community) greater autonomy, sovereignty and choice regarding public expenditure on education. Consumers will, by this analysis, be given greater opportunity to select and 'purchase' the type of education they want. The outcomes of this approach are supposed to include the prime tenets of making the 'producers' of education (professional educators in schools) more directly accountable to their consumers and hence of improving the quality of the educational 'product'.

Of course, underlying the proposals for a consumer-oriented approach and the privatization of educational provision is the stark reality of a reduced funding base for education. This is particularly evident in the case of countries such as New Zealand, in which the country's relative economic standing and performance deteriorated markedly in the late 1980s and early 1990s (although some have discerned an improvement in recent times). In New Zealand, such proposals for reform reflect broader changes in economic policy, variously described as 'liberalization', 'deregulation', or 'more market', and mirror changes in public sector management.

In countries such as France, Norway and Finland, reservations have been expressed regarding the implications of the 'more market' approach for the full range of values and interests vested in a public education system. Moreover, it has been argued, one of the results of the market approach may in fact be the undermining of the vital importance of the provision of funding, necessary not only to provide for and promote the democratic ideal of an informed society of knowledgeable citizens but as a precondition of economic growth.

Yet, even in countries which have not moved so dramatically towards a more market-oriented approach to educational policy and administration, economic forces have impacted on education in various ways. At the present time, in Denmark, for example, economic challenges are demanding new ways of thinking and new initiatives. Improvements in the qualifications of the labour force are regarded as making a significant contribution to an increase in the country's economic possibilities, and a well-functioning educational system is held to be one of the most important conditions for the competitiveness of the Danish economy in the international context. Evaluation and innovation in education are defined as indispensable elements of national welfare, if Denmark is to be able to meet the demands of a modern society able to hold its own in an international economic environment.

Traditionally, the Danish people have stressed the importance of their unique national identity being expressed in the school system. The results of a recent inquiry highlighted the fact that there is, in a most positive way, a deeply rooted image of the 'folkeskole' as a primary school, that distinguishes itself in important respects from schools in other countries, such as Germany, the USA and Japan. Particular reference has been made to the need in Denmark for:

- Pupils to follow a comprehensive line, to learn to co-operate, to be treated as important and valuable. Discrimination is not allowed.
- Pupils not to be singled out as low and high achievers by marks, exams and other indicators.
- Leadership that is not authoritarian. Democracy – in the Danish manner – is of utmost importance.

At the same time as the Danish people are proud of these attitudes, economic pressures and increasing international co-operation and competition are forcing them to question whether they are following the 'right' ideals.

Thus, in considerations of 'quality' more widely, one might ask the central question of national identity and economic viability: Will the independent cultural values and sense of autonomy, upon which nations have traditionally based their education systems, be able to survive when faced with growing pressures for international co-operation and competition?

SYSTEM RESTRUCTURING AND THE STREAMLINING OF DECISION-MAKING

It is clear that in the drive towards increasing the quality of schools a number of policies will have to be adopted and, in consequence, a number of decisions will have to be made. They will include decisions on matters such as: Who is to be the learner? What is to be learned? For what purposes is the teaching/learning to occur? How is the teaching/learning content to be delivered? How are the teaching/learning to be resourced? What resources are needed? How are progress and success to be assessed? By what standards and criteria? What are the appropriate organizational structures and administrative processes to deliver teaching/learning programmes? In other words: How are the efficiency and effectiveness of the whole to be judged?

The levels and loci at which decisions are made vary from country to country and from system to system. The key decisions are likely to be taken by:

- legislative and policy-making bodies (e.g. national government, state, province);
- agencies at the intermediate level (e.g. region, district, municipality);
- members of local community/school constituencies (e.g. school council, school board);
- the school.

In England and Wales, for instance, questions of who is to be taught, what is to be taught, for what purposes, and how learning is to be assessed are now matters for national government (central) determination. The matter of the level of resource supply needed is generally settled at the local area level, while the school governing board, under local management of schools (LMS) decides how teaching and learning processes are to be resourced (though this can include such important matters as the engagement and termination of staff and the negotiation of their salary). The function of the professional educators taking decisions at the school level, under these arrangements, is to determine how the curriculum is to be delivered and what teaching methods are most appropriate for these purposes.

Recent reforms in England and Wales and New Zealand have been designed deliberately to *streamline decision-making*. In several other countries, where the structure of decision-making is still very complex, a similar streamlining process is taking place. In Finland, for example, there have traditionally been seven levels of decision-making: Parliament; Council of State; the Ministry of Education; central agencies such as the National Board of Education; regional administration in provincial offices; local administration in municipalities; and schools. This complex system of administration is now being overhauled and decisions are being delegated to regional and local levels. The former complicated authorization and grading systems are being simplified. To this end, the number of regulations governing administration has been reduced and the planning systems have been integrated. Similarly, in Denmark, previously many different bodies were required to make pronouncements or make recommendations on all sorts of matters pertaining to education, and deliberations in and between such bodies often resulted in protracted decision-making processes and an unclear division of competence. Under new arrangements, influence is centred in the municipal authority as the overall and economically responsible body, and the schools' own boards as the common denominator for parents, staff and pupils.

The streamlining of decision-making is closely connected to other aspects of structural and administrative reform over the last decade. Education authorities in many countries have been undertaking reforms which have had direct implications for the redistribution of administrative power among the various levels within the education system, including the school itself. Although many of these reforms have been undertaken under the overt agendum of 'decentralization', closer examination suggests that any elucidation of the redistribution of power will result in an analysis far more complex than an account based on a one-dimensional conception of changed arrangements along the centralization-decent-ralization continuum.

In an attempt to explain these changes, the authors of a recent OECD report (1988) conclude that current trends in managerial rearrangement and power redistribution seem to show that increased assignment of financial responsibility and resource decision-making to schools is offset by a simultaneous and parallel increase in the arrogation of other major functions of decision-making powers and influence, particularly as they relate to purpose and accountability, to the centre. Thus, terms such as 'centralization' or 'decentralization', in this context, are really too limited to be of any use in giving a complete account of what are far more complex developments, problems and issues.

That OECD report points out that a number of generalizations can be made about the developments in many countries where new patterns of decision-making have emerged. In summary, the report's authors find that among policy-makers and administrators there has been a growing recognition that the key to the success of educational reform is to be found in the implementation and application of policy reform at the school level. This conclusion is consistent with the work of those who have been active in research over two decades on the change effort; it was also the primary assumption underlying the extensive work undertaken by OECD/CERI on the International School Improvement Project (ISIP).

The authors of the OECD report also identify a second trend in what they see as an increasing emphasis laid by policy-makers and administrators on the responsibility, and indeed the 'right', of the 'centre' to govern the formulation of objectives, the provision of guidelines and the monitoring of quality control.

It is not surprising, then, that new arrangements in many countries pose a number of questions for those responsible for quality in the management of schools and school systems. It is reasonable, for example, to ask the following questions:

- What is the balance between centrally determined objectives and priorities as against local requirements considered to be primarily the function of the school?
- How can schools reconcile the tensions between an approach to school improvement aimed at enhancing the capabilities of members of the local school community, and the current politically and economically driven concern for centrally determined quality control?
- What is the acceptable balance between system governors' concern for accountability, and the desire manifested by education service professionals for the empowerment and professional growth of teachers at each school site?
- How do schools address their dual accountability to their superior authorities, and to their constituents and stakeholders in the local school community?
- How may school leaders achieve a more refined and complex understanding of, and power to respond to, the many seemingly conflicting trends in the current educational reform efforts?

- How can a situation in which there is the centralization of control and the decentralization of blame be avoided?

ATTEMPTS TO ACHIEVE THE 'APPROPRIATE BALANCE' BETWEEN CENTRAL AND LOCAL AUTHORITY

In countries such as England, Wales and New Zealand, changes in administrative arrangements have resulted in the 'centre' being seen as responsible for articulating goals in line with government objectives, exercising quality control and providing large-scale policy priorities. The powers of 'intermediary' authorities have been severely reduced, as in England and Wales, or eliminated, as in New Zealand. The school has been granted greater autonomy or 'self-management' in the management of resources, while all the time having to balance this 'local management' with the maintenance of a national curriculum and national standards. Different types of mechanisms for achieving the desired balance or mix of central and local responsibility have emerged. In New Zealand these have been incorporated in the notion of 'School Charters'; in England and Wales, the mechanism is through 'School Development Plans'. In accordance with the new ideology of the market, the assumption underlying these developments in England and Wales and New Zealand is the firm belief that quality will be enhanced by competition at local level among schools.

Elsewhere there has been less emphasis on the 'market', but in Portugal, Spain, Finland, Denmark, Norway and Australia (and, to some extent, in France) the thrust of the reform effort, in response to tighter economic circumstances and an increased concern for community participation and the location of decision-making as close as possible to the place of implementation, has still been to decentralize management decisions to the local level, whilst enabling the 'centre' to retain central control over goal determination and quality.

In Finland, one reason put forward for a centralized system of objective-setting is an interest in securing educational equity and, more concretely, making sure that different school forms and levels can plan their provision on a basis which, to a certain degree, can be anticipated in advance. This, however, does not equal detailed regulation; legislation concerning the comprehensive school stipulates that teaching arrangements must take account of the pupil's age and abilities and that schools must co-operate with pupils' families. This leaves the control of quality to the teacher. One reason given for the present system of *steering curriculum design by objectives* in Finland is the view that the important target for achievement is the objective itself, without necessarily seeking to know what teaching content has led to it. This also stresses the discretion and responsibility of the schools in matters of learning and content and makes it possible for them to provide individual instruction.

Such responses reflect the enduring concern of system authorities: How can schools be released from the costs and constraints of centralized bureaucracies without governments at the same time losing direction in public education? How can detailed control by central authorities be avoided at the same time as ensuring the achievement of central aims and the provision of quality education to all students across the country?

THE THRUST TOWARDS MORE SCHOOL-BASED MANAGEMENT

At the time when the traditional bureaucratic systems of education in many countries were characterized by a high degree of centralized control, a clearly defined hierarchy of authority, and an extensive set of system-wide regulations designed to enforce compliance in curriculum, personnel, finance, facilities and administration, school leaders and teachers had few opportunities to exercise any degree of freedom at the level of the school site. During the 1970s and 1980s, however, although the existence and activity of state bureaucracies continued to be seen as indispensable requirements for the administration of education, there was an increasing momentum in many countries towards more democratic school-based structures and processes. In countries such as Denmark and Australia the impulse was towards democratization of education within government constraints, arising out of concerns for equity and distributive justice.

In the Danish context, local management of schools was based on the view that innovation and quality are best created through decentralization of competence and responsibility to the educational institutions. Given the essentially 'democratic' orientation of the move towards greater school-based management in Denmark, deliberate steps were taken by Danish authorities to avoid those aspects of local management of schools which might promote competition between institutions.

The democratic principle has also been an important aspect of reforms designed to give more autonomy to educational institutions in Italy. It is important to note, however, that in Italy concern has been expressed that giving schools greater autonomy might have the effect of causing disequilibrium across the system: schools that have greater autonomy, it is believed, may be more difficult to control. Moreover, schools with a greater degree of autonomy might make it difficult to achieve the absolute priority of education in Italy – educational access must be the same for all citizens.

In countries such as New Zealand, England and Wales, the educational debate is similarly pervaded by discourse that employs the language of 'school-based management' and 'local management of schools'. In observing this phenomenon, we may believe we can discern at least superficially a straightforward connection with the democratic trends just described. But closer examination reveals fundamental differences in ideology and patterns of control, where school-based management rests just as much, if not more, on the application to education of the values of the market – diversity, competition and choice.

THE OVERRIDING IMPORTANCE ATTACHED TO TEACHING AND LEARNING IN CURRENT REFORM EFFORTS

If a country aspires to provide the best educational service possible, within the limitations of the available resources, then success in achieving that goal will come down to the resolution of questions concerning:

- the setting of priorities for the education system;
- the organization of those priorities;
- the provision of a set of plans and agenda to address the fundamental questions of resource provision and management, the solution of which is necessary to put the social aims, educational vision and resultant economic priorities into effect.

Countries differ in their approach to the development and execution of such a planning and implementation process. In Spain, for example, the approach has been more one of evolutionary problem-solving based on 'rolling reforms'. Whilst the changes in Spain have been far-reaching, the approach to the change process has been significantly different from that of the 'earthquake method' of educational reform adopted in New Zealand, where virtually all major new structures have been erected and changes implemented within the space of one year. The proponents of such a radical approach to the change process in New Zealand have argued that its adoption was essential for the broad-scale reform objectives to be achieved quickly. 'Moving step by step lets vested interests mobilize. Big packages neutralize them', it was argued by those responsible for the New Zealand reform effort.

Assessments of such an approach to change have yet to identify the real benefits and costs, as against those claimed. Attention has already been drawn to some unanticipated consequences of the reform effort in New Zealand: the uncertainty, confusion and resistance experienced by parties at all levels; the difficulty of maintaining adequate communication; the increased workload of principals and trustees; the uncertainty regarding the role of new institutions; and the significant mismatch between the expectations of what the Ministry of Education itself should do and the reality of what it could and did do.

The 'research and development' approach to educational innovation and change is clearly evident in Scandinavian countries. In Finland, the most important experiments are launched centrally, often from initiatives arising from lower levels, and they are monitored by national working groups whose membership usually includes representatives of municipal and teacher organizations. The central administration sets the goal for the experiment and the problem to be studied; the solution is based on the experiences gained by schools and municipalities and the results are used to further develop the whole system. Similarly, in Denmark, changes of legislation and curricula are traditionally made on the background of experience gained from pedagogic innovation projects. Since 1969 the Ministry of Education has been granting support for such projects in the order of approximately four million Danish kroner per year.

But no matter what the approach to the implementation of change, no one can doubt the overriding importance attached by policy-makers, educators and members of the community generally to *teaching and learning outcomes*, in all current reform efforts. This reflects the findings of those who studied administrative restructing in the 1980s and established that restructuring efforts tended more to achieve redistribution of influence and power rather than increase effectiveness of outcomes. After decades of administrative restructuring in education, governments are now refocusing their efforts and placing highest priority on the key matters of *teaching/learning outcomes, curriculum, learning and assessment*.

This focus on teaching and learning characterizes approaches to reform in the 1990s. It is particularly evident in the identification of national curriculum goals and guidelines, and in the increased attention being given to centrally determined quality control of teaching/learning outcomes. It is also evident in debates regarding what counts as appropriate curriculum knowledge.

Thus in Finland, for example, educational authorities have started a debate on what constitutes curriculum knowledge, how knowledge should be conceived, how knowledge should be established and certified, how it should be acquired and employed in a society in which knowledge itself is continually changing and expanding, and how one can determine, in such a case, what knowledge is of most worth for the purpose public institutions have in mind. In Finland, the view has been emphasized that teaching should concentrate on central concepts in knowledge and relations between concepts, and give pupils the necessary tools for acquiring appropriate and useful information. The conclusion drawn from this debate, in Finland, is that curricula and the organization of instruction should be further developed, for instance by taking account of what modern research has revealed about learning in general and about the individual's development.

These epistemological issues, in association with considerations drawn from the psychology of learning, will occupy a central place in discussion about quality schooling in the nineties.

MANAGEMENT OF RESOURCES AND IMPROVEMENTS IN THE QUALITY OF EDUCATION

In most countries, access to a universal public system of education, financed from government revenue, starting at primary level and going right up to the level of university or college, has been widely, if not generally, regarded as a right of all citizens. A sense of collective responsibility for provision and standards of such a system has underpinned the 'free' systems of government education. One of the motivating impulses at work here has been the view that the availability of and freedom to participate in such a system are in the interests of social justice, equity and a fair society.

Such an impulse was certainly observable in government provision of public resources for education until relatively recent times. Now, however, a new element has entered the educational debate on the effectiveness and quality of schooling. Consistent with changes in the concept of 'public service' of late, there has been an increasing interest in and moves towards an approach to the resourcing of education that incorporates and rests upon the ideology of the market. This shift in thinking constitutes a significant challenge to the values and norms underpinning traditional beliefs and the previous approaches to state provision, resourcing and funding for education. The appearance and growing strength of this argument, and the ideology from which it emanates, have added a powerful new dimension to the long-standing debate on 'public' and 'private' education. The conclusion urged by the 'market' argument has tended to be that the responsibility for the resourcing of educational services should move away from agencies of the state towards individuals functioning as buyers in an educational market place.

Some countries, of course, have never accepted the principle that the state has an obligation to subsidize private education. It has been argued in some places that a school that refuses to assume the full responsibilities of a 'public' school should not receive public money. The possibility of the existence of a segregated system of public and private education, in which private educational institutions receive public funds, has been considered in such countries to run counter to the interests of a just and cohesive society.

By contrast, in countries such as Australia, where non-government schools are subsidized by public funds, more than one quarter of students now attend such schools. Of central concern here has been the issue of how the government might respect the rights of particular parent groups to provide the education they want for their children, while at the same time meeting the obligation to ensure that all children receive the best possible education. Although, under the funding arrangements in Australia, higher levels of aid are given to schools and school systems with lower private resource levels, critics of government funding point to continuing problems, such as the 'creaming off' process that functions so as to drain off from government schools a large proportion of academically able middle-class students. This 'creaming off' process explains in part the comparatively high degree of success of private school pupils in public examinations. This phenomenon – public examination success – is regarded as one of the principal marks of effectiveness, justifying the appellation and reputation of many private schools as providing a 'quality education'.

Critics of government subsidies to private schools argue that poor and less affluent students must get first priority in the allocation of government funds for education. It is only when the worst school become 'good schools' that, it is argued, 'freedom of choice' will cease to have class overtones and will become a value available to all.

But private sector growth and government subsidies appear often to go hand in hand. Experience in countries such as Australia suggests that enrolments in private schools are very closely related to the 'private price of private schooling' – that is, to the proportion of a school's costs paid by fees. It is interesting, therefore, to note that in the current reforms in New Zealand an increase in government funding to private schools is seen as an inherent part of the move towards achieving the new policy goal of taking schools into the market place and, at the same time, of course, of reducing the amount of government funds expended on the provision of education and educational services.

Supporters of the 'market' approach adopt the view that the likelihood of a school's succeeding will be directly proportional to the range, quality and delivery of the academic 'products' that it offers. Enduring success, it is believed, will only be achieved by the constant delivery of high-quality products. In this way, quality will be achieved and maintained. Private schools, or schools that are freed from bureaucratic constraints and costs, can, it is argued, accomplish their goals more effectively with minimum interference and danger of resource misuse. In a competitive environment market, pressures will force the school to use its resources in the most economically efficient way and to develop the 'educational product' in accordance with consumer preference. The absence of such competitive pressures in traditional government systems of education, it is claimed, has been to the detriment of achieving 'quality' schools.

Critics of this approach argue that as the market's role increases, the remaining public sector provision becomes 'residualized'. On that model, they claim, the public sector becomes the bottom of the hierarchy – the place for those without capital to exchange for services and goods. Within the public sector, such critics maintain, if competition among public schools is allowed, differentiations and discriminations will tend to be made between schools on the basis of academic and other criteria – and some of these discriminations will, in consequence, be adverse. If additional enterprise is to be allowed for schools to generate further funds on a local basis, inequality within the system of education will almost certainly increase.

Across the world such issues underpin the debates on the provision of quality schooling as policy-makers search for viable options to the present methods of financing and resourcing education. As an example of an approach to this question, reference may be made to proposals in countries such as Russia for the introduction of voucher schemes of various types. Other alternative approaches include proposals for:

- increased private sector contributions or commercializations;
- cost unit saving strategies such as decreasing drop-out rates, fewer and less labour-intensive teaching strategies, amalgamation of smaller institutions and the provision of extension education services; and
- the use of school facilities as a community resource and the community as a resource for school programmes.

In addition to such alternatives, the current tighter economic environment has persuaded many governments of the desirability of a change in policy and administrative arrangements that would give local authorities more financial authority without reducing accountability. This is seen by such governments as providing more cost-efficient management of resources, by freeing schools from the undue restrictions caused by the requirements of ear-marked grants and by enabling decision-making to be more immediately responsive to local needs.

The most radical changes of this type have occurred in England and Wales, where bulk-funding for most aspects of human, financial and physical resource management has been given to the individual school. Bulk-funding to each school board of trustees is also a major aspect of reforms in New Zealand, but in that context such funding is based on a formula calculated by the Ministry of Education and weighted for equity considerations.

As part of the trend towards bulk-funding in the local management of schools, the United Kingdom Education Reform Act of 1988 has devolved to the local school site all powers of decision-making pertaining to teachers' and school heads' salaries. In this way the management of human resources is also clearly included under the rubric of such bulk-funding.

In New Zealand, by contrast, the original government implementation of a policy of bulk-funding to schools did not include teachers' salaries. Allowing principals and school boards the right to make decisions about teachers' pay would, it was claimed in New Zealand, create an adversarial situation in schools, with considerable potential for conflict, the emergence of forces of self-interest, and an undermining of the collaborative relations deemed to be characteristic of effective schools. Strongly and increasingly related to the question of local salary determination is the question of performance-based salary. In the United Kingdom, for instance, many headteachers have been placed on performance-related contracts.

It is yet to be seen whether local negotiation and determination of teachers' salaries and performance-related pay are necessary conditions for the promotion of improved teaching/learning outcomes and the achievement of quality in schooling.

EVALUATION AND ASSESSMENT

In a consideration of the question of the most appropriate form of assessment and evaluation of school quality, it is possible to identify two main approaches in operation. On the one hand, there are those who argue that centrally determined quality control is the most powerful means of ensuring good schools, and there are those, on the other hand, who would maintain that, in the interests of equity and quality, a high degree of professional autonomy is indispensable. According to the latter view, it is the individual teacher who sees most directly the diversity and individual differences that exist among their students at the level of the classroom and the school site.

In some states of Australia, for instance, a long-term commitment to enhancing the quality of schooling has been in evidence, and strategies to achieve it set in operation, based upon the desideratum of the enhancement of the capabilities of the personnel at the school site. In such states there has been very little centralized quality control. This approach is under challenge elsewhere in Australia, reflecting developments in England and Wales, New Zealand, Sweden and Spain, where recent reforms have incorporated, as an essential component, the establishment of bodies to monitor quality and performance evaluation.

In New Zealand, for example, procedures for reviewing and assessing the outcomes and effects of stated goals in the School Charter are required by institutions themselves and their communities every three years. Outcomes are also assessed by external national examinations, nationally moderated internal assessment, and the Educational Review Office, a newly created Crown agency formed as part of the recent reforms, whose task it is to assess the educational effectiveness of schools and to ensure that public funds for education are being used effectively and efficiently. The New Zealand Qualifications Authority has also been established to co-ordinate and rationalize national secondary, vocational and advanced academic qualifications.

In Spain, too, the National Institute of Quality Evaluation has been established, designed to measure the effectiveness of Spain's schools with some rigour, not only from the point of view of pupils' results but from a broader perspective of the concept of school quality, which takes into account school and social circumstances.

In Scotland, the range and quality of resources, the quality of school management, pupil support and school ethos – all of these are measured against criteria drawn up by the Schools Inspectorate in the light of their experience and taking account of the views of regional authorities, schools, teachers and others. It is a responsibility of inspectors to ensure full debate of any educational issues by publishing consultative papers, by maintaining close liaison with education authorities and by discussing them as often as possible with teachers in schools.

Debate on quality within the Schools Inspectorate in Scotland in the last three years – a debate which has been illuminated and more sharply focused as a result of the development of agreed performance indicators and accompanying criteria – has shown up some movement in shifting the focus of attention during inspections away from 'process' and more towards 'product' in *all* stages of schooling. A likely consequence of the present application of performance indicators and their transmission to regional authorities and schools will involve a similar shift in thinking at regional and school levels, to identify outcomes of the teaching and learning process more precisely at all levels. This shift has already been foreshadowed by the Scottish Education Department's introduction of national testing in language and mathematics for 8- and 11-year-olds and of moves to assess pupils informally in all areas of the primary and secondary curriculum.

In the quality debate in Scotland, the strongest argument against the use of performance indicators relates not to their use but to the amount of descriptive writing which needs to be done by inspectors in providing evidence to support a particular judgement. The unresolved argument is whether an evaluation can stand on its own without explanation and, if not, how much explanation is required to be provided, given that every school is unique and every department or stage within it has its own characteristics. This argument is a critical one, in view of the increasing amount of attention being given to the demand for accountability at all levels of the system.

At the same time as there have been all these initiatives with respect to the activity of external evaluation bodies and the utilization of performance indicators in many countries, increasing emphasis is being placed in other countries on the responsibility of the school to develop mechanisms for internal evaluation. This is clearly evident in some Scandinavian countries, particularly Denmark. In Denmark, it is up to the individual school to evaluate the quality of its activities, to set up its goals and plan of procedures, and to assess the outcomes of such endeavours to improve the functions of the institution.

A new understanding of and approach towards the issue of educational and administrative 'control' can be discerned in such developments. In many Scandinavian countries, there has been a movement away from regulatory control towards steering by goals and objectives, with fewer bureaucratic regulations but clearer goals. This is particularly evident in the reforms of previously highly centralized systems such as in Sweden. There, the recent Education Bill states that result-oriented control requires national educational targets to be defined in practical terms at the local level, in the form of specific teaching objectives. Henceforth, in Sweden the terms 'targets and guidelines', 'syllabuses' and 'time-lines' will be used instead of the umbrella term 'curricula'.

Similarly, in Norway, there is a shift in the field of public administration from working according to set rules to working towards set goals. This shift in the broader field of public sector management is seen as relevant to schools also. Consequently, demands have been made for developing systems for follow-up procedures and evaluation to ensure that goals have been met.

In Denmark, where in the past Parliament and Government set goals, defined content, and left it to the local powers to see to it that the tasks were carried through, the authorities have now reached a point where they are showing great interest in developing, at both national and local levels, a base of documentation which proves that goals are being reached.

In Finland, too, where decentralization of administration and delegation of decisions stress results rather than the methods by which they are achieved, measures have been taken to improve the efficiency of both central and local administration by means of management by results. An inherent part of this is budgeting by results, which was adopted by the National Board of Education on a tentative basis from the beginning of 1992. This means that appropriations will be allocated separately to different units, projects and activities. The use of funds will be monitored throughout the budget year, which means a greater responsibility of different officials for the effectiveness of the activities undertaken and for the use of funds. If the projected decentralization is realized, the central administration will be responsible for preparing matters for Parliament and the Government and for introducing management by results in the administration subordinate to it. Consistent with this approach, the curriculum guidelines now constitute the only normative regulation used by the National Board of Education to supervise and control the work of municipalities and schools.

SYSTEM-WIDE ACCOUNTABILITY AND CENTRALIZED QUALITY CONTROL

There are few examples in the world of systematic evaluation of school quality across an entire system. For example, since there is no tradition in Danish educational policy of publishing and comparing academic achievement between schools, and since no external assessment of teachers or school leaders is prac-tised, it is not possible either to compare student performance or to compare work done by one teacher or school leader with work done by colleagues at other schools. In Norway, there is also no systematic collection of records that can yield a satisfactory statistical basis for a thorough and correct evaluation of schools. The Ministry, research institutions, municipal authorities and schools are at present searching for suitable and efficient systems for precise, adequate and unambiguous data registration intended for use in systematic evaluation.

Perhaps the most interesting developments in system-wide evaluation are those evident in New Zealand and France. In New Zealand, the Education Review Office has been established to monitor the effectiveness and efficiency of schools, as agreed between state and school, in meeting their educational objectives set out in charters. This Office has been set up and designed to play a key role in contributing to the government's intended outcome of improving the quality of education for all pupils.

The establishment of an agency independent of the central Ministry of Education to carry out reviews of schools has introduced a new concept into New Zealand education. For the first time in New Zealand an organization exists whose sole task is to *assess the quality of schools*. In addition to providing external review, the Review Office will also visit schools to assist them in improving their own monitoring and reporting systems. Another essential part of its role relates to accountability and the concern to ensure that public funds for education are being effectively used.

In France, it is likely that efforts to improve methods for measurement and evaluation will continue over the next few years, and will be focused mainly on the following aspects. First, it is very probable that surveys of the levels of knowledge of students at key stages in their school career will be carried out systematically and gradually extended to cover aspects hitherto relatively unexplored, such as their abilities, attitudes and patterns of behaviour. Conducted on a more regular and co-ordinated basis, surveys will yield an increasing harvest of information that will enable comparisons to be made over a period of time between the performance of successive intakes of students, and indicate – through analysis of findings – suitable ways of improving methods or curricula. The aim is to build up, by this means, a databank for use by an 'observatory' set up to monitor the knowledge and skills acquired by students.

At the same time, a 'panel' of secondary students – a representative sample of students from a particular intake whose progress is followed from the time they enter a school to the time they leave – is likely to become a permanent feature, and to be expanded so that it can provide other useful information. There is some question whether the panel method might be extended upstream to cover primary education or downstream to cover higher education. The latter possibility is the more likely, since the aim of getting 80 per cent of an age group up to *baccalauréat* level will mean closely monitoring the progress through university of the rapidly increasing number of students entering post-secondary education.

It is clear that such educational innovations in France – whether in the planning, testing or initial implementation phase – will need to be evaluated in order to measure their cost and assess their impact, in both qualitative and quantitative terms, using information already available or gathered by means of specific surveys.

As far as the school itself is concerned, in France, there is a very clear move towards establishing a management information system, i.e. a well-organized set of indicators designed to assist management, provide a basis for informed decisions regarding the use of resources, and underpin the preparation and periodic revision of the school project. As regards the indicators relating to the situation of students on entering and leaving, resources, school functioning and environment, there are still gaps which will gradually be filled with the help of information supplied by the Ministry of Education. This will be the case, for example, with respect to the data regarding parents' socio-economic background and level of education, the language spoken at home, the help given to student learning by parents, the time spent in the classroom on extra-curricular activities, the amount and type of support given to students in difficulty, the teachers' ability to adjust to their students, parents' participation in the educational community, opinions regarding the atmosphere within the school, and the acquisition by students of successful methods of work and a degree of personal autonomy.

In addition, we shall be seeing over the next few years, in France, an increase in the number of studies at national level on the differences and disparities between schools – particularly in resources, recruitment, results and their geographic and social integration. The aim of such studies will be to highlight significant correlations and then establish a typology of schools and the problems they experience as an aid to decision-makers when they are determining how resources should be allocated.

Lastly, in response to a substantial external demand for information on the quality of the education system as a whole, the French government hopes to see, in the very near future, the completion of work begun early in 1990 on a standardized and consistent series of some twenty indicators designed to measure the effectiveness and results of the education system in France, and presented in a form easily understandable by a wide public. The intention is to distribute this information widely and update it regularly so that it will show trends from year to year. Among the key indicators of quality will be: total expenditure on education, all sources of funding combined (plus the breakdown between primary, secondary, higher and continuing education); the enrolment rate in pre-primary schools for children between the ages of two and five; the level of knowledge and skills of children at the start of the college sixth grade and in the third grade; the differences in performance among *lycées* and among colleges; the number and proportion of students reaching *baccalauréat* level; the qualifications obtained by students at the end of their schooling; the effect of having a qualification on the chances of finding a job; enrolments in higher education in absolute figures and percentages; and the proportion of students going on from the first to the second cycle.

The progressive improvement in measurement and evaluation techniques in France will be based on an increasing use of the computer and data-processing equipment. Associated with this development will be the establishment of statistical and analytical databases that can be accessed by those in charge of the education system at the various levels (central government, academy, department and, for schools, local level), and the processing of information that is being obtained in increasing quantities as a by-product of management data files, which will also be welded into a coherent whole.

There will also be attention given to the development of closer international co-operation, so as to permit objective comparisons of standardized data on a bilateral or multilateral basis, the exchange of experience, and joint or convergent action. With this principle in mind, France is participating in the EURYDICE project for a database on education systems in the EU countries. This same objective of closer international co-operation motivates the work that is being done within the OECD on a common set of indicators for evaluating national education systems.

SCHOOL ORGANIZATION, EDUCATIONAL LEADERSHIP AND COMMUNITY RELATIONS

The functions and tasks that have been identified as having to do with, and promoting quality in, education are, in a major way, the responsibility of those who are charged with the exercise of leadership and management in schools and school systems.

In the context of the changing political, social, economic and technical environment, in which altered patterns of educational governance have brought about changes in the decisions to be made at different levels of the school system, it is clear that new qualifications, qualities and competences will be required for those people now responsible for providing educational leadership and sound management. In many countries, the school leader's role is seen as fundamental in enhancing school quality.

Changing patterns of school governance have meant that more responsibility for finance and budget decisions has been relocated to the school site. But there is some concern that the shifting of responsibility for such decisions may distract school leaders from the primary task of schooling, namely learning and teaching. In particular, the fear has been expressed that the relocation of decision-making on such matters may alter the role of the school leader in favour of management and at the expense of educational leadership. In the light of current concerns for school quality, research findings regarding the relationship between improved educational outcomes and the school leader's role in exercising educational leadership, this must constitute a serious cause for concern.

In a few settings such fears have been allayed, to some extent, by the authorities' construction of new patterns of management, on the clear basis of their potential to contribute to the goals of quality schooling. Communicating this purpose, preparing school-based personnel with the skills to exercise their new responsibilities, and providing the administrative and technical support for new aspects of resource management to be properly incorporated into the overall management of the school have, therefore, become important priorities for authorities at the national, system and local levels – though these priorities have added considerably to changes in the powers wielded, and the pressures experienced, by those charged with leadership at the local school level.

Not least of those pressures have been the difficulties in overcoming the inertia of existing institutional arrangements and procedures experienced by school leaders charged with these new missions. The institutional and structural rigidities of long-established procedures of a bureaucratic operation, coupled with lack of experience and knowledge on the part of school leaders and others operating at more intermediate levels of management, have, in many instances, impeded the effective implementation of the appropriate adjustments in management caused by changing patterns of decision-making, the performance of new management functions, and the resolution of the ensuing management challenges and dilemmas.

In addition, many of those charged with the implementation of reform policies have not provided adequate opportunities to expedite and encourage the undertaking of new roles by those to whom the new administrative responsibilities have been transferred. For example, it is not always clear who has ultimate decision-making power, since officials at several decision-making levels are often simultaneously involved in taking or executing particular decisions. Moreover, the new actors are not always prepared, technically or otherwise, to play the new roles. Such omissions on the part of system authorities contribute to the prevailing uncertainties and confusion being experienced and exhibited by some school leaders and managers, and hinder the effective management of schools, educational resources and improvement initiatives.

Adding to the complexities of the school leader's role are the many measures that have been introduced to allow for parents and representatives of the local community to take part in the management and decision-making in schools, in the name of pursuing and achieving quality. These measures have been designed to promote greater empowerment of parents and local communities, in the belief that making the education system more responsive to community needs will make a major contribution to enhancing school effectiveness.

In New Zealand, for instance, this belief can be seen embodied in the increasing powers of Boards of Trustees, the creation of the Parent Advocacy Council and Community Forums and the opting out provisions. In Spain, a similar phenomenon is also evident in the expansion of the powers of the school board to supervise the national resources, the programmes and the effective running of the school. The director and the school administrative team are also appointed at the proposal of the school board in Spain.

In Denmark, one of the most important innovations in the present regulations for the *Folkeskole* is the establishment of a school board for each school. The aim of this administrative reform is to strengthen parental influence in school, presuming this can happen in collaboration with staff and pupils. The proportion of parents and teachers on school boards in Denmark reflects the value attached to the notion of 'partnership' evident in the composition of school boards in other settings, as was the case until recently in Victoria, Australia. This provides a somewhat different basis for relationships between professional educators and the public than is now in evidence in some other settings, such as New Zealand and the United Kingdom, where the notion of community has shifted from an inclusive concept based on partnership among all groups involved in the educative process, to one which emphasizes 'consumers' (including parents, members of local industry and business) as distinct from 'producers' (the professional educators, including school leaders and teachers).

Noticing these changes in the roles of school leaders in today's changed conditions, we may therefore conclude with the following questions:

- What support can be provided to school leaders, and by whom, to enable them to exercise educational leadership in achieving their school's educational goals effectively and in efficient financial and human resource management, especially as these pertain to a changed relationship with the external environment?
- What changes must be made to patterns and courses of teacher education and training to meet the demands of greater independence and increased local responsibility for the administration of each school?

- What additions to programmes of pre-service and in-service professional training need to be made in order to prepare future school
leaders for the plethora of demands and roles they will be increasingly called upon to play in the future, not least in the areas of
implementing reforms designed to achieve the goals of school quality, financial oversight and control, human resource management,
and monitoring and evaluation of the educational process and
product?

CONCLUSION

In this first chapter we have attempted to highlight the importance of quality in
relation to the policy, provision and practicalities of administering schools and
school systems across the world. We have seen how many different topics
and concerns are brought under the rubric of quality: the content of education;
its conception, delivery and assessment; the ways in which teaching and learning
are organized; and the structures and procedures by which schools as educating
institutions are controlled and directed. All of this relates in some way or other
to a range of issues to do with efficiency and effectiveness, excellence and equity,
devolution and responsibility and accountability. We have shown that quality is
very difficult to define precisely, and that it can function very much as a kind of
'hurrah' word, connoting all that is good and all that the proponents of a school's
excellences want to claim to have achieved. But it is also employed by proponents
in many different guises, and for a very large number of different purposes –
economic, political, moral and social.

It is the complexity arising from this variety of concerns and values that
makes investigations of quality schooling so difficult. It is to the analyses of such
difficulties that we now turn.

Chapter 2

The Relationship between Theory, Research, Policy and Practice

A POST-EMPIRICIST ACCOUNT OF QUALITY SCHOOLING

In this chapter we wish to maintain that the complexity of school objectives, the range and modes of their interplay, and the ways in which they are subject to various kinds of forces and pressures – not all of which are readily quantifiable in numerical terms – make many of them unamenable to scientific enquiry, understood in terms of the traditional empirical mode. We believe that a different approach to, and a wider conspectus of, the appropriate modes of research and enquiry into policy and practical theory are required, in the endeavour to give a coherent account of quality in education.

Recent work in the epistemology and methodology of the natural and social sciences has moved decisively away from the emphasis upon measurement and so-called 'value-neutral' description of totally objective 'facts' that was typical of an earlier era in research, when workers believed completely in the academic tenability of the empiricist paradigm and tended only to develop and apply research designs and instruments exclusively based upon it. Modern researchers in the social sciences have now moved much more towards an approach based on advances in epistemology and methodology that arise from post-empiricist work in the philosophy of science and the social sciences, such as that of Quine (1953), Popper (1943, 1949, 1972), Lakatos (1976) and Winch (1958).

This work has made it possible to move beyond the hardline demand for so-called 'value-free' objectivity, typical of former empiricist research, and beyond the untenable relativism of much writing in the social sciences that was too heavily influenced by the work or views of subjectivists and ethnomethodologists of various kinds, to articulate accounts, develop analyses and produce tentative conclusions that are quite as complex, heterogeneous and multiform as the corpus of material upon which they are based and towards the elucidation of which they may be applied.

The 'empirical' approach (particularly that associated with the quantitative model) adopted in much educational research into issues such as school quality, school effectiveness and school improvement is replete with problems of both a methodological and a conceptual kind. But it is possible to go further and maintain that the foundations of that approach rest upon a view of scientific research that amounts to a dogma. This dogma, we believe, incorporates a mistaken view of science and objectivity, and its mistaken character calls into question much enquiry based upon it and hence the conclusions and implications for policy development and management drawn from it, particularly as regards research into quality schooling.

The problem in question is that of empiricism, which, Dewey (1907) showed embodied a major fallacy:

> The fallacy of orthodox logical empiricism is . . . [that] it supposes that there can be 'givens', sensations, percepts, etc., prior to and independent of thought or ideas, and that thought or ideas may be had by some kind of compounding or separating of the givens. But it is the very nature of sensation of perception . . . already to be, in and of itself, something which is so internally fractionalised or perplexed as to suggest and to require an idea, a meaning.
>
> (Dewey, 1907, p. 309)

This point is an elaboration of that position already tellingly summarized by Kant in the well-known aphorism 'No percepts without concepts'.

What Dewey called a fallacy was attacked as one of the two philosophical dogmas exposed to telling refutation by W. V. O. Quine (1953), and ably redirected towards the rebuttal of some key theories of educational policy and administration by Evers and Lakomski (1991). One of the basic tenets of that dogma, according to Quine, is the positing of an absolute divide between what are held to be the 'neutral', factual and 'value-free' statements, regarded as distinctive of mathematics and the natural sciences and thus proffered as paradigms of 'objectivity', and those of other realms of discourse, such as ethics, politics and aesthetics, which are held to be non-factual, value-laden and irredeemably subjective.

Most past investigations and treatments of school quality and effectiveness comprised such dichotomies of description–evaluation, fact–value, quantitative–qualitative analyses as were previously thought to be mutually opposed and exclusive. There is now a need in school quality enquiry to fuse description–evaluation, fact–value, quantitative–qualitative methods in new forms of enquiry that are valuable both for the researcher and the policy-maker. Such an approach will involve both groups in a common enterprise – what Lakatos called a 'progressive research programme' – of understanding and policy generation. Future work in the investigation of school quality, we argue, would be well advised to involve approaches of this kind.

In opposition to the thesis of empiricism, the main burden of the counterarguments has been to show that there is no such distinction as that supposed to subsist between fact and value (or between science and philosophy, or, come to that, between policy examination and policy formation). For Quine, Evers, Lakomski and many others, all language and all enquiries are inescapably and *ab initio* theory-laden, far from value-free, and a mixture of both descriptive and normative elements. Indeed, says Kovesi (1967), in all discourse and enquiry there is an unbroken continuum, at one end of which lies 'fact' and the other end of which lies 'value'. Description, for such thinkers, is a way of evaluating reality; evaluation is a way of describing states of affairs.

Such arguments are used powerfully by Evers and Lakomski (1991) to develop a new approach to the elucidation of problems in educational policy and administration. According to this view, all our talk on these matters is conceived of as being in itself a 'theory', embodying a complex 'web of belief', shot through differentially with descriptive and evaluative elements, according to the contexts and purposes of which our theories of education, policy and administration are brought to bear and applied in our world.

In this enterprise, we do not attempt to reduce everything to some absolute foundations of 'fact' and 'value', 'theory' and 'practice', or 'policy' and 'implementation', in the (vain) attempt to educe some 'analyses' of concepts and theories that can be completely 'correct' or 'true', or to produce some fundamental matters of indisputable research 'findings', about whose objectivity and existence there can be no dispute. We share the Quinean view that what is important is not to establish which analyses are 'true' (in some sort of 'correspondence' sense), or which facts are 'correct' (in some sort of 'positivist' sense), but rather, in our endeavour to identify and promote 'quality':

- *to query which values and which beliefs we should be least willing to give up*, and not simply which unexaminable tenets we should rest on.

Conceived of in this way, educational policy and administration are like any science – an unending quest:

- to grasp the theories determining and predicting advance, and then,
- by critical theory appraisal and comparison, to show which of them is better and for what purpose.

We shall seek to show later how in the field of quality schooling this enterprise might most effectively be engaged in, using an approach derived from the work of one of the most notable exponents of this point of view, the philosopher Karl Popper.

THE RELATIONSHIP BETWEEN RESEARCH, POLICY DEVELOPMENT AND MANAGEMENT

It may be reasonably claimed that the hypothesis of a deliberate or unconscious reliance on empiricism and narrow definitions of 'science' on the part of some workers in the field may serve to explain some of the conceptual confusions and errors apparent in much educational research. But we must now add another set of considerations to our examination of school quality – those embodying the concerns of the applied field of policy development and management.

In these matters it is important to note that there is still controversy as regards the most efficacious means by which any agreed version of quality can be achieved in school systems overall. At the school level, difficulties exist when administrators, often operating in response to political pressure and time constraints but armed with only limited understandings of the conceptual and methodological problems inherent in the school quality research, translate the findings of this research into policy and practice – in some instances adopting simplistic solutions to the complex problems of managing schools for their improvement.

Another major problem arises from traditional notions regarding the nature of the relationship between the researcher and the policy-maker and administrator. Researchers often see themselves bounded by methodological and conceptual constraints which structure and define acceptable parameters for their enquiry;

policy-makers/administrators argue that they have to take into account a wider set of considerations that relate to areas of economic and administrative efficiency and political, moral and social desirability.

In fact, as new developments in the theory and understanding of educational administration will easily demonstrate, the two are not so divided. There is a way of lessening the distance, possibly even of bridging the gap between them. This comes from an appreciation of the value considerations that structure and define their enquiries of and in their field. In educational administration – an applied policy field – research and policy formation show no dichotomy between the claims of the researcher, on the one hand, purporting to enquire into *what is*, and those of the policy-maker, on the other, deliberating about *what ought to be*. They are both, in quite a marked sense, simply working as theorists concerned to address interests that are in many respects different but in one key feature enmeshed: both are seeking to

- understand the causes of success or failure of institutions and their policies, as a necessary prelude to attenuating or eliminating dysfunctions and then establishing or ameliorating structures and procedures that will conduce to betterment.

The criteria for determining improvement and advance in their respective research programmes will require both to attend to the interplay of function and form, with respect to the purposes of the institution in which both are interested and – albeit in different ways and for different purposes – actively engaged. This area of common ground, where agreed interests are enmeshed, provides both sets of researchers with a 'criterion' and a standard against which the success or failure – the progression or degeneration of their ongoing research programmes – can be measured.

This area of engagement, that we have called 'enmeshment', is where the activities of the two coincide. Their common interests provide the area of overlap that Lakatos named the 'touchstone', against which the theories of one and the policy enterprises of the other – and indeed of all other workers in the field – may be tested. It is this that we may call the new 'science' of educational policy administration and management, and the search for school quality is but one part of the overall 'enmeshment' of all similar enquiries.

THE EVOLUTIONARY PROBLEM-SOLVING APPROACH TO RESEARCH, POLICY DEVELOPMENT AND THE ADMINISTRATION OF SCHOOLS

In undertaking this investigation into quality schooling we acknowledge that many of the problems that limit the quality of schooling arise from the fact that in any reform effort there is a multiplicity of desirable priorities. It was perhaps for this reason that, after two decades of studying change in education systems, Fullan (1991) argued that the most realistic model for implementing change (and the one which, according to the perspective adumbrated above, is also the most fecund theoretical model for understanding change) is one that enables people to achieve some balance among values and priorities, facing problems, challenges and dilemmas, consolidating, adapting and building as they go along.

Fullan's suggestion fits in well with the strategy emanating from the evolutionary approach to problem-solving proposed by the philosopher Karl Popper (1949). Popper claims that substantial problems for policy-makers arise from the nature of institutions and the processes undergone by them, not all of which are susceptible to rational investigation. There is, Popper would argue, a recalcitrant, even an irrational, element in such processes, which renders the approach adopted by scientists of the positivist persuasion liable to errors, the least of which would involve sheer simple-mindedness, while the worst would lead to large-scale misunderstanding in anyone's attempt to grasp problem situations and produce tentative solutions for them.

For these reasons Popper advocates a turning away from the millenarianism so enthusiastically espoused by some policy-makers and proposes instead an evolutionary policy construction and pragmatic problem-solving. In Popper's approach, what matters is, first, that the nearest and most readily tractable problem be identified and defined (PS: problem situation). In this process, only a very preliminary part involves the naming of parts, the defining of concepts and the clarification of terms – and this can be simply done on any agreed stipulative basis (DT: Definition of Terms). What follows next is the requirement that a tentative hypothesis be framed as to the ways in which the policy-maker proposes to attempt the solution of that problem (T1: trial solution). After this comes the crucial part – and, for Popper, the most important 'scientific' stage – of the whole process, in which criticism from all quarters is sought in an effort to contest and, if possible, overthrow the trial hypothesis (EE: the stage of error elimination). Finally (should the hypothesis resist all efforts at disconfirmation) comes the point at which the policy-maker is satisfied that the proposed hypothesis may be accorded the status of tentative solution (T2) and go forward as a highly provisional theory, always subject to the expectation that in a few months or years, this too will prove liable to correction or refutation. This approach may thus be represented in the formula: $PS > (DT) > T1 > EE > T2 >$.

An example of the utility of this method in analysing the change process may be found in the United Kingdom approach to the policy problem of a change to the process of secondary education, when it was realized that the tripartite system set up for secondary schools in the 1944 Education Act was gravely dysfunctional, not only to the endeavour to provide the right kind of education for all ranges of ability, but also to such important social goals as increasing access and ensuring equity. Starting with the Labour Party Conference in 1946, the hypothesis was framed that all-inclusive or 'comprehensive' schools would address both needs, and that a wholesale systemic change to the establishment of such schools would effect a high degree of social integration as well as providing a quality education for all. Under a Labour Government in the 1960s, therefore, the process of comprehensivization was instituted on a large scale and brought to completion in the late 1970s.

It was at that point that social scientific investigations began (perhaps the most well-known was that of Dr. Julienne Ford of the London School of Economics) that showed to what extent the original hypothesis was flawed. Ford demonstrated that certain favoured versions of a so-called comprehensive school actually reinforced barriers between social classes rather than removing them. It was only after similar criticisms with respect to academic standards and coverage of syllabus began to be shown up (by such authors as Cox, Dyson and Ford writing [the Black Papers] in the *Critical Quarterly* series in the late 1970s and early 1980s) that proponents of comprehensive education began to realize that their original thesis was in need of amendment and modification in order to ensure that the initial goals could still in some measure be attained.

This led to changes in the structure and internal organization of comprehensive schools, some of the effects of which were beneficial so far as one goal is concerned – social cohesion – but which still fell short of the other, that of heightening academic attainment and maintaining standards for the generality of the school population. It was, perhaps, in the attempt to redress this balance and to promote academic standards that the Thatcher Government in the United Kingdom introduced such measures as the Assisted Places Scheme and, later, a core curriculum and a system of national assessment.

The point of this example is to show that, in a field so complex as school quality, with its range of goals and values (academic, social, moral, emotional, economic, etc.), not only are the understandings required similarly complex, but the processes of policy formation must be highly articulated, evolutionary and always subject to review. In such policy deliberations, proposals, implementations and assessments, it is crucial to point out that (a) the process of change has no *terminus ad quem*; (b) the pace of change is slow and not uniform; (c) a problem solved in one area is liable to generate another in other areas; and (d) there will almost never be a point at which one may confidently say that the evidence is all in.

If one adopts this approach to understanding the change effort, it is clear that making one small alteration in one area will have a 'spreadsheet' effect – a very three-dimensional 'spreadsheet', it would seem – for such is the complexity of the range of problems associated with, and arising from, policy change processes and the multiplicity of levels affected, that even a small functional operation change may impact not only on the horizontal plane but also down the vertical.

It might, of course, be claimed by proponents of the rationalist model of planning that any sophisticated computer program could apply its intelligence to comprehending and representing such effects in a three-dimensional model, and it could be tempting for policy-implementers to try to develop such a model and put it into place. Such a strategy would still be inadequate, however, since what also needs to be considered is the extent to which *intangible factors, arising from human conscious and unconscious attitudes, motives, purposes and drives* will also exert powerful determinative effects on the processes of policy formation and change. Accounting for and handling these factors is, at the moment, beyond the reach of even the most sophisticated devices of artificial intelligence.

As a strategy for working one's way out of problem areas replete with complexities of this kind, we are helped by the proposal of Imre Lakatos, Popper's successor in the Chair of Logic and Methodology at the London School of Economics. He argued that there is a need, in such situations, to establish not only those kinds of knowledge, evidence or solid conjectures about which we can be *reasonably,* even if provisionally, sure and in agreement with others, but also, and much more importantly, those areas in which different approaches to the solution of a policy problem can be *reconciled.* An example of this might be the desire of the Left (as in the United Kingdom in the example cited above) for the promotion of social goals, such as those of increased equity and access, and that of the Right for an emphasis upon the pursuit of academic excellence and the maintenance of academic standards.

Lakatos would suggest that, for both parties in such a dispute over policy priorities, there is in fact, in addition to a body of 'evidence' on which we might all tentatively agree, an area of common interest – what he called the 'touchstone'. In the problem we cite above, this would perhaps reside in the realization that both goals are predicated upon the maximization of schooling for all students from all backgrounds, organized in ways that enable all to capitalize on the widest range of educational opportunity.

Lakatos further added that comparison of and competition between different perspectives and ideologies in such matters may be found both possible and productive, in that their quality may actually be tested against each other in the touchstone area. This would be done by policy-makers looking at what are commonly agreed upon in the community/country in question as desired educational outcomes – in this case, a wider range of educational successes on both grounds, done more efficiently and effectively, and likely to be achieved over a longer time-scale, with an increase in the degree of fecundity as regards other educational, institutional or systemically valuable outcomes.

IMPLICATIONS FOR THEORY DEVELOPMENT AND RESEARCH

The number and complexity of all the foregoing kinds of considerations, as well as their inchoate nature and their resistance to immediately predicable characterizations, underline the difficulty, if not indeed the impossibility, of locating and fully explicating concepts such as 'school quality' under any rationalist rubrics. For the plethora of considerations rendering such concepts amenable to articulation ensures that rationalist accounts of them are likely to be at best partial, and at worst grossly deficient in highlighting their most important aspects. We have to conclude that such 'rationalist' accounts are fraught with the dangers of dubiety and incompleteness.

This might make it seem as though we are agreeing with Reynolds' (1990) suggestion that multi-paradigmatic approaches may be the way to proceed in research addressing issues such as school quality or school effectiveness. But, as Evers and Lakomski (1991) and many others have shown, there is little to be said for the notion of knowledge as partitioned into discrete 'sets', from which different forms of illumination can be focused upon problems, topics and issues and then brought to bear upon practical application. Knowledge does not have that discrete and partitioned rationality: it is much more protean in character.

Better and more plausible is the idea to which reference has already been made: knowledge in educational policy and administration is, like any other cognitive enterprise, a complex web of belief, formed of different elements that interweave and form, in their separate parts, a coherent whole. The notion most helpful here, and one referred to approvingly by Quine, may be drawn from a metaphor employed by Otto Neurath (1932): the theory of educational policy and administration is like unto a boat crossing the sea, which, because of the continuing stresses and strains upon it, has continually to be repaired and rebuilt even as it crosses the ocean, while it is still on the move, so to speak. This repair and rebuilding must be done in a way that will, while still giving overall coherence to the whole, make for a vessel that, at the end of the enterprise of theory-building, is radically different from that 'theoretical vessel' upon which the journey began. For human beings, that 'end' comes when they die: it is part of the human cognitive condition that we are *always* rebuilding our theories. It is the end of our lives that marks the end of theory change.

What is critical to this enterprise of theory/vessel building and repairing is the need continuously to look at other plans, theories and forms of cognitive transport: to see how well they manage to convey their passengers and their intellectual impedimenta across what might be seen as a further example of Don Cupitt's (1985) as yet uncharted 'sea of faith' in any cognitive endeavour; to subject them to critical scrutiny, appraisal and comparison; and to see what elements of utility, fecundity and felicity might be drawn from them and applied to our own theoretical purposes.

This then is the nature of our enterprise. Neither empiricism, such as that associated with rationalism and positivism, neo-Marxism, with its emphasis upon dialectic and eristic models of enquiry, nor ethnomethodological subjectivism will do as a single or 'would-be' comprehensive theory to account for all the phenomena constituting the bases and interstices of our subject of the quality of schooling. What we have adopted, rather, is an 'evolutionary epistemology', one that goes, as Richard Bernstein (1983) puts it, 'beyond objectivism and relativism', enhances and facilitates discriminatory theory construction and comparison, and so makes our own theories meet for application, modification and repair at every stage of our intellectual journey.

It is this theory we propose now to apply to our consideration of the range of questions, the tentative answering of which we take to be directly pertinent to our attempt to analyse, explain and integrate the problems, topics and issues associated with our investigation into the quality of schooling.

OUR APPROACH TO THIS RESEARCH UNDERTAKING

In our research we adopted an approach based upon the above perspective. Working on data collected from interviews conducted with a broad range of stakeholders in education and the community, we attempted to:

1 identify those beliefs and values that, it appeared to us, people were least willing or likely to abandon in their talk of and thinking about quality in schools;

2 grasp the theories which were embodied in these beliefs and values;

3 identify the 'touchstone' areas in which agreement appeared to exist among groups on the criteria, characteristics and distinguishing

marks they sought in schools, to which they would then attach the label of 'good', 'effective', or 'of high quality'.

There might, for instance, be a fair measure of agreement among employers that a characteristic feature of a 'quality' school would have much to do with success in public examinations, and this is a feature that might also be valued and sought by many parents. Others, however, might equally regard it as important that quality schooling would enable children to 'realize all their potential' (whatever that means), or give all children – including the disadvantaged, underprivileged and handicapped – equal access to a challenging and empowering curriculum.

It is the identification of problems and the search for common areas of interest that have defined our research endeavours in this project. What we have been seeking is to achieve some reconciliation, so that we might be able, even-tually, to put forward tentative recommendations about how the quality of school-ing might be enhanced to the satisfaction of as many parties to that undertaking as possible.

Our attempt to identify touchstones was therefore conducted at two levels: the first was to distinguish common areas of interest and shared values and beliefs; the second, to arrive at some agreement about the ways in which current concerns relating to quality of schooling might best be tackled. We accept, for instance, that on some matters, such as government funding of private schools or coeducational arrangements for certain ethnic groups, total agreement might not be possible. In such cases, we have thought it important to seek an area of negotiation, in which an attempt can be made to secure agreement (a) that a problem exists, (b) that it can be resolved, and (c) that there is sufficient good faith between participants to generate possible resolutions, or settle on ways in which negotiations can be conducted.

THE GENERATION OF EFFECTIVE THEORIES FOR DISCUSSING AND RESOLVING ISSUES OF QUALITY SCHOOLING

There remained one final but crucial step. What we still needed was an instrument for checking, comparing and criticizing 'theories', because, as the French physicist Duhem (1914) noted, for every set of phenomena we 'observe', there are a number of possible interpretations and, to that extent, those phenomena are 'under-deter-mined' in respect of a wider set of possible conceptions and interpretations.

The question for us, therefore, is this:

> Of the many possible theoretical accounts of quality we might identify or put forward as explanations of various phenomena, or of the various proposals for dealing with the problems they contain or engender, *how may we determine which is most plausible and which is to be pre-ferred*? We need to establish what it is that makes one theory 'better' than another.

There are numerous possible answers to this question, though for our purposes they seem to amount to much the same thing. Thomas Kuhn's (1973) account of

31

paradigm shift, for example, maintains that the paradigm that succeeds and replaces another generally does so because it is able not only to deal comprehensively with all the material treated in and by the former paradigm, but also to accommodate, explain and cope with all the anomalies thrown up by the former paradigm which the former paradigm was unable to handle, so avoiding the kind of psychological crisis and/or paradigm breakdown commonly experienced by adherents of the outmoded theory.

Another response to this question can be found in Quine's account of the criterion by means of which the preferability of one theory over another may be worked out. It is a fact that the theoretical physics of 'open' Western science is able to succeed in immense enterprises, such as sending human beings to the moon and bringing them back safely, as against the astrophysical theories promulgated by followers of Aristotle and Ptolemy. More importantly, it is the advance of theory in Western medicine that is able, with reasonable confidence, to seek to develop antidotes to and cures for such potentially fatal pathological conditions as AIDS, cancer and asthma – as opposed to the more 'magical' approaches found in the continuing practices of some traditional medicines and their supporting 'theories'. As Quine remarks, 'outmoded theories show the laudable tendency, like dinosaurs, to die out'. Better theories live longer and, crucially, they enable us to predict better.

> We want to maximise prediction; that is, we want a theory that will anticipate as many theories as possible, getting none of them wrong. We develop the theory by progressive observation and correction. When we have to modify the theory to accommodate a wayward observation sentence, we have various possible corrections from which to choose, and here the guiding considerations are simplicity and conservatism. We prefer the correction that makes for the simplest theory, by our subjective standards of simplicity, unless the other alternative is more conservative, that is, a less drastic departure from the old theory. But a big simplification can warrant a fairly drastic departure. We arbitrate between these two interests, simplicity and conservatism.
>
> (Quine, 1974, p. 137)

A mark of a 'better' theory is, therefore, that it has the virtues of simplicity and economy, and accords better with those theories we already hold and have preferred as being themselves more functionally efficient. The better theory also has greater explanatory power; is able to predict better and over a longer time; gives us greater direction and control over the anomalous phenomena we face and the problems with which we have to deal; offers a wider range of insights into those problems and phenomena; and suggests further and more functionally successful ways of approaching them.

It is these kinds of measures that we might usefully employ in following Lakatos and seeking to distinguish between two kinds of research programme – one that is progressing (one 'theory') and one that is plainly degenerating (another 'theory'). A stark example of the latter might be found in the gradual realization in Eastern bloc countries that Marxist economics had outlived its functional usefulness, effectiveness and plausibility, and it was this that led to its abandonment.

Evers and Lakomski take us further by pointing to the work of William Lycan, who proposes five rules for guiding the comparison of the two theories (T1 and T2):

1 Prefer T1 to T2 if T1 is simpler than T2
2 Prefer T1 to T2 if T1 explains more than T2
3 Prefer T1 to T2 if T1 is more readily testable than T2
4 Prefer T1 to T2 if T1 leaves fewer messy unanswered questions behind (especially if T2 itself *raises* messy unanswered questions)
5 Prefer T1 to T2 if T1 squares better with what you already have reason to believe [the principle of 'conservatism' shown above].
(Lycan, 1988, p. 130, cited by Evers and Lakomski, 1991)

Put shortly, we might test the functional utility of one theory over another in terms of its relative simplicity, explanatory potential, testability, comprehensiveness, and 'fit' with existing knowledge. On this basis we can go on to extract from the adoption of one theory in preference to another the implicative practical conclusions it generates for application to a problem situation.

The notion of 'problem situation' is addressed by Popper, who puts the matter of theory preference more simply. The hypothetical solution to any problem that we favour and tentatively adopt as our preferred, though provisional, theory will be the one that has greatest functional effect. In the case of the Lysenko affair, for example, it became plain that the genetic theory operative in the 'open' scientific communities of the West was clearly more productive in the realm of agriculture than the Marxist theory put forward by Lysenko and endorsed by the Soviet Academy of Sciences. The open theory had a 'happier outcome' in that Western agriculture was able to feed more people – and, ironically, the Soviet economy eventually became dependent upon the agricultural production based upon the theory rejected by them, and in so doing was able to feed millions of its own people who might otherwise have starved.

So, functional efficiency becomes the criterion of tentative advance in science for Popper: the best epistemology is the one that, like the advances of organic entities in Darwinian theory, succeeds in adapting best to its changing environment. An evolutionary epistemology produces theories that approach nearer and nearer to 'verisimilitude': our theories grow better and better, approaching more and more to the 'truth'. But truth in this kind of science does not act as a guarantee of the warranted assertabilty of utterances; rather it functions as a regulative principle determining the direction of our enquiries. The more our 'theories' are tried, the more that they seem to 'work' – in the sense of leading to felicitous outcomes – and the longer they resist criticism and refutation, the better they are.

It is on this kind of basis that we believe we may establish a set of criteria for application in the analysis of research data, and for the examination of the validity and utility of theories and recommendations relating to the identification and modelling of 'quality schools'. It is only when the theories underpinning the use of such data and guiding the articulation of recommendations as to the

33

constitution and organization of such schools have been thoroughly tried and tested and have remained unfalsified, that we may feel satisfied in going forward to employ them, with all appropriate diffidence and reservation, as instruments in our identification, elucidation and evaluation of those characteristics, features and virtues that may properly be sought in schools that can be reasonably defined as being of 'high quality'.

Chapter 3

The Quality Debate

In general terms, it would probably be widely agreed that 'quality' in education is something that is worth looking for, to be approved of, promoted and emulated whenever and wherever it is found. This nebulous characteristic 'quality' is identified as a feature of distinctive worth, as setting a standard of excellence among objects, situations or achievements belonging in a particular class of comparison. It is supposed to provide a high point of endeavour or performance, to be lauded, commended and rivalled, and to provide a benchmark against which all other endeavours and imitation might be evaluated or assessed.

In education, 'quality' is a normative feature sought after or claimed to exist in the programmes of those institutions whose representatives wish to associate it with their concentration on particular educational concerns. They do this to demonstrate that the teaching and learning activities they propose, the type of institution they advocate, and the organizational arrangements they advance can and do satisfy external demands for and judgments about 'quality' – whatever that might be taken to mean.

Thus 'quality' is associated variously with 'efficiency', 'effectiveness', 'choice,' 'excellence', 'equity' and 'social justice', among other virtues that are designated as the aims of any system purporting to produce effective learning in 'good' schools. But what any of these terms mean, and how they are translated into operation and practice, are questions for considerable further discussion. They lead us to ask:

> What are the distinctive criteria, the typical features, the identifying characteristics that help us discern those values associated with 'quality' in our assessment of an institution and in the provision of education?

A PRELIMINARY NOTE ABOUT AGREED CORE VALUES

We might perhaps preface our attempt to answer these questions with a preliminary observation. Despite the contested nature of such terms and concepts as 'quality', it could be reasonably claimed, as a prior position, that, in much discourse between professionals and lay people about quality in educational matters, there is actually a wide measure of agreement on certain values, the presence of which helps structure and define many of the enquiries relevant to the search for quality in educational undertakings. Such 'core' values are looked for as characteristic features of the 'quality', 'good' or 'effective' schools, the identification of which is a matter of widespread popular concern, and are also seen as 'ends to be aimed at' or 'worth promoting' in the activities and undertakings of such schools.

One example of such a *core value* might be that schools should be *democratic*; another might be that they *humanize* our students, as well as giving them access and entry into those bodies and kinds of knowledge, skills and attributes that will prepare them for life in today's complex society. Yet a third might be that schools should develop in students a *sense of independence* and of their own worth as human beings, having some confidence in their ability to contribute to the society of which they are a part. A fourth example of a core value might relate to the *quality of interpersonal relationships*, so that schools may prepare our future citizens to conduct their relationships with each other in ways that are not inimical to the health and stability of society or the individuals who compose it. A fifth core value might be a concern for the *cultural enrichment of the community* in which they will ultimately play a part.

We cite these values only as examples; we do not claim the above to be a comprehensive or exhaustive list. No doubt others need to be added to it, as our analysis of data presented below reveals. But what we do claim is that there would be wide and uncontested acceptance that, whatever functions quality schooling might be said to perform, with the promotion of these values at least it is *centrally* concerned. We would also contend that the interests of all involved in the conception, framing and delivery of quality schooling are promoted by attachment to such values and by discussion of the question of how they might best be realized.

It is with a reliance upon the justified assumption of the tenure of an inner core of such agreements on value that we believe we may now proceed to tackle the thornier question of the contested values upon which people place different stress in their searches for quality in education.

This agreement about an inner core of values will provide us with the strength needed to deal with the difficulties, problems and controversies that so beset this whole field. The problems are not only those of the meta-philosophical kind to which we have already referred in Chapter 1, although those problems are substantial; they are also those involving considerable difficulties of operationalization and implementation. It is to the elucidation of some of those difficulties that we now turn.

TENSIONS AND DIFFICULTIES IN THE QUALITY DEBATE

In this chapter we point to some of the tensions and controversies arising from the ways in which members of the educational community attempt to identify and give expression and realization to quality goals of various kinds. For our part, we believe that, using the frameworks and approaches offered to us by Popper and Lakatos, particularly with respect to the Lakatosian 'touchstone' idea – the search to identify common interests and agreed procedures for addressing them – we can, through the examination of the data that have been collected during the course of this study, begin to delineate some areas of common interest and concern that will not only assist us in the development of a new theory regarding 'quality schooling', but may also suggest ways in which that theory might be given practical embodiment in institutional forms.

We might begin by noting that policy-makers, administrators and researchers are being regularly and continually asked to address the implications for schools and school systems of certain antinomies and tensions they see in the quality debate. These include:

- the tension between providing opportunities for all students to do well and encouraging a high standard of specialized knowledge and training;
- the danger that an emphasis on accountability might distort teaching and the curriculum towards an emphasis upon the readily identifiable and testable, at the expense of longer-term and more diffuse goals of education;
- the tension between respect for teacher professionalism and autonomy and the perceived need for central or national guidelines in professional areas;
- the tension between developing a more efficiently regulated system and encouraging a more school-based community/parental involvement and choice.

Addressing such tensions requires considerable discussion of the meanings of many of the terms involved in a debate of such fundamental philosophical importance. It might be thought, therefore, that at an early stage in such a discussion some attempt ought to be made to be clear about such meanings. Some people have suggested ways of doing this, among them conceptual analysis and definition.

We have already claimed, however, that any attempted definition, particularly of terms that are by their very nature contested, is an undertaking fraught with difficulties of both a conceptual and a methodological kind.

To begin with, one of the chief difficulties is that involved in stating and defining educational goals and objectives. And reference to 'goals' brings further difficulties. One is the difficulty arising from the multiplicity of goals, and in the establishment of priorities among goals. Another has to do with the means by which goals are attained. Yet another has to do with the measurement of goals, both in respect to the establishment of criteria for measurement and to the ways and means by which achievements are measured.

Thus when we approach the notion of quality education and its goals, we are immediately confronted with questions such as 'quality of what?'; 'quality for whom?' and 'the pursuit of quality in whose interests?'. This leads to a range of other questions: By what sort of criteria can the quality of a school system (or of an individual school) be assessed? What goals should be aimed for? Is too much being expected of schools? (But then, how much is too much?)

It might be thought that a simple way of clearing up confusion on these and other points is to lay down a clear definition and state a set of standards. We argue, however, that this is too simplistic and misconceived an expedient. What we need is something to get our teeth into, something that will enable us to get a direct bearing upon the problems we all have to deal with. Thus, in the remainder of this chapter, we proceed with an analysis of the data gathered during our discussions with key figures in the provision, planning and delivery of education, concerning their conceptions of 'quality' in the management of educational systems, institutions and schools. Clearly, the views of such agents will provide a solid basis for the development of a theory of quality schooling that will be reality-based, coherent and comprehensive.

DIMENSIONS OF QUALITY: EQUITY, EXCELLENCE, DEMOCRACY AND JUSTICE

Some common understandings and broad general principles that furnish operating guidelines for the assurance of quality may be discerned in the views of many in the educational community with whom we discussed these matters. Thus, as one administrator avers:

> When we talk about a quality schooling, we often have in mind *the best possible, most rounded and complete development for each child.*

This carries, as a consequence, the requirement that we be just as concerned about the optimum development of the migrant, the handicapped, the intellectually impaired, the disabled and the discriminated against as with the rest of a school's population.

It is here, however, where controversy starts as to the nature, substance and criteria of quality in education. For the above view is an example of one concern for quality in education, one that highlights *equity* and *justice* as its chief concerns.

The views of a system official are a further example of this emphasis on equity and justice:

> Teachers will always be concerned with equity because they see things that are hidden from other eyes. They will always tend to resist policies based on the assumption that *all* children are equally able to defend their own interests.

For such people, a requirement of any quality education will be that it presupposes the operation of policies of individual and distributive justice, guaranteed in the adoption of schooling measures incorporating principles of *impartiality* and *fairness*, such as 'No distinctions without relevant differences' – the *principle of distributive justice* – in the treatment of all students.

Another concern is that for *education for excellence.* Many people believe that an overriding preoccupation with and concern for equity in quality education militates against the achievement of excellence. What such educators often mean by this is that schools and school systems should strive to identify those students with a potential for high performance and devote to them the additional resources of time, energy and money that their exceptional abilities, and the ways in which these can be turned to the profit of the economy and the welfare of the community, demand. For such people, the analogy to be adopted is drawn from the factory floor. As one system administrator argues:

It is a hard fact of life that mass production makes it difficult to produce a Mercedes Benz. The increase in retention rates, for example, requires such an enormous budget that one cannot expect to provide an optimal service to everyone.

On such arguments, some *selection* and *exclusivity* are therefore inevitable.

There is, however, a contrary view, that quality lies in providing *excellence in all its forms*. On this basis, quality incorporates notions of equity and individual excellence rather than some sort of externally defined and universally operative notion of quality as supreme levels of performance or achievement. Proponents of this view argue that if one is really committed to equity then one is also committed to quality, for education, they aver, is about the optimum realization of individual potential:

> If we mean by equity that everyone gets the opportunity to develop to the fullest extent of their own capacities, then that is also quality and excellence.

It is interesting to note that, while some maintain that equity, quality and excellence are generally not seen as being in any sort of tension, others maintain that *equity* and *equality* are. Such people argue that quality and equity policies are too often interpreted to mean 'equal treatment', in the sense of 'the same provision for all.' There is a feeling among them that too much money and too many resources have been expended on minority groups generally, to the detriment of the needs and interests of a particular, and especially important, minority group – the high-flyers – whose critical importance to national purposes and planning (especially for economic advance) uniquely requires and justifies special assistance and exceptional (i.e. preferential) treatment. Some supporters of this view also share similar feelings that girls have received too much attention, and that it is not equal treatment to have special programmes for girls when there are not similar programmes for boys. For this group, in order to defend a programme for girls one has to try to argue that any changes that assist girls will also be beneficial for boys. This contention might be seen as a demonstration of the Rawlsian principle (Rawls, 1972) that any unequal redistribution of resources may be properly justified as 'fair' only insofar as it promotes the advantage of those made least well off by its operation, as well as promoting the welfare and advantage of those affected most.

It is around such issues that concerns for equity, equality and excellence appear to run counter to each other, at least prima facie. Some suggest an important qualification, however. Why, they ask, can there not be excellence of different kinds at different levels? In this way, the pursuit of excellence in all its different forms and kinds is believed to ensure equity: equality in schooling is the capacity for every child to develop the best sorts of individual capabilities through the school years.

But this pursuit not only requires commitment to certain values, it also requires excellence and equity in resource provision. Some educators maintain that not nearly enough resources have been devoted to the education of the handicapped and disadvantaged, for example, and so such students have not had an equitable chance to achieve excellence. There are still those groups in the community, such as the Aborigines and other ethnic groups, non-English-speaking background children, girls, students from lower socio-economic groups, that find it very difficult to make progress within the system, and this makes systems both inequitable and short on excellence. As one of the participants in our research claims:

> Everyone should be able and encouraged to achieve excellence at their own level and thus make it possible for schools and the community to profit from the potential contributions of all its future inhabitants.

This view, however, is not merely a function of the critical educational considerations of time, climate and resources; it is also, and centrally, an expression of underlying commitments and political/economic ideologies. These are exemplified in the difference between the political ideology of liberalism on the one hand – which, some modern commentators state, has a far more realistic view of the individual within society and society's obligation to the individual – and that of interventionism on the other, embodying strong and passionately held beliefs as to the need for large-scale state centralist social intervention in what the state claims is in the interests of the collectivity.

As far as liberalism is concerned, some argue that, in the present day, we have moved from liberalism to libertarianism. Libertarianism is still oriented towards the individual, but conceives of a different sort of individual, having a different relationship to society:

> Now the emphasis is on the robust individual who survives within society because of the strength, resilience and independence of his own character, qualities and personal achievements.

The prominence and, in some countries, pre-eminence of versions of such an ideology – called by some 'social Darwinism' – has led to the emergence of a very different milieu within which policies are framed, and in which, at national and local levels, policy-makers have to try to compete for resources on behalf of the weak, the disabled and the disadvantaged.

It has been argued that, given such ideological differences and the substantially altered tasks that schools and teachers are now increasingly being asked to face, educators are being required to get involved in the political, legal and economic issues and problems from which their work in schools has been largely protected hitherto.

Some people are now beginning to question whether schools, given their current expertise, character and modes of organization, are the best places to do some of the things that society wants schools to do. This difficulty becomes especially pointed if the quality of education is seen in economic terms. For many believe that:

> The capacity of the nation to survive and prosper economically depends, crucially, on how well the country develops all its human resources, and schools are increasingly coming to be regarded as

among the prime agencies within which this development can be brought about.

In respect of human resource development, however, and of the economic costs of large-scale 'failures' in education, some point to

> the vagaries of an examination system in which a sizeable proportion of students do not succeed, and a school system from which many students drop out or fail to secure entry into tertiary education. In such cases, the country is not only clearly wasting enormous resources but also risking alienating and failing certain groups of its citizens. In this case, such a country might also inherit huge social costs in antisocial behaviour, heavy dependence upon welfare benefits, and civil tension, division and unrest. This suggests that, even at survival level, there is a dry economic argument for promoting a concern for equity and social justice in educational provision.

At this point it becomes clear that the whole issue of *human rights* and *democratic principles* needs to come to the fore in our consideration of different and competing versions of 'quality.' Central to this debate and these ideological differences are our most cherished notions of a fair society and a strong democracy, secured by and benefiting from the contributions of all its members.

An example of such an ideological commitment would be the view put forward by those who have a particular concern for emancipation. For them:

> If a nation practises elitism and only fully educates the top 10 per cent as being the 'future leaders of the nation', the result is likely to be a very fragile and divided nation and a considerably diminished democracy.

A much better approach, in their eyes, would be to say that a nation is stretching and demanding and expecting the best of all its people. In this way, they conclude, we shall have a society of equity and equality: a resilient, dynamic society where as far as possible everyone is taught to advance as far as they can and to achieve the best they can. The better educated all members of the general mass are, the more widespread and the higher the level of general achievement will be. The way forward, according to such theorists, is to plan for some overall pedagogical reform in the direction of a common curriculum, planned to enhance choice for everyone and enshrining the *principle of inclusivity.*

It is, of course, always possible for such theorists to argue that, as community institutions, schools should be equivalent educationally but able to develop their own special character, perhaps with special subject emphasis. This links well with what Caldwell (1990) has pointed to as the four themes of quality schooling – efficiency, equity, choice and variety – and these will be emphasized in different ways in the particular characters schools adopt or acquire, the subject orientations they have, and the interests of the populations upon whom they draw.

In all such institutions the educational challenge is to do the very best possible for every child. However, if we say that we aspire to provide the best quality of service that we can, within the resources that are available, then the provision of a quality education service predicated upon equity comes down very quickly to questions of priority in the operationalization of the aim. Thus *quality education targeting equity comes back to the priority-setting process, the questions it raises and the values it embodies.* The value placed upon such a goal as equity will remain rhetoric unless we are able to put into place a set of plans for actions that are achievable within a reasonable period of time and a set of limited resources.

QUALITY OF WHAT? THE ENHANCEMENT OF THE INDIVIDUAL AND THE BENEFIT OF THE COMMUNITY

Overwhelmingly, the data upon which this analysis is based reveal that quality in education is seen by many to reside in the quality of the learning experiences and the extent to which teaching–learning activities issue in the outcomes exhibited and successes attained by the students.

These successes are varied. As far as the student outcomes are concerned, many hold that the answer to the question of quality does not necessarily involve a movement away from a holistic type of education to something more narrowly academic or sharply focused upon economic matters only. What is of at least equal, if not greater, importance is the concern for promoting good relations between oneself and others. The central question for such people is: How does a school develop persons who will be sensitive, intimate and humane, in addition to having specific academic skills and knowledge?

The need for an approach to the question of quality based on the concerns of the individual is underlined by a senior administrator of the Catholic system:

> If we ask what is the quality of education, from the perspective of the learner, then we should ask such questions as relate to the understanding of the inner processes of learning: how do people find motivation, what happens when a student finds motivation, what happens when a student is trying to find some direction for their learning, what happens when they are trying to find meaning?

This is the view of those who elevate the *self-reflective* and *self-initiating* powers given by schooling as the hallmark of quality education.

For others, the achievement of quality education for students is also held to consist in the learning and mastery of competences, bodies of content, attitudes and values that will enable them to make an independent and self-sufficient contribution to the enhancement of the community as and when they become fully participant members of it. For these people, quality education empowers students to act autonomously, to make of themselves what they want in the best possible way, in the interests of their own individual pursuits and of society's needs. This requires them to acquire the abilities and the skills so to conduct themselves in society as to enable them to participate in it as autonomous people acting in appropriate social, political and moral ways.

This view sees a quality education as an *enrichment of capacities* for a life of individual quality *and capabilities* to exercise skills that will contribute to the social whole. But such contributions do not necessarily require more than the mastery of certain skills or competences; it says nothing about cognitive content. Moreover, it is quite unclear as to which capacities are supposed to conduce to what sort of quality; clearly the capacity for communication and controlled movement is an indispensable pre-condition for all developments leading to a good life and for effective community action. But of what other 'capacities' are we to speak, in terms that are not trivial, when showing how their fostering and realization will bring about 'quality' in life and benefit for society?

One senior administrator puts these points in a discussion of the different demands of education for individual excellence and education for social utility, employing the 'excellent product' analogy, and stressing the choice between two kinds and classes of product:

> A lot of people have almost an automotive [*sic*] syndrome for quality: a Jaguar represents quality while a VW represents utility. *Relevance* and *appropriateness* can be dimensions of quality as well. One of the things that has driven [our] considerations over the last decade is in fact [the aim of] an education relevant for students and the circumstances in which they find themselves and will find themselves. Is it appropriate? [Emphasis added].

For their part, very many parents believe that one of the chief marks of quality in a school is provided by success in achieving examination results, conferring qualifications that will guarantee some sort of employability. But even though many agree on the importance of good examination results, they also agree that this criterion is not the only feature that characterizes quality schooling. They are sometimes worried by what they see as an increasing emphasis on the very easily measurable outcomes of education: examination results, tertiary entrance, basic literacy tests, and the like. When many parents are asked what they want from school for their children, they remark, 'I want them to be happy there'.

What many parents want, then, is not only success at school (judged in terms of examination success) but a growing experience in a caring atmosphere, leading to the ability to get on with other people. They also look for growth in non-tangible qualities that, they are clear, are immensely important, though very difficult to measure, such as respect for other people, concern and consideration for others' interests, tolerance, sensitivity, an ability to put oneself in others' shoes, warmth and approachability – in short, all the humane qualities called for in the interwoven interactions and relationships of individuals in the various networks of obligation, responsibility and interpersonal engagement involved in relating to other people in the community.

A clear-sighted view of the range of the whole spectrum separating but also conjoining education for individuals and education for community enmeshment, education for personal autonomy and education for social contribution, is put by those who are concerned for the growth of young people into, and their gradual involvement in, communities within the community. Here the key notion relates to the ideal of 'life-long learning' particularly, though not exclusively, exemplified by the person who moves out of school into tertiary studies or other forms of study. This is a form of learning that stresses ways in which people come especially to value, within and during the overall span of their lives, the various elements that arise from educational and physical activity – the enjoyment of artistic and expressive experience, in addition to the acquisition of knowledge and its employment.

Such growth and gradual enmeshment lead on to the notion that the quality of education and experience ends up as contributing to good, both for enhancement of the life of the individual person over his or her lifetime, and for the benefit of the community. A well-educated community is a pleasant place to live in, and a place where people can make intelligent judgments about the running of institutions in their society. In this way, quality is related to what the school is trying to do for the students and for the community, both locally and in a larger society.

TOWARDS A THEORY OF QUALITY SCHOOLING: THE NATURE OF GOALS

From this examination of the data, it is apparent that different goals relating to quality can be clearly delineated and differentiated, thereby laying the basis for a common set of agreements upon which we can develop our theory of quality schooling to cover all these obligations and enmeshments:

- One set of goals sees the school as a centre for *communicating civilization*. A quality education seen from this perspective would include a school's concern to communicate to students knowledge of and love for a wide range of cultural practices and achievements, including the worlds of aesthetic values, the arts, literature, music, drama and creativity.
- A second set of quality goals involves *meeting the immediate personal needs of the students*, so that all students are enabled to become everything they want, to have sources of activity and pleasure that will enable them to reach acceptable levels of personal satisfaction in their lives.
- Finally, the quality goals for a community ensure that *students are responsive to the needs of society* and try to play a part in answering those needs in various forms of social, economic, communal and cultural action.

These three goals are interrelated. For a community, a quality education is one that will succeed in communicating civilization, in ensuring that all students are equipped to gain all that they can from life, and that they are also contributing through their education to meeting the needs of society at large; it is through the enrichment of the individual that the whole community is enriched.

The individual's responsibility to society, however, must be seen in the broadest of terms. It is for this reason that the domination of particular interest groups is something to be avoided and, if encountered, to be argued against and diminished. Although the interests of the individual have to be placed in a social context, an apprehension exists about the control and direction of those processes and ends that some special sections of society contend are in the society's interests. Powerful pressure to accept such a sectional view comes from the perceived insistence of business, for example, many agents of which have considerable expectations that education should be primarily concerned with producing and furnishing the kinds of people that industry wants and needs in order to bring about economic advance.

In addition to the need to resist the ascendancy of such a view, or at least to set it in the wider social context and work with it, emphasis must be placed on *the development of the individual as a critical and responsible member of the body politic*. As a senior administrator highlights:

> The great deal of concern exists as a result of the [state] inquiry into corruption; a concern about the degree of malaise that has been found within politics and institutions, of organization and government. All of this is a fundamental criticism of the quality of education that has gone on in the past; that it has not necessarily created people with integrity to stand against the problems that have emerged or even the perception to understand the problems. So the quality of the body politic, the quality of the nation, are of concern.

Thus quality schooling is not so much about being equipped to operate as a successfully qualified functionary in society, having the capacity to respond to economic norms and to perform competently in various modes of economic production. It is much more about the capacity of the individual to enhance and enrich the society of which he or she is being educated to become a part – someone who is going to be a giver, an enlarger and an enhancer, as well as an inheritor and recipient. Quality schooling is as much about the future of the society we see for ourselves, even if at several generations hence removed: a world better and richer than the one we currently inhabit.

REFUTING THE NOTION OF INDIVIDUAL POTENTIAL

At this point, however, we must point to a disturbing aspect of the data examined in this enquiry. Clearly there is some differentiation between quality of outcomes, as indicated by the mastery of some skills and the power to engage in certain sorts of intellectual activities, and the quality of life in respect of other, intangible virtues, although both are widely seen as crucial quotients of quality in schooling for students.

It is with respect to this second notion of quality that the idea of an individual 'reaching or realizing his or her potential' seems to have emerged and assumed an enormous importance in the educational community. This leads to statements such as 'A quality education is whatever can be done to improve the chance of a person, male or female, to reach his or her potential.' However, the contentious nature of references to 'potential' must be noted. The notion of 'realizing potential' is seen by some to be rather unhelpful in talking realistically about quality as an outcome of education:

> It is possible to talk in general terms about those programmes likely to develop the potential of all students to the utmost, but a student's

potential could be anywhere between Charles Manson and Arnold Schwarzenegger.

More can be said on this matter. Indeed it must be. It is a matter of considerable puzzlement to us that talk of 'potential' has assumed such a place in educational discourse that the idea that education is about people being helped to 'realize their potential' has been accorded the status of a self-evident and unquestionable truth – one that we see as a patent truism or a myth.

It is a truism in the sense that all human beings have 'potential' in the Aristotelian sense of an organism's growth from potency to actuality. An acorn has in it the seeds of the oak. 'Large oaks from little acorns grow' – and acorns have in them the attributes that will eventually be realized in the maturing of the fully grown oak tree, with its branches, leaves and other differentiae. So it is with human beings: the fertilized ovum in the womb already has the potential for controlled and highly sophisticated movement, speech, conceptual thinking and affection, and this is true for all examples of the species *Homo sapiens*.

What differentiates one oak tree from another, and one human being from another, is the ways in which and the extent to which the various potencies inherent in them develop and mature. Oaks will have more or fewer leaves and branches, larger trunks, higher tops; human beings will have different-coloured eyes, hair, length of leg, heart-beat rates, breathing capacity, and so on. But – and here is where our refutation of the myth starts – they will also have different capacities for language, reasoning and affection. The potency for all of these is shared by human beings, but the development of these distinguishing character-istics of human-being status will be different. Some of those differences will be genetic in their aetiology, some the result of environmental influences and experiences, but in none of them will it be the case that the potential for develop-ment in those key areas of human identity is irretrievably fixed. To think that it is would be to fall into what we call the 'the jug fallacy'.

According to the view enshrined in this fallacy, the contents of an individual's mind and growth potential are like those of a vessel. The myth is that some people are born with bigger, some with smaller 'potentials'; some with jugs made out of clay, some out of china, and some out of bronze. Plato's myth of the three classes of people – Gold, Silver and Bronze – in his dialogue *The Republic* is an exemplification of this fallacy applied to education. Another example is the theor-ies of intelligence propounded by Sir Cyril Burt, upon which the 1944 Education Act in the UK instituted a tripartite system of public schooling. According to the myth, once enough 'education' has been given to people to enable them to achieve the full complement of learning, training, maturation or growth, to the levels that their vessels will permit, they have then 'reached their full potential', and all future efforts at educating will be redundant, wasteful and indeed counter-productive. They could not reach beyond the final actualization of their potentials if they tried. Their natures would prevent it.

It is plain that this myth may be rejected as a figment of metaphysical imagination. We do not need to engage in a search for Burt's mythical 56 pairs of identical twins to associate ourselves with the famous, if apocryphal, rebuttal reportedly made by Günther Zuntz: 'Intelligence is a metaphysical notion.' To say that educability is limited is as easy to say as that it is not. On the contrary, there is quite as much evidence, as Bruner (1966) would claim, that an individual's powers of learning are almost infinitely elastic, and their progress depends as much on factors such as motivation, quality of teaching, frequency of engagement, amount of repetition, the support and richness of domestic background, and so on, as on those of genetics.

And we might assert all this in rebuttal of the myth, without needing to take the additional step of remarking, as scholars such as Labov (1972) would, that 'intelligence' is in any case a highly culture-specific notion. We need not remind ourselves that, even if we accept the notion of 'intelligence', the Harvard Growth Study of many years ago demonstrated that an individual's measured intelligence score could vary over the years by as much as twenty points.

'Potential,' therefore, we take to belong to the same class of concept as 'giftedness': the idea that individuals are like vessels that can be filled only to certain limits is quite as inane as the contention that certain individuals have been in some way or other, and by some higher power or other, 'marked out' by the bestowal of special powers of performance, achievement or excellence on them. Both notions run counter to the hypothesis of the almost infinite powers of educability that environmentalists would want to assert. There are problems with that thesis, too, of course. but environmentalism has much more that is plausible to say about an individual's capacity for growth and development than the Platonic myth has to say about potential. Our conclusion is that the latter should be given up and decently laid to rest, for the purpose of intelligibility and plausibility in discussions seeking to appraise 'quality' in education.

The major point in this argument is that, like 'education', 'potential' or 'intelligence', 'quality' is not an absolute: 'It is there for every student and different for each one.' The critical point is to underline the need for quality considerations to encompass not merely the academic and economic but also the moral, cultural and aesthetic concerns and values that students and society pursue, and to do so on the assumption that quality can be strengthened in learning to the same extent that it can be enhanced and pursued in life – to the end. The same goes for the protraction of excellence in those aspects of personal growth and development that some choose to call 'the realization of potential'.

FURTHER CHALLENGES IN THEORY DEVELOPMENT

The analysis of our data suggests that, in our attempt to develop a theory of 'quality schooling', there are further problems to be tackled: the ability to identify the major goals that we are setting at the school level; having good reasons for these goals; deciding which achievements at system and school level can be approximated most easily to the goals; establishing how a system or school can best use the resources available to it and attract further resources if that is at all possible; and looking to increasing the efficiency and effectiveness of the procedures and activities aimed at achieving those goals.

Therein lies the next challenge in our desire to develop and articulate a theory of quality schooling and, in so doing, assist in the attainment of quality in education. Quality resides as much as anything else in the consonance between

47

the plans, goals and objectives within a school setting, and the goals, objectives and processes put in place to achieve them at a systemic level. It is to the search for this consonance, particularly as it finds expression in curriculum, teaching and learning, that we turn in the next chapter.

Chapter 4

The Search for Quality: Curriculum, Teaching and Learning

In this chapter we continue our analysis of data assembled during the study. Here we are concerned to describe and analyse the views of the principal actors and representatives of the various constituencies involved in the present debate about quality in education. We do so by reflecting on that range of matters in which they felt that quality issues were embedded or made manifest, through *curriculum*, *teaching* and *learning*. For it is primarily on these areas of school activity that many of those concerned with the search for quality in schooling believe that attention should be most sharply focused. What should children learn; how should they be taught; what form of learning is best; how might students' knowledge and understanding best be acquired; over what range of knowledge, skills and values should the impacts and outcomes of schooling extend? The answers to these questions seem to go to the heart of modern concerns about quality schooling.

FINDING A DIRECTION

Perhaps a good point to begin our discussion on these matters would be the observation of one director-general: 'Some of the best things being done in individual schools and classrooms are based on hunches rather than a highly developed or clearly articulated educational theory.' We take this comment as a starting point in our discussion, since it seems to us to illustrate a widely held attitude among many important actors in education: namely, that there is a *gap* between theory and really effective practice, and that teachers in classrooms simply 'know better' when it comes to questions of effective pedagogy. Others who are not directly involved in teaching in schools as the principal forum for the delivery of education are often perceived as indulging in fanciful and self-indulgent 'theorizing' – a word that almost always carries pejorative connotations.

These connotations relate to an activity – educational 'theorizing' – that is regarded by some teachers and many politicians as only barely relevant to the real work of classrooms, and liable to grave suspicion on the grounds of the supposed ideological or doctrinal biases and intentions for which such activity is supposed to be a cover.

We take the previous comment on 'hunches', however, not necessarily to contain a denigration of theory, for work with hunches generally presupposes that the operator does work with some theoretical commitments. These might, of course, be operating at the tacit level, functioning as the presumed theoretical under-girding of the practical endeavour. Thus, if people produce a spectacularly successful golf swing, they do not simply produce it by instinct. So it is that the successful teacher of reading in a primary classroom has some fairly solid theoretical bases for her activity in knowing what counts as good reading, and a willingness to experiment with methods as to how to bring it about. The same is true of the surgeon at the operating table, the barrister pleading in court, or the engineer building a bridge. All operate with a high level of theory–practice integration.

It is important at this point to confirm that in this work we are not operating with the supposed theory–practice dichotomy that we believe has so bedevilled talk about quality schooling these many years now. We consider it not only odd, but educationally disastrous, that very many people in education, and certainly many in the broader community, seem to have the view that educators can be divided into two classes – one of them theorists and another practitioners. Of these, the former have traditionally borne the brunt of a fair degree of public odium, even opprobrium: 'If we could only get rid of "theories" of education, everything in the classroom would be all right' is a refrain of many politicians, businessmen and the educational Mrs Grundys.

It has certainly been strongly argued in a number of countries in recent years – in the UK, for instance – that one of the motivating forces behind the move to take teacher education out of the universities and other tertiary institutions and relocate it in the school has been the determination to diminish the influence of so-called educational 'theorists' – particularly those coming from the direction of the social sciences – who were regarded by some leading politicians of the Right as so pernicious. And in this belief such politicians were often, and surprisingly, supported by many members of the teaching profession itself.

We note with regret that many in positions of influence, who have the power to shape and redirect education and teacher professional renewal, hold such a Neanderthal view of the bifurcation of theory and practice (what Aristotle rendered by the one word *praxis*) in professional matters. It is odd that such people do not make similar distinctions in the case of successful surgeons, barristers and engineers – all of whom must by definition be operating with a clear grasp of what it is that they are about, what counts as good progress within their professional activities, when that activity might be said to have concluded, and with what kind of good or bad result – and to whose ministrations members of the lay community would not remotely contemplate offering their abdomens for incision, legal cases for handling, or persons for safe carriage unless they had complete confidence in their professional knowledge, competence and experience.

Such competence includes an amalgam of theory and practice: such experts' professional actions are an intelligent operation in which critical reflection is necessarily embodied. Aristotle called this particular quality *phronesis* – practical wisdom – that is, wisdom instantiated in the very act of achieving valued ends. That concept of practical wisdom – the work engaged in by what Schon (1987) and others have called 'the successful self-reflective practitioner – we seek to identify and characterize in our appraisal of the evidence we have assembled in this research. In our quest to develop a coherent theory and find direction in quality schooling, it is this feature of *practical wisdom* that we shall employ as our guide – and our goal.

Of course other directions for quality schooling have been identified. For some politicians and policy-makers, the direction lies in the provision of centrally determined quality control. Within the educational community of Australia, however, there are considerable reservations about this approach. Many fear that a national curriculum assessed by a national system of testing may result in success-ful teaching strategies and approaches, based upon extensive professional knowl-edge and experience, being subordinated to the overt demands of external imposition. It is for this reason that one senior administrator speaks apprehen-sively about 'the possibility of teaching to tests'. This view embodies the wide-spread belief that good teaching of a subject may well suffer by being subjected to excessive external teaching and assessment ordinances, which will then distort and redirect individual classroom teaching towards producing only the results that figure in the pantheon of particular national or state Ministers of Education. The problem is that these can change – sometimes remarkably rapidly, in response to economic, social and political pressures or, more simply, to alterations in political standing and popularity. As Harold Wilson remarked: 'A week is a long time in politics'. Three years for a government's educational agenda must therefore seem to some politicians like a lifetime.

Fear of external imposition links in with another cause for concern among professional educators. Many of them are worried about the general perception of the work of schools held in the broader community, and the impact that these views might have on fundamental issues of direction, professional knowledge and accountability. A high school principal with experience throughout Australia expressed this anxiety in this warning: 'The community perception of schools is that they are out of touch, when in fact it is more the case of the community being out of touch.'

Notwithstanding the understandable sensitivity of the educational community on these matters, however, there is nowadays an increasingly widening and, many would say, totally justified interest expressed by the broader community in the nature and purpose of schooling. The debate in the community over the goals of schooling and the need for schools to be in some way accountable to the demands and expectations of that community has boosted the ever-present requirement for schools and systems, funded out of public resources, to justify and defend what they are doing, especially in the light of the powerful external influences to which they are increasingly subject.

It has been pointed out by those involved in this study that, in responding to these pressures, those speaking on behalf of educators and the educational pro-fession have to exercise caution to avoid accusations of 'resisting accountability and protecting the continuing presence and inertia-exerting force of mediocrity in schools and the educational system'.

In the endeavours of professional educators to find a direction for quality schooling, we have seen that it is incumbent on them fully and properly to inform outside interest groups about all those aspects of their work in which the wider community might have a legitimate interest. In this way such groups might see more clearly and precisely, and receive the appropriate informed comment on, what schools are doing in the name of quality. That will obviate the likelihood of the 'lay' community relying on their untutored perceptions or (sometimes heavily) 'interested' apprehensions of what is happening now, or on their selective mem-ories of what used to happen, in their own school experience, in the past.

SETTING ABOUT ESTABLISHING GOALS

Many school-based educators who have been associated with this research activity appear to be clear in their goals: they do not want streaming and highly competitive learning, but desire all their students to feel in some way or other challenged, involved, and to have a sense of success. The majority of teachers do not believe in 'singling out students for special commendation on grounds of some excellence and thereby showing others up'. A commitment to this kind of democratic spirit and egalitarian endeavour, which is a marked feature of Australian education, promotes the notion of schools as places where there is co-operative decision-making in all aspects of schooling, including the setting of goals. Schools are, in this sense and to this extent, places where the democratic enterprise can begin. We shall have more to say about this in Chapter 7.

While this is all very well for those in schools, increasingly, however, the broader community is insisting that *its* needs and concerns are of equal importance and must be addressed: it wishes to pose and have answered the question of what it wants the school to do within the community, and what purposes, generally, educational agencies and systems should serve.

In particular, representatives of the business and industrial communities want to be assured that their potential workers, whom they want to see as active participants in the joint endeavour of securing their own undertakings and contributing more widely to securing their country's economic future, will come to them possessed of those skills and competences that will enable firms to assure their customers of quality goods, products and services. Politicians echo this demand, at the same time wanting their nation's schools to produce citizens who will be able to play an informed and responsible part in the country's political processes.

What is critical is the integration of all these various elements into policies and programmes for schooling, in the shaping and agreement of which all parts of the educational and lay communities can feel they have had a share, and over which they now possess some measure of ownership and justified control.

Within much of the education profession, teachers are beginning to hold the view that it is now pressingly incumbent upon educators to assume a leading role in this debate, and in the exercise of delivering education in accordance with these demands and expectations. If educators do not take this responsibility as a matter of their professional right, then, in the eyes of many, much of the education debate, and the power of autonomous action and judgement with it, will have been taken out of the hands of the profession. One educator put this succinctly: 'Principals, teachers and education professionals need to stand up and debate some of the education issues rather than just accept what passes for "lay" wisdom.'

In the attempt to achieve a measure of integration in this undertaking, perhaps we might look to one guiding principle: schools and teachers need to look at the goals the school sets for itself and attempt to ascertain whether they fit in with the expectations that the school community has of them – that is, those expectations that the school community believes are conceivable and practicable. In this endeavour, one foundation, one basic principle, on which many of the undertakings of the school are based, needs perhaps to be restated: the school exists primarily to promote knowledge, learning, understanding, and it is these cognitive increments in a person's development that lead to growth in all its various aspects.

It has been pointed out that this principle appears often to have been lost sight of in some schools, where the emphasis on co-operative endeavour has resulted in a tendency for goals expressed in terms such as 'the mutual learning experience of children and teachers' to emerge. One principal of a primary school comments caustically upon the conceptual appropriateness and validity of this approach:

> Now, while at one level I accept that one goal of a dynamic teaching process is that you are learning all the time, I'm not paid by the state to be taught by the children. We as teachers are expected to have expertise to teach their children or to facilitate their learning. It has been suggested that we come to learn and play together. I don't. I come to work.

It is this kind of statement from a principal that makes one appreciate how much is at stake when the system delegates the setting of goals to the local level. Schools in devolved systems are given (and expected by the community to have) greater responsibility to set their own goals, to make sure that they meet the needs of their own students in their own community. Even in a devolved system, however, schools must function within a framework of agreed policies and guide-lines – and this enmeshes them within a whole network of demands emanating from the wider community to be responsive to their needs and interests, and then be accountable to them for the discharge of those responsibilities.

The reality that schools are not operating in a completely autonomous manner, in a completely independent environment and a completely self-chosen context, has a direct bearing, not only on the question of the setting of goals that will take in a system's demands and a community's requirements and aspirations, but also on that of the justification and employment of appropriate methods and approaches to enable those goals to be achieved and the school's educational/community missions and responsibilities to be delivered.

One of the ways in which schools may seek to accomplish this integration, and secure that kind of enmeshment between themselves and all their proper stake-holders, is to involve representatives of the local community in the goal-setting and mission-writing process. To achieve closure in these matters, however, requires time, energy, resources and, above all, a commitment to consensus. Moreover, it is important to point out that, although the commitment to agreed closures is fine from the democratic point of view, it does have its administrative and implementational problems. Such problems are shown up graphically by a teacher describing the participative decision-making process in a government school:

> The protracted nature of the process has stemmed from a commitment to consensus, I guess. We'd get to the point where we'd say in the writing group, 'Can you live with it?' After another glass of wine some-one might say, 'Frank's not happy', so we couldn't go on until everyone was happy with it, until we took the core of what was bothering

someone and dealt with it. The positions were rarely directly contradictory and could generally be worked around to be acceptable to both sides. Had there been a less homogeneous school community there might have been irreconcilable differences. Certainly, the parent response to the survey raised a number of points that were accommodated by us sufficiently to stop further reaction at the final meeting where someone might otherwise have jumped up and said, 'There's still too much soft option, we've got to compete with Japan', which is the sort of stuff people are concerned about and want to discuss. We could say that there's nothing in the policy to prevent that emphasis . . . Because of the tensions in past years people have learnt things. A lot of things were hard won and people were very committed to them and there's a strong feeling about it. A lot of things were resolved where other schools might tinker around and never resolve them. There were enough processes to accommodate different views and sufficient talent in the writing group to translate those concerns into a written statement. The final statement has a harder edge about learning and about educational expertise.

What is daunting about this is to consider how long that 'democratic process' might have taken, and how protracted the attempt to arrive at agreed goals might have been in a school where there was not such identity of aspirations or sense of common purpose. Clearly, in this instance, the outcome justified the expenditure of the time, energy and resources involved, for it gave a community a set of criteria on which to base their judgements as to whether or not 'their' school was succeeding in meeting 'their' expectations.

ADDRESSING THE MULTIPLICITY OF GOALS AND EXPECTATIONS

Clearly, part of the drive to develop and deliver mechanisms for quality learning and quality outcomes originates from within the broader community, which believes it has some justification for having a variety of expectations of schools. As a teacher's union official argues, however, community expectations of schooling are becoming extremely diverse:

The world is becoming a more difficult, frightening place with the pace of change. Schooling is the only institution which has a role in shaping society that can be pointed to and identified. People in their anxiety and fear of what is happening around them tend to impose on schools the requirement to solve problems. They even blame schools for creating such problems – though any logical analysis would quickly show that such could not be the case.

In face of such wide-ranging and heterogeneous community expectations, it might not be thought unreasonable to query whether too much these days is being expected of schools.

The danger implicitly contained in or hiding behind such views as are expressed above is that schools may often become diverted from their chief *educational* task – among them, that of inducting students into *knowledge* – when they are seeking to address the demands posed by a wide and varied range of expectations. As one administrator argues, when pointing out the danger of schools becoming overly concerned with addressing and responding to external pressures: 'We can lead ourselves off the track if we are too concerned with meeting all the expectations placed upon us.'

The point that emerges strongly in our research is the widely held belief that in the present day too much is *indeed* being expected of schools. This becomes clear from a rehearsal of only some of the demands being imposed on schools at the present time:

> Drug education, sex education, road safety education – they seem to become broader all the time and there is this attitude that something must be done at school; you have to catch them at school. Sadly there are many areas that in some ways encompass the whole of life. They relate to matters that should be the responsibility of the parent. But because of changes in our social structure these needs are not being met. [Instead] schools are standing on their heads trying to work out what to put in and where.

Many of the problems arise from the expectation that schools will serve to provide role model, moral, disciplinary and other functions that, it might be argued, more properly belong to the family and/or to other social and community welfare agencies. In addition to this, schools know only too well that business, commerce and industry have additional expectations and demands: 'Every time reference is made to the need for a new skill or a new development, schools are expected to pick up the burden of helping a community's young to acquire it.' From this, some might conclude that there is a need to limit the breadth and diverse range of aims and expectations to which a school is required by its community to conform.

This is a point made by one director-general, who wants to get back to limiting what schooling can do and do well. He argues that for too long education and schools have been expected just to respond to all the changes in society, expand and do everything that people require of it. But he points out that concern for approaches to such large-scale problems as AIDS and road safety, although serious problems, are community problems calling for community solutions, and not solely the preserve or responsibility of schools. For this reason, he believes that there is a need for schools and the education system to 'get back to defining what it is going to do and do it well'. We shall consider whether or not this is feasible or conceptually appropriate in the latter part of this chapter.

ACKNOWLEDGING THE TENSIONS AMONG GOALS AND EXPECTATIONS

At the same time as schools are expected to take on more and more of the community cares and concerns, however, their centrally granted finances and other resources are being continually trimmed. On the one hand, students are now expected and indeed encouraged to stay longer at school, yet, on the other, the provision of public resources to enable that to occur is more and more restricted. This highlights the whole issue of commonwealth and state government resource restriction, as against the legitimate economic, social and cultural aspirations of the community and the expectations of schools arising therefrom. Such conflicting expectations – and the tensions they generate – often come about as a result of wider movements on the political–economic front. The community's expectations are changing, and often in line with, sometimes as a direct result of, the restructuring of industry, business and commerce.

As the community's view of what it wants for its young is changing, this brings about corresponding changes in important centres such as a Ministry of Education. There, the system officials have to respond in a flexible manner to the new political climate. As one official commented:

> Such concerns express themselves in a greater pressure to meet the new requirements of skills and competencies in the work-place – the need to spell, to comprehend, to write a letter, to take a message and to communicate clearly and intelligently – all the pressure for the increase of literacy for living.

Often the community outside schools finds what it sees as the defensiveness of education professionals in the face of these demands and their desire to 'educate' their students in what *they* regard as a less narrowly conceived range of subjects and skills, as a cause for real concern. This too is a source of tension.

For their part, teachers often feel threatened by community pressures. One principal noted: 'They [teachers] feel they are not held in high esteem, and that they are targets for continual public criticism, in the face of which they adopt a "siege" mentality.' Most teachers acknowledge that, in today's harsh economic climate, people have become apprehensive about what is happening to and around them, and so tend to visit on schools their anxieties about their children's future and the demand that teachers and educationalists should take the lead in solving their problems. Teachers, too, are aware that people outside education may even blame schools for allegedly creating the problems, though in their eyes such scapegoating as they are constantly exposed to is quite illogical:

> The blame should be laid upon a far wider nexus of causes, conditions and phenomena than merely the education service. The causes often have to do with large-scale and worldwide economic movements and changes that are quite beyond the scope or power of any education system to foresee, much less respond to individually or bring under control.

Teachers point to the kinds of criticisms that tend to be made of members of the eduction profession, some of them quite at variance with each other, yet often coming from the mouth of the same person:

> Some critics make statements such as 'Teachers are not as dedicated as they used to be', or 'Kids are not as well taught as they used to be'. Yet such critics often qualify such generalizations with other

apparently contradictory comments: 'But my child's teachers are all right!'

In this respect there seems to be a widespread and commonly held dichotomy in public perceptions of teachers as individuals and teachers *en masse* – itself a cause of tension and conflict.

From a parent's point of view, a difficulty arises from the pressures that they in their turn feel coming from the importance attached to employment in today's society. The labour market today seems shorter on opportunities for those young people who do not handle well the academic activities that allow them entry to colleges or universities, and success which will equip them with the extra edge that parents believe their children need in the search for employment. Perhaps it is their subjection to such feelings of pressure that engenders in many parents the desire to compare the progress of their child with that of others. Teachers report that the usual question parents ask in such cases is 'How are all the other children going?' or 'How many are there at that level – and above it?'.

Another source of tension comes about in the area of employer expectations. In addition to looking for potential employees possessing an appropriate range of skills and competencies, employers seek and value people capable of accepting and exercising responsibility, working as a member of a team, and being able to communicate clearly and easily. As noted by a member of a Chamber of Commerce:

> Employers want students to emerge with a basic education comprising at least a range of basic skills and competencies, but with the ability to think and analyse so as to be adaptable to change, and trainable as far as the employers' industrial and commercial needs are concerned.

School-based educators respond differently to the pressures being exerted on them by such expectations. If they believe that such forces require of them outcomes that will benefit children, then, it is generally believed, they will respond positively. School-based educators tend to respond negatively if they perceive that the external forces are trying to influence what they are doing in a very marked way, and in pursuit of goals which they do not believe are in the best interests of the school, the students or of education more broadly conceived. Such a pressure is felt to be exerted by an externally imposed system of examinations, for example, one to which schools have somehow to try to adjust and accommodate their larger educational and social agenda. These larger agenda are often concerned with such matters as promoting social justice through increasing participation and access rates for students who were previously disadvantaged. Such goals are often seen as inimical or not susceptible to current forms of external evaluation or supposed public accountability.

At the same time, however, some members of the community point to modern approaches towards school-leaving examinations as embodying shifts on the part of some schools or teachers towards goals of trying to accommodate the needs and interests of non-tertiary-bound and/or low-performing students. Such orientations are often believed to have come about at the expense of preserving intellectual standards and academic rigour. This antinomy has been an enormous source of tension between schools and the outside community, not least between examination boards and some tertiary education institutions.

At the school level, it is the school principals who have to try to moderate and manage such tensions between the internal and external environment. Increasingly, principals are recognizing the need to make some forceful points against pressures exerted on their schools by the outside community. One principal put it this way:

> Schools may need to point out that, on many issues, parts of the community are out of touch with things that have been coming to the fore, with respect to curriculum developments, social justice initiatives, and theoretically sound models of assessment, that have been happening internationally over recent years.

Such phenomena suggest that educational leaders nationally have to take on a greater role in dealing with, answering and rebutting public criticism from the media, from some employer groups, and from generally uninformed comments or judgments made by or emanating from those outsider groups who have access to those public forums which ensure that their views get a hearing, while those of the schools and school systems do not.

This will then enable educational leaders to point to those areas of real tension that arise from the key questions concerning the nature and purposes of schooling. Among these would certainly figure the short-term goals for schools that some politicians and employers want to see put into place, the most common and obvious ones being those directed towards improving productivity as the saviour of the economy. There is clearly a tension between that view and what educators see as the longer-term goals of education.

The tension that many teachers see in this antinomy concerns the question of how a society can continue to grow in the larger and wider sense by concentrating on going down what they see as a narrow economic path. They point to ways in which some of the current dysfunctional phenomena and antisocial tendencies, of which there is increasing evidence from countries such as Japan and Germany, are now making themselves manifest; they ask politicians, economists and business people whether the economies and socio-political structures of such countries provide us with models that are really worthy of emulation.

In all this, teachers will point out that teaching is not a 'commodity' or 'market place' activity: it is to do much more with caring about people. What they want is to see our government leaders associating education with an emphasis on personal values and the importance of adding quality and value to people's lives – and this, they contend, does not come about by a simplistic linking of education with the economic gains of lowering inflation or diminishing the public sector borrowing requirement.

ACHIEVING GOALS THROUGH THE CURRICULUM

Within this context of multiple goals and expectations, one of the first questions for educationalists constructing curricula is that posed a century ago by Herbert Spencer – what knowledge is of most worth? And it is to the task of providing answers to this question and justifications for the curriculum choices and decisions that systems and schools make, that philosophers, policy-makers and educators have struggled, proposing various kinds of conceptual, moral and instrumental arguments for the construction, application and justification of educational curricula for today's schools.

As a preliminary to such attempts at justification, many philosophers have also thought it a vital part of designating a quality curriculum to grapple with the prior question of what counts as knowledge, what as belief, and what as mere opinion or even prejudice. Many philosophers see education as centrally concerned with the transmission of and initiation of our coming generation of future citizens into those forms and fields of knowledge – substantive, procedural, personal – that are valued by society today, embodied in its various intellectual traditions, and made communicable according to the norms and conventions constituting intelligibility within its varied and different forms of discourse, cultures and communities.

Matters relating to the transmission of beliefs of various kinds are regarded as much more difficult, while opinion and prejudice are counted as the currency of indoctrination, and therefore to be excluded from the staple of the curriculum diet of educating institutions. It would make little sense to talk of a 'quality-*indoctrinating* institution'; 'quality' in *education* has much more to do with those key epistemological concepts, truth, evidence, objectivity and warranted assertability. To that extent, therefore, the prime debate about quality in the curriculum is directly related to the problem of knowledge. Enquiries around this matter will be related to such question as:

- the relationship of knowledge to truth;
- the validation of knowledge claims;
- the relevance and adequacy of diverse appeals to knowledge;
- the particular procedures enshrining the various tests for truth;
- the networks of categories and concepts constituting the different kinds of knowledge;
- the logical and psychological characteristics of what might be claimed to be the different ways of knowing and, therefore, of the different ways of teaching and learning them; and
- the kinds of consideration that allow certain moves to be made, and define those that shall be decisive in a particular form of thought or discourse.

A second part of that debate about quality in the curriculum is the axiological question posed by Spencer: for the purposes of education, which shall be the parts, aspects or forms of knowledge that we shall select for the edification of our younger generation? Such an enquiry will be devoted to the articulation of those arguments that might be properly deployed within the framework of the educational endeavour of a school or a system to justify the selection of particular kinds or areas of knowledge and understanding that we believe will best and most effectively lead to the educational outcomes we have in mind. Here, the question will revolve around kinds of value judgment and their justification, whether intrinsic or instrumental, moral or prudential.

To the discussion of these larger and prior questions we shall return later in Chapter 6. Before that, however, it will be useful to adumbrate some of the preconceptions and curriculum notions that emerge from our data, and are currently animating the curricular and other concerns of leaders in the debate about the production, promotion and assurance of quality in schooling. It is important to note that, according to our data, few of these concerns focus on the major epistemological questions just delineated; many more centre around the questions of curriculum selection, prescription, control, delivery and assessment.

CONCERNS AND BELIEFS UNDERPINNING THE CURRICULUM DEBATE

Curriculum for the Compulsory Years

One authority official felt that the main thrust of the curriculum debate for the compulsory years of schooling lay in settling the question of the range of subjects taught and options available:

> Systems have to be prepared to say that if secondary schools are going to offer a quality education, then they have got to be prepared to offer a central core of subjects with a range of alternatives that will offer and cater for a reasonable number of options at different levels.

An administrator in a different system considered the main thrust of the curriculum debate to be about who *controls* the curriculum – the teachers, the school or the system centre – and noted that:

> Some people at the centre had felt that, educationally speaking, things got out of hand when curriculum development was given to the school. The thrust is now towards more centrally prescribed selection and direction of curriculum and planning, but with resource decisions being given to schools to determine implementation. By imposing that kind of central control over the curriculum, the system believes it can get a better control over quality.

Yet another system administrator thought that quality had much more to do with style of curriculum delivery and method of teaching, the key questions being:

> What do we teach? How do we teach it? Is it more pedagogically effective to engage students in group discussion and enquiry learning that it is to sit them in four rows of desks and teach them?

This view argues that education is enquiry-centred and forces a search for meaning and personal understanding, and that this is personally more meaningful than an approach to curriculum that simply passes material on or presents precast conclusions to somebody. This style of curriculum delivery is built on the hope that it will challenge teachers to reconsider the approaches of effective methods and practices of teaching.

Elsewhere, the concerns are for the content and structure of the curriculum, with particular stress, on the part of some, being laid on the idea of a core curriculum. Numerous arguments have been advanced for the requirement of all schools in a system, state or country to adopt and conform to a particular set of norms for subject selection; these range from the promotion of national identity, to economic self-sufficiency, to such concerns as the avoidance of the existence, never mind the proliferation, of different forms of spelling and handwriting.

In one system, other arguments for a common curriculum appeared to be tacitly at work: it was alleged by one principal that, although some system officials denied their support for such a notion for a long time, the truth about the value they assigned to a centrally dictated curriculum was always there. As the principal described it:

> [The core curriculum] was cut and dried and was very easy to super-vise. It was easy for teachers to write programmes – work programmes – and they could slot it in for half an hour here and half an hour there, and they knew they were on the right track. Because of the commit-ment to enhanced professionalism, however, teachers decided that wasn't the way to go – the unions told us we should be rejecting that approach – teachers got on the bandwagon and wanted to devise their own programmes. We then went into a new era where every school sat down and made its own programme. The problem was time – in school and out of school – the system flogged teachers pretty solidly, quite frankly, to make sure documents were available for assessment when the time came. We are now at the point of saying – we wasted an awful lot of time, didn't we? and it is about time we came through with statewide and, some people are saying, national standards: that there should be a national core curriculum. Yet the perception is that the Minister is one of the people who is fighting tooth and nail to make sure that doesn't happen.

One other system, in which the idea of a prescribed core curriculum received widespread support, has a much more comprehensive view of curriculum – similar to that in which a curriculum is defined as the sum of all the various experiences, formal and informal, that are planned or, in a very wide sense, intended to contribute to a student's learning. An official from this system maintained that:

> The whole curriculum, that is, the whole school life, not just subjects taught, produces other areas of quality that cannot be assessed by tests in academic achievement. What is important is how the sum of all those experiences contribute to developing the whole person . . . the growth of the individual into becoming an autonomous person in his or her own right.

This official saw a danger in the role being currently taken by politicians, whom he saw as key players in the curriculum debate. In his view, politicians employ economic reasons to advocate proposals to construct a national curriculum, under the guise of its being for the good of the country. Yet, as he saw it, economic pressures must be not allowed to drive curriculum:

> The current emphasis on technology, science and maths will lose for

us the cultural history of the country and a lot of areas of curriculum that cannot be measured. For this reason curriculum and, indeed, education must be depoliticized.

Another system official was concerned about the way in which curricula are constructed and curriculum choices made. He believed the education system has a responsibility to encourage parents to be involved in curriculum choice for their children on more than peripheral matters:

> The curriculum is likely to be affected by increased retention rates, and if there is an increased retention rate in secondary schools, then questions of equity – in provision, access and participation – come more to the fore, and the necessity of giving to all students access to a high-quality and empowering curriculum becomes of prime importance.

One teacher pointed to the expectations held by some sections of the community for their various concerns to be catered for in curriculum terms, and noted that, if one puts a good idea before the community, they will immediately expect it to be taught in schools. Moreover:

> Schools are guilty themselves of taking on programmes because the pressure often exists within the school to address issues beyond those that might be seen to be appropriate for the pedagogic function of schools. On certain matters this turns out to be unavoidable. Teachers find themselves under pressure to address the human, social and welfare needs of children, in addition to the educational ones.

Very often the programmes that might be seen to fringe the school curriculum – driver education, for instance – are seen as important, yet their provision often adds pressure to schools. Not that such programmes are unnecessary. The question is whether the school can manage to provide the additional teaching time, personnel and resources for the attention they feel they are under a moral obligation to pay to these larger-scale needs, at the same time as they are attending to the requirements of the established curriculum.

The Post-compulsory Curriculum

The pressures for redefining the curriculum have been most intense in the area of post-compulsory education. Much of the recent drive for curricular change in post-compulsory education has come from national reports detailing those skills and competences which, they argue, it is incumbent on educating institutions to provide for the preparation of a national workforce, ready, equipped and able to 'bring home the bacon' for the country's economic needs. The views embodied in these reports have often been at variance with those views which have traditionally driven the curriculum in the senior years of schooling. One principal points to outside forces and agencies which have traditionally played a powerful determinative force in shaping, even dictating, the curriculum at the post-compulsory level:

Schools historically have had an obligation to see that students meet the standards for the Tertiary Entrance Scores and entry to tertiary institutions. It has been the tertiary institutions, and particularly the universities, that have set the so-called standards for students leaving at Year 12 and going on to first-year university courses. The prerequisites university courses require – particularly in the high-prestige faculties of Law, Medicine or Computing and Information Technology – often determine what sort of curriculum schools feel that they should provide, not merely for students working in Years 11 and 12 but further down the school too.

One effect of this university-governed curriculum provision has been the creation of an elite group in a school society that has access to the high-prestige subjects of Mathematics, Physics and Chemistry. Such subjects, in consequence, assume a high status in the curriculum hierarchy, as against some of those subjects currently on offer – such as in the Arts or Australian Studies – in the newly expanded range of subjects available to the larger cohort of Year 11 and 12 students, subjects that are then regarded by the elite group as being of dubious import and value.

This raises the larger questions to be addressed concerning schooling in the later years. Economic pressures and the reality of high youth unemployment mean there is no longer a question of which students should be catered for in schools after the compulsory leaving age. The educational and curriculum question is now much more one of what to do to offer all students a range of subjects from which they can choose or construct promising and rewarding sets of life options for themselves in a worthwhile and productive learning environment.

For many of the newer and wider range of students staying on in schools, it has been widely thought – Bantock (1971) was one example of this tendency – that there has to be a bias towards the affective and adaptive curriculum rather than the cognitive curriculum. The new circumstances of increased retention rates and a wider spread of ability in the later years of schooling have seemed to some to demand a slightly different orientation in curriculum planning, because, previously, the usual education provided in those years tended to place emphasis solely on the cognitive dimensions of the curriculum, and this was thought, traditionally, to be the preserve of the academically interested elite. It seems to us that this 'Bantock-like' view of an altered orientation in curriculum provision, offering a more affectively based curriculum to students of lesser- or non-intellectual interest (rather than potential!), is based upon exactly the same 'faculty psychology' premise that we have already refuted in the previous chapter.

One principal tackles this point vigorously, pointing out that for the new range of students staying on at school in the later years, one does not start out with a blank page:

It is important that the curriculum framework and goals are strong. One has to acknowledge that there are bodies of knowledge and skills that are indispensable, values that are unshakeable no matter what era one lives in

To this we would add that perceptions derived from previous experiences teaching extremely able students, who typically were the only ones to stay on to the end of Year 12, should not necessarily form the total base of the preconceptions brought by such teachers to their education of newer and larger cohorts of students with a wider spread of ability. It does not follow that such students should automatically be offered a different or diluted curriculum diet.

On the contrary, modern methods of pedagogy and the kinds of teaching resources to which schools have access these days – computers, telematics, research-based learning – could be brought into play to allow students from disadvantaged or minority backgrounds life chances, through curriculum experience, that have hitherto been the preserve of only a few. 'Any subject can be taught in an intellectually respectable manner to any group of children at any stage of development' was a remark made, and a motto held, by Bruner (1966), one of the pioneers of modern cognitive psychology.

Whether all students remaining to Year 12 could eventually secure employment and, if so, of what type, is another question, with wide implications for curriculum design. It is to the redefining of the curriculum to meet these students' needs, interests and capacities that we turn in Chapter 6. An official of a teachers' union pointed out that:

> Whenever a country is in some social or economic difficulty, it seems constantly to turn upon the outcomes and products of its education system. Businessmen and industrialists will proclaim that somewhere along the line education has failed, then politicians for the most part scramble around and try to find some quick fixes. In education you cannot find quick fixes. Instead we should be looking at where we want our 15–20-year-olds to be at some longer time in the future, adjusting our programmes and our educational thinking towards that long-term end, rather than trying to provide some knee-jerk reactions to difficulties that some people perceive in current economic circumstances – many of the principal factors of which are brought into play by causes largely outside education's control.

The long-term evolutionary view of the process of education that tends to be held by members of the teaching profession has its critics in the wider community. Some of that criticism is well-intentioned: parents want very much to support schools and to assist them in developing their children as stable persons and mature citizens, but, at the same time, they want schools to prepare them to earn a living and to maintain themselves in a satisfactory quality of life. Business leaders and politicians latch on only to the latter part of this and use it as a rod for schools' backs. Unfortunately teachers have to recognize that – to change the metaphor – the common coinage of this anti-educational animus appears to enjoy wide currency, certainly among some members of Parliament and some leaders of commerce, business and industry. From their perspective, education should be narrowed down and, instead of education's larger-scope and longer-term visions, there should be a reversion to, and perhaps a revision of, what they perceive as being the basics and the real business of education and the curriculum – what they regard as the necessity of preparing for earning a living and helping their country provide and maintain the material circumstances in which that living can be provided. Other pursuits – culture, the arts and personal growth – come a long way behind these more pressing concerns.

This idea of 'the basics' can often be distilled down to a dozen or so subjects at Year 12 level, success in which would lead to admission into most 'proper' faculties at university level. The result of that kind of thinking is often a tendency to stress as curriculum *basics* only those subjects in which progress is readily measurable, to reduce the scope, size and potential of the curriculum, and to oversimplify teaching and educational processes, in the hope that, miraculously, the community will see all its problems resolved by ensuring that most people get to university, or undergo highly specific skills training or something of the kind. This notion unfortunately ignores the inconvenient fact that, as things stand, not all of the Year 12 population is going to gain entrance to university or other institutions of education. Some will certainly secure entrance, perhaps even an increased number of them; the others will be looking for something within our schools that will enhance their opportunities for employment, offer more and more opportunities to spend their leisure time gainfully, productively and enjoyably, and improve and reinforce their own self-esteem.

For these young people their education is headed (and most educationalists are trying to direct this appropriately) along a fairly broad track of curriculum offerings, which must also contain within it the narrow path the critics want to highlight – not only for the elite group of academically oriented students, but also for those among the broader cohort of students at that level who might conceivably become interested in *and good at* higher-order thinking, understanding and skills. According to this view:

> The main thing for schools now is to get programmes in such a form that there is that clear core running through them, but that there is flexibility to enable teachers and schools to make adjustments for local needs and needs of individual students.

For the main thrust of the educational enterprise, our data would suggest that in these times most educationalists want:

> education to keep on the broad road, to provide as many opportunities as possible for all the youngsters in the various school systems. Curricula nowadays need to provide a greater number and a wider range of subjects based on employment prospects or clear technical links *and* the enhancement of personal lifestyle choices.

Along with this must come – and indeed it is coming – quite clear guidance and instruction in the principles of positive social behaviour and right moral conduct as well. For it is of prime importance that, as well as establishing the mental, physical and social health and well-being of today's young people, fifteen years from now we shall have the sort of society people would want their children to grow up in. There would be few who would want to see a continuation of some of the more depressing and disturbing aspects of life in parts of our society, where the incidence of domestic violence, child abuse, workplace discord and teenage suicide seems to be increasing.

Many critics of education believe that their preferred society can be brought about in the here and now if only teachers and schools would do their 'proper work'. Those who have been in education a long time, however, know that the instant creation of such a society is not possible. Preoccupation with the provision of instant solutions does not solve longer-term problems, most of which arise from deep-seated causes. It may well silence the critics for a while to have the assurance that the narrow aspects of curriculum upon which they place supreme value are indeed being addressed; however, educationalists argue:

> It is not that [these] narrow aspects should not be addressed but that they should be placed within the context of the whole educational programme. The educational endeavour has to be aimed at the total individual and the total population we have in schools, as well as at what we can assess of the future needs of the whole community.

This does not just mean employment of economic self-sufficiency: it means people having the chance to live in a society that offers them safety, security, dignity – and beauty.

Speaking more optimistically to this end, a union official noted that:

> Most politicians today accept that human resources and their powers of critical and creative imagination are the greatest resources that countries and systems have, and for this reason politicians are placing great priority on the provision of good, sound educational services. One can talk with any Minister of Education across Australia and one will discover that those Ministers hold that view, even though they have to work within the constraints of their own Cabinet's thinking. One has only to look at issues being raised at the federal and state elections when all the parties seem to have education in the forefront of their political programmes as major agenda items, even though the parties may have different ways of addressing them.

The problem is how to translate this concern into curriculum action and extend the implications into the provision of resources and the improvement of what happens – or should happen – in the classroom. Attention now has to be focused on the kinds of curriculum structure that exist at federal and state levels; how they work; what input teachers have into them; how local schools manage them for their own particular needs, so as to secure teacher involvement in translating broad curriculum goals into specific curriculum behaviours in the classroom.

One of the successes of some state education systems has been the ability of teachers in schools to design courses that reflect their perceptions of the needs of the particular clientele. This is perhaps one of the reasons why some states have higher retention rates, because of the diversity of course offerings for students. As one official noted: 'Students these days are staying at school, not solely for reasons of employment but also because they can find a mixture of courses to suit them.' To facilitate this, schools must leave room within the curriculum framework for individual students or individual parents to make an informed curriculum choice. If that framework becomes frustrating or coercive, then the institution is in effect wasting students' and parents' time.

This means that there have now to be different, better, more flexible ways of imparting mainstream knowledge – ways of enabling students to acquire and use it. But there also has to be curriculum subject content to which students can respond positively, and can negotiate, not merely access to the subjects that they and their advisers believe would be in their best long-term interest, but also their own preferred learning styles and end-points. This is where the vitally important process of the negotiated curriculum comes in and gets its main point of purchase.

Negotiation is a two-way street, however: teachers must negotiate to meet students' needs, but students, in turn, have to come to accept the teacher's expert knowledge and professionalism in pedagogy. The adult teacher must know how students can get from A to B and, crucially, must know how to *motivate* them to do so, not just how to allow them to continue to be happy at A. It is a main concern of all educators, not only, as Ryle (1949) remarked, to show their students the ropes, but to challenge them to climb higher and faster – and sometimes to accept that they will climb further and faster than the teachers themselves. This says something about the quality of the teaching – learning interaction: the quality of education depends very much on the quality of relationships in educational institutions, and chiefly and fundamentally those between learner and teacher.

The teacher is of course only one part of a set of extremely complex relationships, another part of which is the relationship between the learner and the learning experience itself, and the drive of the educating institution, especially at the post-compulsory level, to grant the student the empowerment that comes about through the pursuit of truth and knowledge in their various forms. This concern for the empowerment of students through knowledge goes to the heart not only of what is taught and how it is taught, but also how arrangements are made for the delivery of the curriculum, and the organization of teaching and learning at the post-compulsory level.

But schools cannot have students involved democratically in decision-making about the organization and negotiation of what they shall learn and the character of the learning experience they shall undergo if their teachers are not also involved. Both must have a feeling of the ownership of decisions about the structure and shape of educational activities and learning experiences; for this, a sense of commitment to joint cognitive undertakings and the school's educational direction is important. The benefit of seeing both teachers and students as participants in the democracy of learning carries its own sense of shared adventure and enjoyment. As one principal said: 'It is a joy to experience initiative born of collaborative processes.' That is why cognitive empowerment is such a key notion in the pursuit of quality schooling: empowering schools relates positively to the quality debate; schools can organize their own programmes and so cater more for the needs and interests of a particular school population, while still remaining within broad curriculum guidelines.

For many people, then, it is from the curriculum, and from effective programmes and patterns of teaching and learning, that quality should be generated. One administrator put it this way:

> The critical change leading to the promotion and achievement of quality in the whole system needs to come from curriculum, teaching and learning. All the pressures that have come to be exercised in the pursuit of quality, such as parent involvement, school organization [and] system change, have not really got down to looking at the whole question of implementation in schemes of quality teaching and learning.

There is a sense in which the curriculum is the *whole* life of the school – the social aspects, and extracurricular pursuits as well as the academic – for it is largely, though not exclusively, through the curriculum that the educational goals are realized, and it is in the delivery of the curriculum that quality education is attained.

We conclude, then, that the main focus and target for everything provided as an activity of an educational institution, as part of the total experience of the child in the course of his or her education, is the promotion of quality learning. By that it is meant that all students need access to and engagement in a broad, inclusive and empowering curriculum, and that this must be a major preoccupation of the system, institution or school. Part of that emphasis on quality for students will be a concern on the part of teachers to provide for the needs of the underachievers, the students in the broad general bands of competence and ability, and the most able.

EMPOWERMENT OF STUDENTS IN THE ADVANCE OF QUALITY TEACHING AND LEARNING

We may lay it down that quality education is where all students are empowered, through their education, to a realization of their own freedom, to determine issues and choices for themselves and by their own action. They will, as a result of their educational experiences, have acquired the abilities and the skills to influence their own future and that of those with whom they share the community in a personal, social, political and moral way.

If we accept this premise, the question then remains: within their school experience, what form should student involvement and empowerment take? It is difficult, as one principal believed, to involve students in complete curriculum negotiation – curriculum construction from scratch, so to speak – as that involves considerable academic expertise and mature professional judgments. They can, however, contribute 'to knowledge about teaching strategies – though often teachers are too scared to listen because the students are too accurate!'

A student council is a useful medium of communication here: its members can tell principals and teachers what students think about what is taught and their feelings about programmes offered, in an impersonal and non-threatening way. Such councils can negotiate themes: the 'embodiment of student thought can generate some excellent ideas into learning approaches'. One system official saw the advantages of allowing students to negotiate on these matters:

> A part of the empowering process is to involve students as active partners in negotiating a curriculum. At what stage this begins could

be a difficult question. It is a gradual process of empowerment. Even from the initial stages of the educational process, students should be empowered to have some say in the type of schooling and curriculum they have.

Students and student representative councils can also undertake negotiations on resources and types of equipment. This might be a minor role but important, for all participation in decisions of this kind leads to a sense of empowerment for the students working in the institutions that will treat them in such ways.

Empowerment through education brings students to the point at which they can assume responsibility for the exercise of their own freedom, and where they can be autonomous in achieving the goal of being the person that they want to be. Nowadays, there is a sound social and political argument for schools seeing their curricula and learning activities and experiences in this way: educational empowerment is closely tied to the question of equity and social justice. This comes particularly to the fore when there is an increased rate of retention in secondary schools.

Of course this is all very well in a school where the atmosphere and approaches are conducive to student involvement and empowerment. In many schools, however, empowerment is still a very revolutionary concept, especially where there is a strongly authoritative, possibly even authoritarian, approach towards students, one that sees them still as children even at Year 12. Sadly, too, the past experience of some students with student representative councils has not been either happy or strong; in some places there is a tendency for their membership to be selected by principals and staff, who want to retain the right of veto over topics to be discussed, modes of procedure to be adopted, or outcomes to be 'allowed'. One teacher added a further cautionary note:

> Staff presence at meetings can also tend to stifle discussions. Students themselves can have ambivalent attitudes to being on such bodies: often students get themselves elected as a way to escape lessons because the principal allows it to meet in school time. It does not mean that schools get those students on such councils who have real potential for leadership. In such circumstances it is hardly surprising that not too many parents and citizens associations or school councils have students attending for decision-making.

However, one senior system officer was clear about the importance of student involvement in planning their own learning and engagement in their own curricula. He commented that:

> [Student involvement] is important in secondary schools, but the framework and goals have to be strong. You have to acknowledge from years of experience that there are bodies of knowledge and skills that are indispensable, values that are unshakeable no matter what era you live in, and they should be there whether children want it or not. Student involvement can come more on content, the textbooks, and how they want to shape their assessment pieces.

A senior academic made an important point here – the necessity of involving students in school decision-making and curriculum negotiation as a crucial issue for education. We are seeing a change in the notion of what it is to be a person and the nature of personhood; and with this, to some extent, the disappearance of childhood:

> We are now beginning to see young people right down as far as primary school in the light of what we used to talk about as an adult learner. The child is being viewed as much more responsible for his or her own learning. That is, we are starting to talk in terms of a student's taking responsibility for learning; we are beginning to teach in a problem-oriented way as we would with adults; we are saying that we must start with where the student is, be less inclined to impose a curriculum, but instead build on what a student knows already – and go on from there.

This change in our view of the student, and what counts as being a person, parallels a shift in the view of learning, because we now understand a little more about how children learn and what it means for things to be relevant. The empowerment of students to become active participants in curriculum negotiation is an absolutely crucial factor in enhancing the quality of schools.

CURRICULUM DESIGN AND DELIVERY

Curriculum design is a sophisticated activity and, given the complexities of all the issues involved, and the various interests and concerns of the diverse groups of stakeholders, it is going to be almost impossible for the average teacher working with students and parents in the individual school to have the time to work out a framework that has broad community support. The generally accepted belief is that:

> School-based curriculum development needs to continue, but within the context of a statewide framework. This means that the Ministry negotiates with groups like the Confederation of Industry, the Chamber of Commerce, the trade unions and professional bodies, and all other interest groups, and then sets out general parameters about the breadth and depth of student studies and the key areas that children learn in them.

That is perhaps the area in which one can discern a role for the central office in a system, one that can be expressed in curriculum policy statements and curriculum frameworks, allowing a very strong role for teachers and school-based personnel in adapting to a local context, taking a bare central framework and fleshing it out in negotiation with students and parents so that it is suitable for the particular school.

After a decade of experimentation with school-based curriculum development, there is now a widespread belief that, in the process of curriculum realization, teachers are better modulators, adaptors and providers than curriculum designers. But the issue is a complex one. One system official comments:

> If teachers feel uncertain in the new curriculum area, they look for someone to give them the answers in a ready-packaged curriculum. The push to a more centralized curriculum will meet with a ready response by teachers who have been asking what to do and seeking information. But at the same time this disempowers them. They no longer have control over what happens and where it goes.

That is important, for evidence suggests that the curriculum packages generated and deployed in the 1960s did not work well in the hands of those teachers who had not been directly involved in their development. As always, there is a question of process and product here, in both of which those teachers who are to apply them successfully have to have a sense of co-ownership and commitment. One principal commented:

> If you are not engaged in the process of developing [a curriculum], then it is very difficult for you to implement the product, because you do not have the same sense of commitment and you have not thought it through in detail. It is very important for teachers to be involved [in curriculum] appropriately.

Teachers could, of course, be extremely effective curriculum designers, because they know what will work, pedagogically speaking, and what will not. However, there is at least one reason offered as to why teachers are, more generally speaking, ineffective curriculum designers: they do not normally have enough opportunities to develop expertise in that area. There is a widespread agreement that, at present, there is not much done or much direction offered in pre-service training as regards curriculum design; moreover, there appears to be little support available within school time. As one principal put it:

> They [teachers] would be capable of doing these things and effecting those transformations, given some leadership in such matters. For that reason it would be advantageous if schools could programme teachers by allowing an extensive period of time – perhaps half a day per fortnight or month – to attend to acquiring competence, even mastery, in curriculum design, development, innovation and change, just as other professions do.

But, we may ask, is this practical within a period of budget constraint? It appears that politicians and system officials think not. However, one system official has suggested that a way of practical implementation for the development of such curriculum thinking could be for an integration of system support for teachers with more formal study in tertiary institutions:

> Those involved in higher degrees [that] focus on curriculum design and development should have the knowledge, insights and skills to be effective. But once again, if you are going to ask people to carry out jobs that involve a great deal of skill, then there is an obligation for the system to make provision for them to acquire those skills.

For some teachers, however, designing curriculum is seen as a waste of time,

71

effort, skills and energy. It is often regarded, and indeed experienced by them, as an activity that can cause burn-out. Many teachers see no need to design or develop curricula themselves when so many excellent and commercially produced curriculum or subject packages, plans and schemes are already available. Indeed, one academic working in the area argued that, in fact, most teachers should probably not be required to be curriculum designers. In so far as teachers are good curriculum adaptors, they are already effective curriculum developers working within a curriculum framework – 'That indeed is the pattern that has now emerged':

> As the twentieth century closes there will probably be real opportunities for entrepreneurial curriculum designers among some teachers. Given the fact that schools will generally have control of their own resources, you will probably get schools buying the expertise of curriculum developers in other schools, because specific teachers will get the reputation of being good in this area and so will be highly valued.

THE PROFESSIONAL STATUS OF TEACHERS AND QUALITY TEACHING AND LEARNING

One critical factor in obtaining the best kind of performance from teachers is to give them a supportive and professionally conducive environment in which to work. A good-quality work life is important for teachers, to enhance the quality of their performance and enable them to pass on their knowledge, values and philosophies of learning to their students. Part of teachers' sense of the value of the contributions they are making to helping their students achieve a good quality of life will come from a sense of their own professional value and status.

However, a number of factors impinge adversely on teacher status. Some parents argue that among these have been teachers' own contribution to a loss of status in the public eye. It is also argued that, nowadays, teachers are closer to the community than they were years ago when, as a result of their very remoteness, they were held in greater regard and even reverence by the community. That has certainly changed; as one teachers' union officer put it: 'Public perceptions of the teaching profession have now taken a turn towards the much more critical, even in some cases to the downright hostile.' This phenomenon is attributed to a number of factors: teachers' increasing militancy in pursuit of improvements in their terms and conditions of service; the association of teachers in the public's mind with particular sets of social and political agenda; the comments of business and industry who lay the blame on the lack of competence of teachers for what they see as a decline in the necessary skills, attitudes and knowledge exhibited by those seeking employment with them; the low academic regard in which teachers are held by other members of the academic community, probably arising from the low level of entry scores needed for admission to faculties and departments of teacher education.

One system officer makes the interesting comment that there is a different clientele entering teaching now:

Teaching used to be the path to social mobility. It attracted bright students from less wealthy families. It was also a socially acceptable career for girls and many very talented girls became teachers. The concern now is about the quality of entrants: other careers have opened up for girls and, comparatively speaking, teaching has lower status and salaries.

It is also widely believed that the quality of some entrants to the teaching service has declined, because of the perception that, generally, students with a high academic ability are not choosing teaching. The comparatively lower entrance standards for Education in some institutions, against the high-demand faculties of Medicine and Law may, of course, have more than a little to do with the need to keep up faculty quotas and the amount of funding per capita in institutions operating with some form of relative funding model. The salary rewards at the end of training are low in comparison with the equal or smaller number of years of training in subjects and disciplines required for other professions: yet in those professions the remuneration, even on entrance, is much higher than that obtainable in teaching. Award restructuring exercises will, it is hoped, attract higher-quality entrants to the education service, retain effective teachers in the classroom, and thus improve the status of teaching.

It is certainly a matter of great importance to the future of society that by some means, including an increase in remuneration, the most able and committed among our young people are attracted towards teaching and away from other occupations. One industrialist and businessman participating in this research was very vocal on this point. He saw the lower entry mark for teaching as the lowest of any profession, and as constituting a real problem for recruitment to a vitally important profession: 'It seems ludicrous that in the most important discipline (because on that depends our greatest resource) the entry standard is so low.' It is clear that the salary, working conditions and public perceptions of the teaching profession all need to be raised, for in these ways we might hope to improve the quality of entrants to the profession. There is a real need now to focus on the quality of the candidates seeking admission to the teaching profession, given the critical importance of the task it performs. Remuneration, both on entry and then within the service, should be improved. But one senior system administrator sounded a note of caution:

> It is a sheer assumption that a different career structure, remuneration and devolution of decision-making as an enhancement of community participation will be enough to overcome the disincentives faced by those considering entering teaching at present.

As an illustration of one of these disincentives, a noted female educationalist pointed to a major area of difficulty that meets new entrants to the profession and that presents them with a daunting and often unattractive set of challenges. Teachers, she remarked, get exposed:

> There is no way one can cover up a bad teacher. Each teacher has to take a certain number of classes – meet the mandatory 180 students a week – and this is a task that is demanding enough in itself . . . A

fresh graduate – a new entrant to the profession – has to meet all these people and staff in the first week of teaching and be able to interact intelligently all the day with them and others. This is an extraordinary demand, and one the burden of which we should be disinclined to lay on other vital professions, such as, say, medicine, the law or engineering. Yet, in addition to this, the level of scrutiny for beginning teachers is very high: they are in front of 30 students all day, in the school ground as they walk, or go to lunch. They are still in the public eye to an extent that people in public service, business offices or elsewhere aren't – and this can constitute a marked disincentive for some young teachers who might be able, with help, to develop into real quality teachers later on.

There is a further factor to be taken into account, relevant to the search for quality entrants to the profession, that could well function as an additional disincentive. What must be a major concern at the present time is the question of how the recent changes that have been made or have taken place in the tertiary sector, such as amalgamations, strongly biased and inequitable applications of relative funding models, academic concentration and selectivity in both teaching and research, the emergence of *de jure* or *de facto* league tables of institutions, will impact upon teacher education programmes. There is a strong concern in the education service, and particularly among those involved in teacher education and training, that, even during and perhaps notwithstanding all the changes that have taken place in the higher education sector, the same high quality of teacher education and preparation will be maintained and not watered down. One teacher educator in such an institution expressed this concern in this way:

It is essential to have teachers who have done major studies in curriculum subjects such as history, literature, economics, politics, maths and science, not simply because they have to teach these as school subjects, but because their studies in them *educate* them as human beings, and in this way has a beneficial effect on students in the classroom. It is to be hoped the amalgamations won't just give teacher education students access to and practice in improved techniques for the classroom, but will produce people with broad educational backgrounds.

Once the teachers have been trained, however, they still have to secure employment and be selected for service in schools. Many are clear that, given recent moves towards the introduction of principles and procedures of local school management, the time is coming when schools will have more autonomy in relation to the selection, engagement and even dismissal of staff. In this matter, geographical considerations will certainly play a part; but what is chiefly brought into question is the range and quality of systemwide and statewide provision, and the responses one must make to questions thrown up by the demographics of supply and demand, as well as the questions of curriculum change and of a changing professional age profile. If address is to be made to these questions, then there will have to be some co-ordination and liaison on questions of teacher training and education, supply and demand, relocation or redeployment, on a much wider basis than that merely of the individual school. And that means looking at past performance as well as present needs, and likely future demands across a system.

All this leads many to conclude that there needs to be some form of appraisal of teachers' past performance, monitoring of their present activities and planning for their future development – and this means some form of performance review, to cover both past activities and future development potential. It is widely believed that performance review is probably best done by someone within the school, who will see to it that guidelines are prepared and, in general, an approach adopted that will make the whole process as little of a threat and as much of a help as possible. However, there is one feature of performance review and teacher appraisal about which teachers are justified in entertaining some reservations. As one of them remarked: 'The reality is that there will be individuals who make this a chance to be power agents and controlling agents. It will be interesting to see what this does to professional relationships in schools.'

Yet another powerful source of apprehension about appraisal is the fear that teacher appraisal will be linked causally with student outcome data and the publication of results, and will be used by system authorities to control and direct teachers' future behaviour, even to the point of dismissal. There is some justification for this concern. As one system official confirmed: 'Criterion-referenced outcomes and publicly recorded results act as a powerful agent to motivate teachers to do things that they would not normally do.' Nevertheless, as another senior official commented, schools have to respect teachers' professional judgements on matters to do with the delivery of the curriculum, with effective styles of teaching and learning, and with appropriate forms of examination and assessment.

In this context, the term 'professional judgment' enjoys wide currency and considerable normative power in this debate. It is usually employed to refer to the craft or science of teaching and the judgments teachers have to make at classroom level on such matters as:

- what content to offer to students and at what stage;
- how much challenge to put before individual students;
- how much support to give individuals;
- what kind of modality teaching should occur in.

In addressing the pedagogical imperatives arising from the professional judgments on such matters, teachers, it would appear, prefer to join with their peers in monitoring each other's work and ensuring professional standards and comparability in ways that do not detract from or distort their obligation to meet the needs of children: 'After all, teachers are directors and heads of their classrooms and they have a great deal to say about what they teach and how they teach it.' This belief on the part of the teachers in the primacy of their pedagogical rights in their own classrooms results from a strong sense of their professional standing, competence and autonomy. It is supported by the attitude of many system officials that, if teachers are in control of the delivery of education in their own classrooms, they will do a better job and be more productive in their teaching than if they are working at the instigation of someone operating by remote control from central office.

That view emanates from, and is an expression of, a professionalizing argument, based on the view that teachers and principals can, on site, make better and more educationally sound decisions than bureaucrats at head office: 'Changes in education dictated from the top will never be as successful as changes instituted and developed from the bottom up.' There is, however, another side to teachers' increasing recourse to their professionalism, and that is a strong industrial element. Indeed, one representative of commerce, business and industry sees the change in teaching associations and unions from being embodiments and preservers of professional standards and values to now being a set of industrial organizations as arising from and related to the attitude of teachers towards themselves:

> The whole issue of whether a teacher is a professional or is working for award wages is shifting. If that shift does in fact occur, then it is probably not reasonable to be looking at the establishment of national guidelines for what counts as appropriate behaviours for a professional body over against what might be expected from an industrial organization.

For teachers to retain their professional status, according to this view, their unions and associations have to be seen as bodies that deserve that kind of regard.

There is, of course, a great deal involved in being a member of a profession. But at least part of being professional is the realization that the true professional can only achieve so much with limited resources, support and previous education and training. For this reason: 'One of the crucial things is to limit what is expected to be done in any given time ... teachers are expected to know too much, to attend to too much and to do too much. So little change occurs.' One system official noted that:

> With the increase of social demands on schools we now need teachers with a stronger background in counselling as part of their necessary post-initial learning. Increasingly, nowadays, teachers are expected to be social workers, counsellers, to run 'before-school programmes', and even provide for breakfast. Parents expect teachers to bring a sense of discipline to their 'undisciplined' children: teachers are seen as police and probation officers as well as exercising the role of social case worker – even though not much sympathy and empathy is accorded to teachers on the basis of what is expected of them. Now, and much more, they [teachers] have to give both education and training on one hand, and counselling and practical personal help on the other.

This is a phenomenon arising from the present state of society. Opportunities for leadership in academic vision and professional development can become subject to constraint as teachers come increasingly under pressure to address the social and individual human needs of children. Some of the wider social programmes being set up as a result of trying to address these wider needs add considerable pressure to the academic and training missions of schools, even though the additional programmes are necessary in today's changing society. The question is whether teachers have the resources, expertise and social remit to manage all these additional loadings of social responsibility.

To these societal changes have been added system-wide changes associated with policies of decentralization and devolution. Indeed, one of the major issues facing education at the present time is the significant impact that change is having on teachers and their toleration of increased levels of stress:

> There are teachers who seem to have been uncomfortable with change, its extent, range and complexity; some have been adversely affected by the mere thought or the experienced pressures of all that change.

This signals the need for clear, understandable processes, and reasonable time-frames for the introduction of any system-wide change. As one teachers' union official put it: 'Systems should not be failing to put in place proper processes for change and/or allow the fear of the unknown to impact on teachers and classrooms unnecessarily or adversely.'

For some teachers, of course, supported by more caring and responsive system policy-makers, officers and administrators, the effect of ongoing system change has been to offer them a wealth of opportunities for professional and personal career development. For others, unfortunately, the effect has been to make them unsure in their job, not knowing what is happening to them, and this has the effect of making some of them professionally very discontented. A teachers' representative stated:

> Discontented people blame the system rather than themselves usually, and a fairly persistent and consistent complaint to some head offices is that far too much is expected of teachers and principals. Some of this has, of course, to be taken with a grain of salt, because when people are pressured that is one of the reactions. Some of the adverse reactions might have to do with the lack of inefficiency of appropriate management skills.

One system official says:

> There is also a danger that a school cannot keep control of all the things that it would want to address in any one year and so ends up doing very little . . . Schools have to prioritize – limit the number of courses they undertake so as to get real depth in what they do. Stress is not unique to teachers, but those teachers that cope with it better are generally in schools where principals know and care about those conditions that impinge adversely upon teachers and try to help them handle the dysfunctional phenomena of change.

An academic and former system superintendent noted that a major source of stress for teachers is found in their preparedness for and competence in handling problems of discipline. Many of these problems, and the anxieties they occasion, may well arise from the increased Year 11–12 retention rate:

> The curriculum at that level is not geared to cope with increasing

numbers and levels of ability. Teachers in the state system have done an incredible job in the last few years in coping with major changes at lower and upper levels in a way that compels admiration. Indeed, teachers seem to like change. They do not, however, like unsupported change, where they have to do all the thinking, developing and carrying through of everything. Such a necessity puts them in impossible situations ... As against this, if they have ownership, the change is usually much more successful, but again they need guidance in exercising that ownership. That is one of the problems of the school-based decision-making groups. People do not know how to get things done. They can be aimless groups and very frustrating for participants unless they are well led and well guided. So just giving ownership is not enough. Teachers need to be trained to exercise ownership. It then makes [change] constructive and beneficial to them, and not just in terms of the instrumental sort of outcomes, but emotional as well.

A different source of stress was pointed out by an officer of another system, who saw a dilemma for many teachers in the number, range and complexity of the value judgments they are called upon to make, some of which are probably always going to be in conflict with those of local communities. This is, then, another area in which teachers have to learn to enhance their skills of effective communication and negotiation with their own students and members of the wider community. Otherwise such situations involve potentially a deal of conflict, and can become yet another cause of demands and stress on teachers.

For this reason, among many others, teachers have to be more adept in their skills of communication and in interpersonal relations. But in the secondary system, it is argued:

Teachers still tend not to develop those interpersonal skills, because they often still see themselves as being teachers of subjects and disseminators of knowledge rather than knowing how to handle different opinions, values and conflict on matters about which many people in the community care passionately and might well hold views that are opposed to those they themselves hold dear.

Such comments underline the view articulated by many professionals, namely, that teachers are (a) first and foremost teachers of subjects; and (b) ill-equipped in time, training or resources to respond to the demands for the wider type of personal and social development, and the moral guidance or counselling role that many parents and other community agencies have either tacitly or overtly assigned them. In some sense, teachers are justified in taking this view, as one remarked:

My qualifications in English and History equip me only to induct my students into those bodies of content and modes of enquiry that typify understanding in and mastery of those subjects: I am not a personal counsellor, family therapist, or social welfare officer.

But the fact is that being teachers of these subjects in an educational institution already disposes them in those directions, whether they like it or not. In educational institutions, we do not condition, indoctrinate or brainwash, but initiate our students into the ways in which the knowledge we are employed and committed, as their teachers, to impart is publicly established, developed, verified and assessed (knowledge being directly connected to truth and objectivity). These commitments inevitably require of us that we treat our students as moral beings and not as candidates for indoctrinatory treatments of various non-moral kinds. Moreover, we initiate our students into knowledge and understanding in an institution whose principal underlying motive is the moral one of helping our charges understand and cope better with the exigencies of the society they currently inhabit, and preparing them for all the opportunities and possible threats of the future. As Warnock (1978) argues, we are, in a quite decided way, working out by our efforts as teachers in schools of today, the shape, form and content of the society in which future generations of our successors shall live, even if in times considerably different from those in which we presently operate.

EDUCATION AS A COGNITIVE AND MORAL ENTERPRISE

Education is, as Daveney (1973) remarked, a moral concept; so, notwithstanding the feelings of some teachers that they are not doing anything except offering instruction in a non-evaluative environment, the conceptual consequences and requirements arising from their employment in an institution that is absolutely shot through with moral intentions and purposes makes them – whether they know it or not – responsible for much more than their pupils' academic development. For such development can take place only in a context of institutional concern for students' overall equilibrium and personal development, in ways that will enable students to capitalize on all the opportunities offered them in that institution for individual enrichment and social progress. The work of teachers in a quality educational environment is, therefore, and paradoxically, not far removed from that of the roles and functions taken by social workers and family case-workers, or, at least, of being the near-standing assistants of the professionals actually employed in those positions and for those purposes.

Thus the basic and indispensable virtue required of and expected in quality teachers working in a school devoted to the education of coming generations of citizens is their cognitive and moral commitments. Teachers have a cognitive commitment in that they are themselves committed to the world of knowing and understanding, and, because of that, to getting their students to know and to understand things too. One of the academics associated with this research developed this point further:

> The attempt to engage their students intellectually must take place within a context of moral commitment: teachers want a student to know but, within the climate and context of an institution's being *edu-cational*, they realize they have to try to help them to acquire their knowledge in morally acceptable ways . . . Students come to know about the world within a framework of morally acceptable values and norms. That is the essence of teaching.

79

Generating advance towards the production and further development of teachers ready to offer quality teaching and learning in a caring and supportive environment requires able, highly trained, knowledgeable and morally committed personnel, backed up with the requisite kinds and levels of resources, advice and assistance from the schools and school systems in which they work.

Chapter 5

Restructuring Education in the Interests of Quality: The School, the Community and the System

We ended the last chapter by pointing to the cognitive and moral commitments for which teachers, as agents operating in institutions established and directed with educational purposes and intentions in mind, are necessarily engaged. We noted that this expectation in their conception and operation required schools and school systems to provide teachers with the circumstances and resources in which their commitments might find expression. In this chapter we continue with an examination of our data, with particular emphasis on the restructuring of education and the changing relationship between the school, the community and the various educating agencies, whether they be state or religious systems or loose forms of organization, as in the independent sector. We are concerned now to examine the impact of such restructuring and change on the provision of quality education.

THE FOCUS OF THE CHANGE EFFORT: RESTRUCTURING AND THE QUALITY OF EDUCATION

There has been little evaluation of the ways in which the restructuring of education has impacted on the delivery of educational programmes at the classroom level. It is perhaps still too early to say. Indeed, in some systems it has been argued that excessive preoccupation with structural reform, especially that which begins at the central offices of ministries of education, misses the central point of meaningful educational change. As one leading educationalist comments:

> There has been little or no debate as to where change should start. One could argue that it ought to be in the classroom. Systems might build new structures around what they believe a school must do and *then* try to deliver the change and to achieve its hoped-for outcomes in the classrooms and the school.

Clearly, then, there are problems with a traditional top-down approach to educational change: it is much to be doubted whether reforms that are conceived at the centre and then disseminated outward and downward are ever going to be implemented at the local level in exactly the form in which central office believes they will be – even supposing the absence of any local considerations or difficulties that add further to the inevitable distortion effect. As one system official commented: 'The department started by restructuring Central Office, then divisions and regions. By the time it reached schools, it ran out of breath.' Another official remarked that 'top-down changes are never as successful as bottom-up', particularly with respect to the obvious need to give all those involved and affected by the change a sense of involvement in and ownership of the change. If members of the community, and particularly teachers, do not feel that they own at least an important part of the change, and are not prepared by the appropriate in-service education courses for their part in implementing and monitoring it, then the changes proposed are not going to have the effect of promoting quality in the way that was originally intended.

It appears that those concerned only with applying a structural approach to educational change and improvement risk shirking many of the most important issues. For example, the real issue for many teachers and members of the community is whether, given the current expertise and resources assigned to schools and the ways in which schools are organized and managed, schools are the best places to do some of the things and achieve some of the outcomes that society is currently expecting of them. Certainly, the apparent lack of evidence of a direct causal relationship between structural rearrangement and improved classroom performance makes many educationalists suspicious. As an official of one state system argued: 'Unless all the administrative reorganization has an impact on classrooms then it was all a waste of time.'

But is this what restructuring is all about anyway? From our data, we consider it worthwhile remarking that, if it is the case that systems are concerned to redistribute responsibility for educational decision-making to local initiatives, on the grounds that such devolution actually enhances the quality of education, particularly in regard to teaching and learning, then they seem to have failed to communicate this belief and intention effectively to the educational community.

Why Restructure?

One former system official echoed the view of many educators who saw the shift towards devolution in negative terms:

> Nobody seems to shift authority when there is plenty of money around. As soon as the budget is a bit tight you find that devolution is the in-thing. This is cynical but true. In any matter that really means something, that involves big spending, the school does not have a say. There is still a great deal of central authority *despite* the devolution. It is only the implementation of those hard decisions that will be passed out to schools.

Another system official commented that devolved local arrangements can be supported for a variety of political reasons, but, principally, devolution has been introduced because to a large degree it is seen as a means of solving, or at any rate transferring, the economic problems:

> Head office can give a budget to schools to manage. Schools cannot then come back and say that they were not given enough teachers. The introduction of the policy of devolution puts the politics of decision-making, the economics of education, right back in the school.

An official in another state also believed that the motivation for devolution in his system was basically economic:

> In this system, the real political force and impulse for the change came from the Finance Minister who saw school devolution as a budget issue. Devolution [in the education system] was introduced as a result of a decision made by the group within Cabinet.

Such a change was then publicly justified by reference to supposed educational values:

> The proposal was to give schools a theme for the future: 'Working together' . . . This means that schools have to start building partnerships and supportive relationships with all elements in their local communities. So a lot of leeway had to be made up: suddenly parents had to be made to feel welcome, had to be enthused, had to feel that they were deeply involved with the school on more than peripheral matters – one of which would be the matter of curriculum implementation.

A union representative also spoke with some reservations about the supposed motivation for the introduction of devolution. He regretted that, along with the announcement of the new plans about devolution, there came no concomitant restoration of funding to the education system as a whole, much less to schools. In his view, devolution in the state was too hastily done; too ham-fistedly done; and largely motivated by the need to direct attention away from a funding crisis. He reported that what the government presented as one of the arguments for the introduction of devolution – the opportunity for the introduction of flexible staffing policies – the union saw as involving, in reality, a staffing trade-off:

> The Government that introduced it really wanted school-based budgeting within certain limits that would enable it to collapse all grants into one, with the motto of 'Let schools spend their funds on what they want'. The idea was to give schools a total complement of human resources expressed in unit terms – mix and match as you wish. That is a problem, owing to context – a context of not enough of anything to go around. They [the Government] had halved the teacher aide hours in the budget, and now they were saying to schools that they could have anything that they wanted. Just trade off what you have to get it. So you can have a music teacher but you lose a classroom teacher because it all must add up to X.

What really occurred in that system was, in the view of this union official, a devolution of problems rather than of responsibility: devolution was a way for the government to make financial cuts or to evade or avoid accountability. The Department of Education wanted parents to have a role in decision-making in such a way as to break the previous union alliance with parents.

Another teacher union official emphasized that the union was not against restructuring, but commented that what the union wanted was a change in the management structure in education, driven not by economic considerations but by notions of democratic management and teacher professionalism:

> Teachers need to be involved in the development of educational initiatives at central level through their unions. At school level, structures are needed to empower teachers to help set the directions of the schools. These are based on principles of professional activity and modern management methods to which the union is strongly committed. Many schools still have medieval notions of management. The principals make all the decisions and the teachers are not involved . . . You cannot have students involved democratically in decision-making if their teachers are not . . . Everyone seems to be frantically decentralizing the school system. It involves a major educational exercise in itself to make sure that things work, otherwise you end up with a few people (say the principals and the deputy principals) running things, and sometimes everybody being disturbed and disaffected by the exercise.

The professionalizing argument is also important to some system officials, especially in states where there has in the past been a history of connection between appointment to senior administrative positions in the Ministry of Education and the holding of official positions in the various teacher and professional associations. A system official in one such state commented:

> The key element [about that system's improving schools document] is that it is based on the belief that if teachers are in control of their own situation they will do a better job and be more productive in their teaching or more able to give sense and purpose to it than if they operated by remote control from the directives of someone at head office. This view is based on a professionalizing argument that focuses on the belief that teachers and principals make better decisions and more educationally sound ones than bureaucrats at head office.

This is one of the more educationally sound motives behind restructuring: not merely to avoid the harsher implications of economic management decisions by transferring them to those responsible for their delivery and implementation at the school site, but to improve education by providing an arena for education decisions to be made as close as possible to the point of their application. Regrettably, however, these more educationally informed intentions appear not to have been well or widely communicated in the complex process of restructuring schools and school systems. Without clear indications of goals and intents, many people at the local level, who are having to carry the burdens of restructuring, are often forced back to their own resources to explain these changes to the constituencies most closely affected by them; and it is inevitable that, in attempting to frame such explanations without having been given clear indications by the centre of the reasons for their introduction, some school-based personnel become suspicious and may indeed resort to cynical interpretations of what they imagine to have been the motivation and purposes of those at the centre.

Implementation Issues at the School Site

Just as the more educationally sound motivations for the introduction of restructuring have not been clear or not sufficiently fully communicated to those charged with its implementation, so the implementation itself has been a process fraught with difficulty and confusion. One commonwealth official spoke of the indecent haste with which the restructuring has been introduced:

> It was driven by various state committees of review intent on restructuring and concerned to bring about a move to self-governing schools. But it was done too quickly and some systems and schools did not get it right.

In this regard it is worth noting the wide agreement that the introduction of any kind of change, particularly that of the magnitude accompanying educational restructuring, will usually be much more successful if those involved in its implementation feel a sense of ownership of the process and of their own part in it. What emerges from this study is a need for guidance to be offered to those who are charged with responsibility for implementing and monitoring the change, in ways that will enable them to claim and to exercise their sense of involvement in and ownership of the whole process. The lack of guidance offered on such matters has been a problem for school-based decision-making groups:

> Many people working in school-based decision-making groups do not know how to get things done. Such groups, and their activities, can be aimless and lead to very frustrating experiences for participants unless they are well led and well guided.

Parents and outside members of the community also have only limited experience in participative decision-making. If, therefore, we want devolution to succeed, and local school decision-making to issue good-quality decisions, then system and schools

> have to make very deliberate attempts to provide all school governors with sufficient and appropriate information to allow them to see a range of options and allow them to canvass opinions . . . to make up their minds and take their own decisions.

The sorts of decisions that school councils are to take will depend very much on the knowledge base and on deciding and knowing who are the people most suited to take the decisions and to be responsible for their forward carriage. Members of school councils must also realize that their decisions have both magnitude and effect and must be willing to take them seriously: one system official reported that, in the implementation of school development plans, many parents were not so ready to talk about curriculum as about matters of the school uniform, the tuck shop and the state of the grounds. It is important to note, however, that, in the same system, one of the concerns of teachers has not been realized: that with devolution parents would take over and actually run the schools. Instead they have discovered that 'the rabble-rousers and ratbags drop out soon and you are left with the well-intentioned parents'. One principal gave

85

an account of the power, utility and contribution to the implementation of policy in his school of an articulate parent group:

> The worldly-wiseness of the parents was due to political contacts which were brought to the school operations. This school knows how to squeak. They know how to lobby and do it happily. They broadened the whole expectations of what the school could be about. They raised issues, such as social justice and integration, before they were widely disseminated in the community. These parents wouldn't allow themselves to be manipulated. They had a real commitment to their children and have extrapolated this to say 'this is the way education should be'.

For one senior state policy director, the best way to develop this kind of community participation is through a problem-solving approach based on activities such as the formation and implementation of a school plan:

> The school development plan is a way to get increased strength in the school community in its fullest sense. The school development plan, used well, by a principal committed to parent involvement, is a way of saying to the school community: 'Students, parents and teachers, this is the department's three-year development plan. We have to come up with a local realization of that plan. We have to take that plan into account, but we have the opportunity to give a particular and local manifestation of and modification to that. We may now ask some key questions: what kind of school do we want? What kinds of things do we want to see as priorities within the overall system plan?' Thus, inviting parents in to debate these matters and to get them to help set the plans in train could be a very realistic way to empower them and not just to indulge in tokenism. It is vital to a school's future to get parents in there on more than just cake days and for fund-raising.

Of course such an approach can lead to tensions if the parents turn out to be arguing for unusual or unconventional educational programmes or practices. In those circumstances, the central office of a system will probably have to override their wishes, in the wider educational interest. But experience has shown that it will need to do so only rarely, and then as a last resort, when discussion and negotiation have proved fruitless.

Generally, it is believed that, given parent input, devolved schools are more democratic places than schools used to be. Indeed, nowadays there are few schools without a decision-making group, formal or not. As one principal put it: 'The days when the few could make dictatorial decisions are just about gone. Consensus is in.' Most schools these days have a school council of some description, and are anxious to get parents involved a little more formally than was the case in the past:

> Such councils have been found to assist schools with the framing, implementing and assessment of their policies long before official documents came in and required them to do so. Thus the idea to

devolve responsibility to schools is very soundly based in concepts and versions of modern community democracy and social responsibility.

One senior system administrator averred that one of the benefits of devolution has been that schools seem to be all the time trying to ensure that quality is a part of daily experience. They work at it informally and formally, in structured and unstructured ways, through decision-making, school improvement, school reviews, staff development, attempts to involve parents and the wider school community in the life of the school and in exploring school ethos and culture. Nevertheless, unless there is quality in relationships between principals and central office, schools are not going to be such effective quality schools as the system's central office would like; nor will there be quality education offices without it. So a great deal of time has been invested in building and confirming this relationship.

Devolution to local level had its attractions, another official from the same state agreed. It is attractive to professionals, for now they can do the things that the system may have hitherto constrained them from doing. It is attractive to parents: they can get the interests of their lobby aired and heard locally, and their projects funded at school level, whereas previously, at system level, there was no hope of getting them resourced or even given a priority. However, he went on, it will take time for people to realize the implications of devolution: the local school community will have to make unpalatable priority choices:

> Hitherto most parents and friends committees have been preoccupied with fund-raising and so have never engaged in profound educational debate about priorities of education at the local level. Only in sensitive areas have they been involved, such as in human relations, sex and AIDS education, drugs education and the like.

Another system administrator agreed with this proposition, and argued that one factor contributing to the problem of school renewal and change came from the fact that, at the present juncture, the education community basically lacks the skills of self-management or philosophical debate. This is an important deficiency, if the contention is true, since self-managing schools are being adopted, or their institution is being recommended, in many systems around the world. The point here is that change must be consistent with certain agreed principles and an overall philosophy understood and owned by all parties in the process. If school-based personnel are poorly equipped to develop such philosophical underpinnings, a sense of direction for effective school operation and school change is in danger of being lost.

School-based decision-making throws up a number of issues for consideration and radical reappraisal: it also calls a number of long-standing assumptions into question. It demands a deal of hard explaining to parents and the community as to why one should want to institute changes, and it requires much solid reasoning and political work to get their acceptance. One comment we heard was that:

> Lack of clarity on important matters of procedure and direction can lead to a situation in which participants simply coalesce into aimless

groups; this can be very frustrating for participants unless such groups are well led, well guided, and given a clear set of terms of reference, objectives and time-lines.

It is clear that, in the process towards increased school-based decision-making involving all interested constituents, there needs, therefore, to be an informed understanding of democratic decision-making. Participants in all processes have to know who makes which decisions, and this must be clearly defined. Control and a sense of common purpose and shared objectives in this endeavour are everything. If the people who are working the changes are doing so with a clear sense of purpose and for the good of the school, then there is a strong chance of good things being done and shared aims being achieved. However, the commitment to improvement and change is also important:

> If one allows people whose characteristic preferences are oriented towards the preservation of the status quo to join the important school-management and decision-making committees, then the conservation of the status quo is likely to be the outcome.

Of course, for the purposes of managing effective and positive change there are always individuals who are going to be influential. In one school, for instance, it was reported that:

> In the school's governance structure, persons such as the deputy principal [DP] or the curriculum co-ordinator, the timetabler and level co-ordinators will be highly influential in getting change through. The DP knows the workings of the school, the procedures that will work to get things done; he will have a grasp of the overall picture and can assess whether the change will fit into this or not – and, if the latter, what further adjustments or accommodations might be needed.

In regard to the work of important and influential committees in a school setting, it would appear that, from the point of view of staff in many schools, the curriculum committee (or its equivalent) is the most powerful decision-making committee and agent of change, for its decisions affect so many areas in the school. However, it is equally important to note that one further element of real influence in the successful implementation of changes sponsored and agreed upon by that committee will be the expertise of staff, their knowledge of the most effective ways to deal with people, and their ability to come up with innovative curriculum or pedagogically novel ideas.

The problem with statutory committees, such as the administrative and curriculum committees, is that often they have elected staff representatives who do not find it easy to put aside their faculty biases to see what is good for students and the school. Furthermore, the power network often does not quite correspond with the official hierarchy. Some people are listened to and others not – though this may have nothing to do with their staff position. It is a truism that some colleagues are seen as being more worth listening to, and this has mostly to do with the hidden criteria by which people are judged and so supported:

> Some people who might be given power officially by the administration

have absolutely no influence; indeed, they probably influence people against what they say by the mere fact that it is they who are saying it.

In such cases there is a need for balance in consulting the range of interests involved, while still giving power to the decision of the whole committee – and then supporting it.

Of course the participative approach is not without its political elements or problems. For instance, if a teacher or group of teachers has political influence within the hierarchy of the school, they will often know how to get things done by circumventing the system that has been set up:

> Most people, however, know they have to go through the system of line progression for handling proposals for innovation and change: individual teacher to subject department – to faculty co-ordinator, to faculty meeting, submission to the administrative committee or curriculum committee, and finally to school council, unless the principal intervenes in some way. In some respects, however, it is often better to go the other way – the faculty co-ordinator goes to the principal to get support for an idea, then all concerned work out how to get through the formal processes in order to institute the innovation. In this process, very often if an individual teacher or faculty are seen as important, then rules can be accommodated or invented to handle the proposed change quickly; for example, courses that don't meet the set deadlines but still get included for the next year.

The point is that, nowadays, although the influence of individuals and sectional interests still obviously forms part of the environment in which decisions are made, nevertheless, if the appropriate structures and processes are in place, clear and adhered to, such influence can be reduced to a realistic level of manageability. There are now public and objective processes and protocols in decision-making that rise above and beyond the fiat of individuals or sectional interests. Decision-making has the potential to become less personalized but more structured; however, success in managing the structures and procedures involves knowing how to use them properly:

> This means that in the final analysis one must formally approach committees or authorities, such as curriculum committee, administrative committee or principal, for final decisions and the school council for ratification. These days, one may have to go through a number of committees to get changes: to influence changes means presence and presentations at a lot of meetings, and preparation of papers and political initiatives in order to give point and purpose to being on committees.

Consultation and collaborative decision-making necessarily involve meetings. But this requirement of participative democracy, of course, brings problems with it. One deputy principal commented 'there are too many meetings now. This has become a perennial complaint that has arisen since greater degrees of responsibility for aspects of administration have been left with a wider group of staff.'

Moreover there are differences of approach on the part of staff members towards the exercise of these new responsibilities:

> Some people carefully choose what they want their role in the school to be, as far as decision-making goes. They will not take on too much, though they are quite prepared to attend all the meetings. Others try to be involved in everything, though cannot do so all that successfully. Some staff colleagues do not see their role as being anything more than a classroom educator, and thus neither participate in school decision-making nor even attend meetings.

In this way, and for these reasons, the introduction of increased collaboration has not been without its problems or its costs. One principal commented that, with the existence of a network of committees in a school and the necessity to service them, there is an expectation that staff will participate on committees. The business and management of such committees may be rendered more speedy and efficient if care is taken to ensure that there is as little overlap as possible between the levels and realms of responsibilities of committees. This will avoid the otherwise inimical situation whereby matters can be referred from one committee to another, so that decisions are deferred, or indeed never get taken.

RESTRUCTURING: DECISIONS ALONG THE CENTRALIZATION–DECENTRALIZATION CONTINUUM

An obvious source of tension can arise in some of the approaches being adopted to restructuring by some systems, particularly those which devolve the implementation of decisions to schools whilst maintaining the policy-making and prime decision-making functions at the centre.

It is argued by some, for instance, that if a system has decentralization of delivery but centralization of curriculum policy, construction and development, this enables those in administration to maintain a form of tight control, both centrally and at the local school site. This may well militate against the need or aim to preserve an adaptable, flexible and rapidly responsive model of management. One state system official gives an example of this:

> When devolution and the concept of school development plans were instituted as the future model of management, it was accepted that the process should carry on within a framework of agreed curriculum documentation, and a framework of a particular departmental policy on curriculum. The tensions arose when the frame started to get altered, when the centre started to change the ground rules for local curriculum implementation suddenly, which made colleagues at local site level ask about the function, utility and responsibility of school development planning. In reply, they were simply told that they had the responsibility to implement the change, not to determine it. Obviously this made people question how real was the degree of devolution they were supposed to enjoy.

Indeed, on occasion, such uncertainties and tensions can lead to conflict. One case where conflict can arise, for example, is when the central policy writers fail to keep in touch with what is happening in schools. This situation is exacerbated by apprehensions entertained by officials at the centre about the competences and roles to be exercised by parents and other groups in the new model of devolved power and responsibility:

> Because parents have not previously been involved in genuine planning for school development or monitoring what has happened at the school level, there is little real feeling of confidence in the department that local school councils can really manage the resulting complexities of school direction, control and evaluation. So the department gives power with one hand and takes it away with the other: on the one hand, schools have been told to develop programmes, but, on the other hand, there have been strong controls over what the Government or department would accept. Ministries and departments have negotiated their way through the devolution requirements very successfully and managed to hold on to a good deal of power and control.

One principal gave an account of some of the more subtle ways in which this central control is maintained: 'Schools are funded for autocratic decision-making and not democratic decision-making. So you have people [in schools] awfully stressed to participate over and above time allotment.' One system officer had a graphic illustration of what this aspect of restructuring meant, and how it was working:

> There is a very good analogy between what is happening to schools now in devolution and the fast food industry. It is like buying a Kentucky Fried or a McDonald's franchise. You buy the franchise, you own the business, you are the manager – you have absolute right to manage that as your business. You have to make a profit and presumably give a good service to the community, and it is private enterprise-run. You can't of course change the product; you can't add new lines; you can't change your suppliers because the quality of the product isn't there. You can change the advertising, the building structure, employment conditions, the salaries, because it is either built into your company contract or the statement that you do that – it gives you a string of restrictions and then points out that, apart from those few things, it is your business and you run it.

This analogy enabled the officer to keep saying to local principals:

> This is what is happening to you. You will run the school, you will be responsible for making the profit – which is the educational outcomes – you will manage your staff within certain industrial and institutional parameters, but you will be implementing things and doing things which will be pretty well directed from the top, and that is the flavour of the whole business. That is Margaret Thatcher's London.

And, of course, there have been many commentators who have pointed to the similarity of the realities of devolution in Australia and the obvious analogies that can be drawn between developments in that category here and what has happened elsewhere in the world – principally in the United Kingdom and New Zealand.

INVOLVING THE COMMUNITY IN THE DECISION-MAKING OF SCHOOLS

In the restructuring effort, there is increasing value attached to the relationship between the school and the community. One very senior system administrator went so far as to suggest that the relationship between schools and the community is the most important relationship in the provision of quality. In his view, this is the key relationship to work on – not the relationship of school with the state or federal government. He added:

> Building up the capacity of the families to understand what is going on with their children and to make serious inputs into the educational process; building up the capacity of teachers to cope with children and to relate to the families: that is the essence of quality control.

Some argue that it is only through improved community involvement that government schools will remain a strong, viable and attractive option compared with private schools and school systems:

> The state system is going to have to go to a model where there is active partnership between parents and teachers. They have to be active partners in fashioning or re-fashioning either the system or the school. This is the only way the state system is going to survive in its current form – to open itself up to influence and change by parents, so that they have the scope and real chance to influence the system and to make the real changes. The results of such change efforts will involve a compromise between teachers and parents, but they will have significantly influenced the education which the children are getting.

The driving forces behind community involvement and the nature of that involvement are identified by members of the education community as a potential source of problems. An indication of some of the dangers which arise when prejudiced attitudes drive the move towards changed governance relationships with increased community involvement has been highlighted from the experience in the United Kingdom. A senior administrator commented:

> Thatcher empowered parents over the heads of teachers who did not want to give parents much of a say. She empowered them to make teachers teach what she thought should be taught – she attempted to use the mass of parents to discipline teachers.

For the purpose of arming schools against the imposition of such attitudes, many better-informed educators are firm in asserting that teachers have to get involved in their school's governance and create partnerships at school or system level.

Among other reasons, in the view of educational experts we consulted, they will do so:

- to improve the schools, in so far as parent input will help make schools better – enable the school to operate in greater synchrony with the home to achieve greater educational success;
- to establish a political alliance at school level against anybody who wants to take it over or change, cut back or foist things on it.

One teacher commented on the need for such alliances: 'So that is the race – either we get in there and establish the partnership, or government will purport to empower parents over our heads.'

Yet, among many educators, caution regarding community involvement remains. Australia, it must be remembered, adopted a highly centralized and bureaucratic approach to the administration of schools on the assumption that a centralized education system would better ensure the equitable provision of education to all students. The fear is that greater community involvement in school decision-making will undermine the concern for equity, and instead promote greater individualism and competition:

> The school becomes concerned with building itself up and occasionally this is done at the expense of other schools. It is not obvious that this contributes to improvement of the system as a whole, as against the pre-eminence of one particular excellent school. Excessive individualism carries the risk that states will end up with a diversity of state schools that reflect the aspirations and beliefs of a range of individual parents. This risk has to be modified and moderated by state guidelines and equity considerations, comprehensiveness in the curriculum – a balance between what needs to be determined and insisted upon centrally, and what can be determined locally. To this extent we must adopt a supportive but cautious attitude towards parent empowerment.

Within the school, this means democratic empowerment for the whole of a school's community, not the capturing of the school council by a clique or one particular type of parent community. Community involvement in school decision-making has to be genuinely broad and democratic.

Regarding community involvement, however, there is another set of constraints and difficulties. For instance, with respect to parent–teacher co-operation: in meetings between parents and teachers, the issue of confidentiality will often arise. One principal commented:

> [This] still rears its head every now and again, because sometimes you really want to unleash tension about a kid who's giving you a hard time and all of a sudden you realize that there's half a dozen parents there. Our problem has been that we don't have enough room. As a result, a little room off the library was cleared out completely and we used to have staff meetings down there as no one else would be around . . . The other side of the coin is that you've got parents up

here working in classrooms and contributing to the school and you can't not say 'come in and have a cup of coffee'. But when the school council made a ruling that the staffroom should be a community room, that caused heaps of friction.

Yet another teacher remarked that some teachers feel overwhelmed by some of the parents: 'There are some teachers who are very insecure in the context of having to articulate their own theories and positions.'

There will also be some difficulty in attempting to educate parents to have an interest in school development beyond their personal interest in their own child. Indeed, one system official, reflecting the views of many professional educators, offered the cautionary reminder that, though parental involvement is a worthwhile goal, it is difficult to achieve. 'Parents are only really interested in their own child, and too busy in their daily lives to give real commitment to schools.' Clearly, then, the attempt must be made to get a wide circle of community members interested and involved in the school's doings, if the whole community is to assist in school improvement.

There are, of course, other tensions in these new relationships between schools and the community, particularly with respect to the powers now given in recent legislation to parent members of the school council. Some principals are concerned whether or not a lot of authority is going away from them towards people who are not trained and have little or no expertise in educational and professional matters. Another source of tension can come from the fact that some parents have strong views on schooling – in spite of the policies of the school rather than in co-operation with them – particularly where there is on the school council a group of parents who are articulate and intelligent enough to see a determinative role for parents in schools and to work towards grasping it. It is for this reason, perhaps, that many principals and teachers consciously or unconsciously create barriers in their schools which block the positive participation and helpful and supportive contributions from their parents.

One senior commonwealth administrator pointed out the lack of wisdom in this approach, by observing that public accountability often centres on questions of financial competence and the integrity of systems, officials and procedures:

> The way the world is going, with concern for economic conservatism (shared by both major parties now), the only hope of maintaining a strong public system is to keep the government accountable for a list of things, hard things, funding- and philosophy-driven. There is a need for the public to be able to have the finger on them – and this again means a greater amount of preparation and education of the populace, to be able to deploy, require and understand the processes of accountability. This generates yet another role and responsibility for schools in modern political economies.

SCHOOL LEADERSHIP AND MANAGEMENT

In all this, the important thing to remember is that in recent times schools have definitely become more democratic places – as well as becoming more autonomous from 'the system'. A major feature of the change has been the imparting of increased authority to principals. One principal comments:

> At the moment principals' authority in their schools has probably been greater than the principals ever realized. Principals are no longer bound by rigid guidelines from a central authority and they are able to make more decisions with accountability built in . . . New systems of financial delegation will mean that principals can spend their delegated funds on what they like, but they will be held accountable for the outcomes. Principals will have to justify educational outcomes to a regional director and to school councils on how they propose to spend the funds. This means there is less chance for a principal to be autocratic; nor will they be able to be erratic leaders either. In future there will be school renewal plans which set a school's priorities at the beginning. These will have been determined democratically with school council and the school's full understanding and acceptance of them. In this way, principals will be more or less locked into a situation in which they cannot autocratically change their minds (though the rest of the management group can't either). In this state of affairs, it would be very hard for a principal to say, once the school plan was printed, 'I'm going to throw all that out and do something else!'

There is now a new vision of the role and responsibility of a principal:

> Principals are now not so much autocratic head teachers as chief executive officers to school councils, and the preparation for meetings, summaries, and executive implementation means that principals will now do a lot of the writing and the executive follow-up, as well as the administrative oversight. It will not be fair to ask parents to do all the hack work. Their role lies now in giving ideas, providing support and exercising scrutiny in policy evaluation and assessment.

At least one principal saw this change in lines of accountability responsibilities to the principal as also affecting system-wide relationships and structures, especially in respect of the intermediary bodies in the system, such as the region. The concept of the autonomous principal in the self-managing school (an aim of the director-general in this principal's system) means that the relationship between principal and region is a collegial relationship, not a supervised one:

> As the concept of self-managing school and autonomous principal flows through the system, there is ultimately no place for an intermediary level of system officers at the regional level. Now that there is more direct funding from the centre to the schools, and schools can make their own political decisions according to certain priorities within central parameters, there is very little need for an intermediary level.

Moreover, in some systems:

> Principals are now the largest group of experienced administrators left in the system, whereas those making decisions from head office

now are not necessarily experienced people with school-based experience. It is the principal now who has to wear the responsibility for the ordinances of the system and their successful implementation.

However, their new roles and responsibilities have their complexities. As one principal commented:

> I sometimes feel we are really looked at as branch managers, where you are just there to repeat and carry out the instructions of a central hierarchy. I also see, in the new look of the people who are in the so-called key decision positions, very much the business manager – male, pinstriped suit brigade, middle/upper 30–40 age bracket, who like making similarities with [the activities between] a business or a private enterprise organization and the teaching profession. I think they miss the point of most fundamental importance, that teachers are professionals. They might be salaried professionals, but they are professionals; the teacher steps into the classroom, closes the door, and then he or she is professionally autonomous.

One system official confirmed that, in the changed arrangements, the role of the principal was in danger of being treated more as a management issue than a leadership one:

> Financial responsibilities and budget management have been thrust upon principals of schools, even to such minute levels of activity as ordering and paying for all goods used, needing to use careful choice and to pay directly for such items of expenditure as the telephone. Textbook monies, too, are a large area of responsibility, with some schools being accountable for sums up to $500 000. The pushing down of these management tasks on to the principal threatens to detract from leadership in curriculum, teaching and instruction matters.

An administrator notes that global budgeting and its responsibilities worry principals, who see this as an added financial responsibility, rather than seeing its potential to enhance educational goals:

> Until they have some practice at it, become familiar with it and adept at it, they will not realize that it really is just a tool to let them carry out the policies they want to institute, and to pursue their educational goals. It is an activity that is not like simply holding the purse strings, but is a creative way of moulding the planning and distribution of resources to provide an impetus and support for a school's educational policies. That is its chief *raison d'être*.

The common note of all the foregoing, and the underlying motif of the search for quality in schooling, is that the role of the principal is vital. It is the principal's task to use resources to create, in the school, an atmosphere in which people (students and teachers or school council) can perform well. One system administrator remarks:

It seems to me that the creation of an environment or culture in which people have the same sorts of objectives and are aiming for the same sorts of goals is perhaps the most significant role of the principal, and . . . he or she will be able to do that a bit better by holding the purse strings.

But the widespread fear is that in the changing arrangements the principal's role as educational leader will be diminished. In this regard:

The key role of the principal in this aspect of quality assurance lies in being able to facilitate and allow quality to happen in the classroom, and to set up procedures so that it can come about and be fostered.

Many principals involved in this research reported on the stress that they now experienced in association with the changed structural arrangements and their new responsibilities. One authority points out, however, that the pressures principals claim they are feeling about changes are often self-imposed. For example, principals will often feel that they should pick up and run with a new curriculum programme as quickly as possible. Yet there is no compulsion on them to do this:

They don't have to keep up with the curriculum Joneses. Instead, it is the principal and members of the school community who should determine the rate of change in a school. They should realize that if they are retaining students there must not be much wrong with the programmes their school is already offering. Thus instead of trying to implement whole new curriculum programmes, they should simply look at the framework of what they have and adjust existing programmes to it, gradually feeding in changes in curriculum. They should forget time-lines and consider instead what resources they have (human and non-human) and where they are coming from. They should be content with some degree of change but not look for total change. While doing that, they need to forget the claims being made by the fellow down the street: much of what people claim they are doing only exists in their minds. In implementing change it is often the principals and teachers themselves who are their own worst enemies: they have to be convinced that the system is not pressing down upon them.

Some principals are hoping that there might be a limit to how far devolution in some states might go. The concern of these principals is whether or not a degree of authority might be slipping away from them towards people who are not trained and do not have their expertise and knowledge. Their worry is that the power is going away from the principal's area into an area he or she cannot manage. This introduces an element of insecurity into the principal's role, especially when the principal retains ultimate responsibility to the system. A system official commented:

A school principal is handicapped by pressure groups and commit-tees telling him what to do. One cannot simply consult experts and get on with the job: one has to conform to pressure groups. Principals should have the power to see that the word of experts should take precedence over that of non-experts.

In addition to the professional difficulties experienced by principals in times of restructuring, one principal pointed to the personal costs sustained:

> A principal can be under enormous criticism in day-to-day things, such as offending someone or other because one might not have referred something to someone. This saps morale . . . Power can be in the hands of a small group of a few 'pushy people'.

By contrast, it has been pointed out, things can go the other way, too. A system official draws attention to the tendency of some principals to overrule committee decisions, thereby undermining the role of the administrative committee or blocking the power of the curriculum committee. This can be both frustrating and disillusioning. Indeed, the way ideas are sometimes overriden at the top – and collaboration thwarted – often causes people to quit the attempt at innovation. The allegation concerning the tendency of some principals to override committee decisions is, however disputed by a deputy principal: 'The time has gone when school administrators can make changes single-handed. Teachers do not work unless they see that you have commitment to them.' The trend now is for principals and others in school administration to share the load and share the decision-making; in today's school, management for quality education has become strongly democratic and consensual. However, principals need to develop models for the emergence and management of such consensus. Further, they need to learn that effective management means giving authority and freedom to operate, on a plenipotentiary basis, to all members of a management team to whom authority can be properly delegated. It is in this re-allocation of responsibilites that the principal has a key role.

In addition, there is a strong need for management skills linking strategic planning to the whole issue of policy conception and implementation. In creating a structure and system of management for policy conception and implementation, leadership is required which provides clear goals, high expectations, with a stress on teachers serving the needs of students, a school that is open to other professionals and, above all, that respects teachers' professional judgment. Another system official commented on what is expected of a principal:

> Good principals are good because they are able to help create a situation which maximizes the performance of all the teachers, gives them both the greatest space to move and the greatest motivation, and at the same time helps create *esprit de corps* – the feeling of being part of something and that is a shared vision where everyone knows where they are going and they are going there together as part of a team. That is the key to leadership; it is very hard to achieve that [shared vision] without a principal who can do it.

A system administator emphasized the importance of vision and the need to ensure that visionary leadership and effective management of processes and resources are properly integrated:

You have a vision of what you want your school to be, and you know about curriculum, and you know about pedagogy, and you know the direction you'd like your school to go, and you're a good manager of people and those sorts of things. It seems to me that the whole business of having to sort out a budget or whatever will never get to the stage of being the be-all and end-all [of a principal's educational mission]. Those people that are losing sight of the purpose of their organization are the people who are going to have problems . . . If you let those sorts of things divert you from what you're on about, which is educational leadership, then you're going to have problems . . . we're saying that [principals] have got to be educationalists first, and maybe managers second.

This administrator pointed to the problems of morale for principals in relation to this visionary role, referring to the protest of one principal who said: 'When you're down on the ground, with your head right down after being belted, it's pretty hard to get your head up and start talking about a vision.'

To maintain the role of educational leader, one system official remarked, principals have to be alert to what is happening in many aspects of contemporary life, without at the same time being so caught up in the day-to-day nuts and bolts part of their job that they do not really think beyond that: it is frightening that some principals have not thought for some time about what education is:

There has to be a balance between internal involvement and external vision, and there has to be an emphasis on the principal's establishing a shared vision in broad terms, so that changes can be made in a coherent direction, according to values and philosophies agreed between staff, parents and the wider community of the school. In this way changes can become more easily institutionalized.

One part of this successful implementation of a shared vision emanates from the way in which a principal is able to select and form his or her own school team. Yet, on this vitally important matter, in most government systems at the present time a principal can be hamstrung. One principal felt in a foolish position, in that the principal does not at the moment have the power to hire and fire: 'It's all very well to put a person in a school and tell them to clean it up. How can you if you don't have authority to do it?'

There is a potential danger here, however. Prima facie, it seems contradictory for principals to work in democratic decision-making mode and in an open climate, yet at the same time to have to conduct appraisal and assessment – particularly if this requires critical comments and negative judgments to be made on people's performance in the past – and then to have to turn around and be responsible for developing that staff member's future career path and for lifting and encouraging them positively in the direction of improvement for the future. The paradox here lies in the principal's having to be both judge and supporter at the same time.

All this leads us to conclude that, of the many forces making for quality in schooling, the role of the principal is crucial, in so far as the principal is in a position to:

- *empower people*; thus the principal needs to be intelligent, confident and energetic, and to relate well to people;
- *transform the school*;
- *be a catalyst and agent for change* able to enthuse others with *a vision* of what can be achieved in a school;
- *take wise and well-informed decisions* because he or she is a good listener to what is said in the school and community.

In this endeavour, the principal and teachers must profess commitment to the values that are agreed to as part of the purposes of the school. This will mean that principals and teachers have a commitment to encourage all the other people in their care to give of their best. Too often principals are seen as giving too many directions, and as not sufficiently helping and enabling other staff to express their real professionalism: when their staff colleagues can do that, such staff are challenged to grow themselves. This then requires that principals will:

- have administrative ability;
- be efficient and well-organized;
- recognize the needs of individuals within the organization;
- be an enabler and facilitator;
- not be the sole source of all new ideas;
- encourage the broad, encompassing curriculum, and have an enrolment policy that is not exclusive;
- exhibit strength of purpose and firmness of values.

Commitment to the professionalism of the teaching service means that the leadership of the school should constantly present challenges to the staff. Principals need to know each person in the organization and what each is doing, jointly set goals with them, see that there is an agreed process of moving towards the realization of goals, that there are changes being made in the right direction, that the needs of staff and students are being met, and that people get the opportunity to develop.

SYSTEM SUPPORT

In the previous sections we have discussed changed arrangements in the internal functioning of the school. However, schools located within systems of education must still engage in a complex range of activities and play their part in a complex set of relationships, all of which emanate from, and have a bearing upon, the ways in which those activities and relationships operate and interact within the system in order to promote and secure the system's overall goals.

A major preoccupation of our interlocutors in this study concerns the ways in which education systems, during times of educational reform and restructuring, support or fail to support schools and school-based personnel in their drive towards quality delivery and assurance. One senior administrator commented:

> there is often considerable distrust from school-based personnel towards those who work at the centre. This often arises from central

personnel not having a broad experience in teaching and in schools. They are regarded instead as having a *bureaucratic mentality* that distorts or blocks their perceptions of real problems and possibilities at school-site level. This perception of the present is contrasted with past times when inspectors used to know the schools and teachers and helped personalize the bureaucracy.

In contrast to the way in which inspectors and system officials in former times were often seen as sponsors and protectors of their regions, districts and local schools, in present times it is often believed that, at system level, personnel *fail to get out into the public arena and defend schools* and the system. There is also a widespread perception of a *lack of consultation* with school-based personnel on the part of system officials concerning the questions of what changes are to be introduced, when and how. One teacher commented:

> Those who suggest changes have not got their act together. Change is not threatening if it is explained and if it is seen as necessary. Changes that do not seem necessary, or are unexplained and sudden, make a recipe for disaster.

Problems arising from the speed, kind and degree of change have particularly impacted on the implementation of the devolution process. A system administrator commented on the difficulty where:

> one day the department has complete control and the next day the school thinks it is in charge of running itself. Parents, principals and teachers often have only limited understanding and experience, and initially face considerable problems of adjustment.

This problem is compounded when information about changes often seems to come more fully from the media and other sources, and not through the official channels of the Education Department:

> Schools receive phone calls from parents requesting an explanation, but in many cases schools have not been informed and cannot answer, not having been provided with information of the requisite type, range and complexity.

Thus one barrier to the achievement of quality is clearly a *lack of communication* between the administrative centre and the local school site.

A further barrier is seen as arising from a *lack of support* to schools and teachers, whether in respect of adequate and appropriate teacher work conditions, resources in schools, opportunities and arrangements for professional development, support for young teachers in the country or curriculum development. Certainly the types of curriculum changes now under way require appropriate and effective preparation and training. Yet, in one state, we were told:

> The teachers in [the initial stages of a particular curriculum innovation] were thrown into curriculum development and implementation with little trialing. There were no resource packages provided for them to

turn to; teachers felt they were being left to do all the thinking, developing and carrying through of all parts of the innovation.

This kind of approach puts school-based personnel in impossible situations: in introducing and implementing large-scale and sometimes quite radical programmes of change, they need to feel valued and supported, not to be working on their own unaided. Any such lack of support will clearly affect the quality and extent of any outcome that may be expected to emerge from proposals for innovation and change.

There is a clear need, therefore, to support principals, teachers and parents in their need and desire to make quality decisions in all matters and areas of new responsibility. For this reason, deliberate attempts have to be made to provide information and allow school personnel to see options, canvass opinions and assess a range of possible outcomes. This means providing school staff with the appropriate information and training in the skills of decision-making and evaluation. The sorts of decisions that can and should be made depend very heavily on the knowledge base that school personnel work from, who takes the decisions on important issues, and on the basis of what criteria.

The above holds true particularly with respect to the introduction of programmes of curriculum development and innovation. In one system, some teachers made a distinction between those agents of the system who participated actively in the delivery of schemes of curriculum development at school level in ways that required active curriculum intervention, and those officials who were concerned merely with the administration of their delivery. These teachers welcomed the system's commitment to:

- running in-service activities and programmes,
- getting into classrooms;
- trying to encourage teachers;
- seeing that teachers have appropriate materials;
- providing manageable challenges;
- letting principals see that leadership is called for in the drive to improve curriculum content and pedagogy.

Regrettably, responses indicate that such support from a school system is not perceived to exist widely across the country.

System Support for Principals

It is perhaps worthwhile for system officials and others charged with managing restructuring to remember that, in the undertaking of educational restructuring and reform, one cannot change the system without changing the people. As one system official remarked:

> Our principals have been used to following fairly close directions and working within a fairly tight framework, but in future they are going to have to work differently and will need a lot of professional help. In providing for support and assistance for principals, there will be no substitute for face-to-face encounter and getting together with col-

leagues in small groups, to avoid or mitigate that worst of all aspects of leadership–isolation. We do not mean by this merely geographical isolation, though that is also part of the problem. It is often difficult to provide experienced support, assistance and advice to principals in remote areas. One is conscious that, often, remote areas are serviced by volunteers or who are in the first years of a contract; geography can pose a major problem regarding the pressure for quality in remoter areas. But what we mean is that larger isolation – the isolation of the principal in office and the need for positive feedback, support and encouragement from above, and sideways from the school's wider community. For us, the isolation of the principal presents the greatest challenge to the successful implementation of those policies and plans that will make for quality in schooling.

There is general agreement that system support for principals is a requirement:

First, to bolster spirit and morale, particularly when they often feel themselves embattled and struggling for survival rather than happily being astride the scene, with the pleasure of shaping things through empathy; and second, to restore trust and rapport between teacher, student and parent – what has been termed 'the triangle of trust'.

Indeed, the idea of support for principals is past being a mere requirement: it is now regarded as an absolute necessity. Principals need from the system more time, money and acknowledgment of their efforts if they are to cope successfully with the management of reform and the improvement of quality in their schools.

For providing leadership, however, principals need not only resources, but training and professional preparation. Increasingly, professional development for principals is seen as needing to focus on developing skills for whole-school change. Features of such programmes are seen to include: personnel management; understanding adults in the work-place; the psychology of adult behaviour; team building; and the skills of marketing an institution and communicating with its stakeholders and constituency.

In addition to professional development, part of the process of encouraging quality in educational leadership is an increasing reliance upon performance review of principals. The process can be simple, supportive, yet vigorous enough to pick up areas or functions where there might be major problems. The Catholic system has very much led the way in this regard. For instance:

Performance review in the first year of their service can be quite simple. The school management and personnel/resource services [of a system] get their people to work with the principals to establish some goals at the beginning of each year, and then some agreed understanding of how principals are going to carry these out. Such central services support principals in their role, and at the end of the year there is a review of the goals, which can then be reset for the next year. This is an iterative process that can be done over a cycle of, say, four or five years. During the fifth year of a principal's contract, another agent can come in and bring together the achievement of the

103

past four years, talk with the school council, the staff and some local community people, and then a summative review is written. On the basis of this, principals might or might not then be offered a further contract. In this way, principals can find out that there are things that the system, the school council and the local community believe have not been done well enough, what things need to be confirmed, and what improved.

System Support for Teachers

All system officials would agree that ensuring quality in schools is as much a function of the work of good teachers as of any other factor. This requires the training and provision of quality teachers in systems and schools. This means, in turn, that positive efforts have to be made by school systems to attract teachers to the profession. Perhaps this is why professional associations and teacher unions place so much stress on the appropriate professional training and the achievement of effective and appropriate terms and conditions of service. But payment is not the only criterion: 'Teaching is not a market place activity; much more is it to do with caring about people. We want to give teaching back to teachers.'

Perhaps the professional answer lies more in getting through to teachers (initially or at retraining) that teaching is a particular sort of profession, having enormous personal responsibilities, but also offering immense rewards above and beyond the merely pecuniary – important though those are. One official comments:

> It is fairly easy and simplistic to fix on wanting more time from teachers in exchange for increased salary. Teaching has to be reconnected to people. The whole business of teaching being a human activity, one that involves constant connections with people, is extraordinarily important in addressing teachers' current problems.

It is agreed throughout the profession that teachers need much more appropriate remuneration and public regard. However, they also require advice, assistance and support from the systems within which they work. Indeed, there is a need to maximize the support given by the system to classroom teachers, particularly in respect of provision of resources and opportunities for them to enjoy professional development and career advancement, by conducting research into *how* to support teachers and what professional development is required. Discussion of these issues needs to be much clearer and more co-ordinated.

In some state government systems, unfortunately, teachers often see themselves as little more than paid functionaries – mere staff numbers – despite any attempt on the part of the Ministry to show them otherwise. One teachers' representative who had intensive experience in government and non-government systems expressed it thus: 'Some teachers in government schools often feel that they have no one who knows their history and who has a concern for them.' We must then ask, in what ways and from what sources can teachers be helped to lose that feeling, and to acquire a sense of being esteemed colleagues in an organization and an undertaking that places high value on their academic contribution and cares for them as individuals? In this regard, the principal of a school has an enormous responsibility that can be used to pave the way towards helping teachers retain their commitment to quality teaching and learning. He or she can serve as a starting point for the development of a sense of professional identity and value, and can provide much psychological and collegial support.

Another source of support arises from how and how much teachers can profit from courses of further academic and professional development. These can be provided by system or school. Some tension does arise from the question of how to provide teachers with in-service education and training (INSET) without causing too much disruption to their school's programmes. However, there is widespread agreement that systems, like schools, have a responsibility to provide INSET to their teachers, for it is only as a result of effective INSET that teachers are able continually to update their curriculum knowledge and improve their pedagogy in their attempt to enhance quality in the achievement of the goals the community sets for its young.

As the ones charged with that direct responsibility at the front line, so to speak, teachers have the right to be involved in goal determination, even though they do not – and probably should not – have the right to decide on the goals entirely by themselves. Their key professional responsibility is to decide how to translate the goals on which governments, systems and school councils have decided into teaching and learning strategies which work well and have a real point of purchase in the school setting. If the school community (particularly the teachers) does not have a sense of control over, and ownership of, the major part of the changes currently coming about in education, and is not going to be given the appropriate INSET and professional preparation, then the changes will not be implemented in ways that will contribute to quality. And it is with this last that teachers' sense of professionalism is, at root, primarily concerned.

In all this, inspectors and system officials can provide system support. As an example, we may refer to the way in which one system has encouraged inspectors to establish:

- cluster groups (secondary and feeder primaries) and meetings within clusters;
- inter-school visits for teachers; and
- exchange teaching (primary and secondary) for a couple of days at a time.

The success of this system support strategy was seen as being largely due to the Education Department pushing the dual role of its inspectors and officials – a duality concerned with the encouragement of development as well as the scrutiny of accountability: 'In this system inspectors are not seen as monitors or spies but are there to support; elsewhere the inspector is seen as having a role and function related only to accountability.'

The developmental-accountability model described above works well in the use it makes of a multi-level, multi-skill inspectorate. One of the system officials describes how it operates:

It is possible now for a district inspector to go in and ask for a teacher to tell of their concerns, and then for him to find someone within the inspectorial team to help, say, as a consultant. So, at a review stage, the inspector is not trying to review the work he has done himself, but he is the co-ordinating person, a link to help and then later look at how it all worked out.

An official of another system refers to the role of the supervisor of studies in regions and describes how this links in with the activities of district inspectors, among whom a main concern is for the curriculum development undertakings of the system. If these two groups understand the developmental role they have been assigned, then they are able significantly to influence action and also ensure effective monitoring.

Nevertheless, complaints abound that systems have not put sufficient resources into professional development activities for teachers.

> Staff have had to use their own time for professional development by 'the trickle down method', whereby they 'fossick around', find out opportunities and possibilities for their own advantage, and then tell others about them ... the lack of state- and centre-provided professional development programmes has been seen as a source of great frustration.

Alternatives and Complements to System Support

The question of system support in these days of restricted budgets highlights a need for additional resource support from external sources. In this context, it is important that schools and systems have the ability to develop good projects which will attract outside funding and external support:

> System authorities and school principals need to learn how to ferret out money and use it well. Increasingly, nowadays, schools and systems realize they have to attract grants to set up the projects they want to undertake and to service them appropriately. Most of all they realize that they have to develop programmes which are not just about engaging more teachers, since that of course creates redundancy problems when funding runs out or is withdrawn. A strong base for development and innovation in any system will be provided by research and development programmes. When money is spent on research, and when funds run out or money is withdrawn, at least it is possible for the learning to continue.

One resource which is in very short supply, however, is teacher time. It is thought almost impossible for the average teacher to have the time to conceive, develop and work through the establishment of a framework for curriculum innovation that will have broad community support. There are just not enough hours in a professional day to accomplish this. If that task is to be done, it will necessitate the freeing up of some teachers' time for the purpose, and their release from other constraints.

In association with the work of the system and any support it may provide for such purposes, one can observe another source of considerable assistance in the support available from and provided by subject associations, particularly in the implementation stages of new courses. The importance is clearly established of co-ordination between both central office and subject association in assisting teachers with curriculum materials and special seminars; in timetabling; and in 'selling' courses to teachers, parents and students.

Important sources of support for principal professional development do still come from central, regional or local sources and centres. Increasingly, however, principals are also seeking support from private non-governmental agencies. Principals report that, faced with the necessity of seeking such support, additional burdens are placed upon them to engage in the requisite explorations, discussions and negotiations, and to prepare and present the submissions involved. The carrying of these burdens needs to be managed and resourced. Again it is systems and schools which are most likely to foot the bill for the time and costs involved, and thus function as a hidden source of further subsidy for those necessary undertakings.

System Support for School Renewal

Most policy-makers and administrative officials of systems, nowadays, ascribe a central importance, among all the patterns and elements making for improvements in the quality of schooling, to a set of strategic academic and educational development plans. The presence and power of such plans in a school, together with an institutional profile and mission statement, can serve to identify the needs of the school and the individual teacher or principal, and position them appropriately in the context of system and government requirements and priorities. About the utility and importance of such plans for the self-renewal of a school, one principal commented:

> It should be possible to have a simple structure whereby those needs come together and priorities are established from year to year. One of the crucial things in that is that you limit what is expected to be done in any given time.

Principals and teachers make it quite clear that they have strong views about what time and energy should be given to the preparation of plans and programmes for system-mandated school self-renewal. School-based personnel have priorities for school renewal that they will insist upon being present in such plans; in particular, they have a very clear-sighted view of the extent to which, and the ways in which, the implementation of a school development plan affects what happens in the classroom, and they are right to insist that this be taken into account in the preparation of such plans.

A major factor in school renewal will, of course, be the provision and availability of the requisite information. One system provides a whole package of such information containing: a summary of current practices and policies; the consultative structures; excellence of specialist services; individualized educational planning; protocols for regional–central interface of services; school development planning; school-based curriculum development; and strategic planning for special education services. The provision of such detail underlines the point that there is a need for constant updating of information and directions coming from the system. As one teacher said: 'Most information comes to teachers informally and from the very strong teacher networks; clearly more information is needed from formal sources.'

In addition to support for improved decision-making and planning arrangements, some systems realize that quality also resides in and can be improved by the physical environment, the capital structures and infrastructure, and the range and type of equipment provided. Such systems make sure that very good buildings, modern technical facilities and fully landscaped grounds are all being supplied to new schools. They make sure that these new schools cater for new technology in teaching and learning. Some systems also realize that additional increments of teacher-aide time, and the availability of accounting staff for larger schools, will give the professional educators more instructional time and opportunity for curriculum leadership, as well as time to liaise with parents, all aspects of those vital concerns from which they have been deflected through preoccupation with these other concerns.

SYSTEM-WIDE ACCOUNTABILITY AND QUALITY CONTROL

In some of our respondents' views, some types of centrally determined assessment schemes are concerned as much with public perceptions of educational achievement and with the politics of assessment schemes as with the quality of education. There are, of course, some excellent models of system assessment in operation, and perhaps the best of them is in one state which has a full-scale pattern of activity in this area, involving research, survey and collection of data, which is then interrogated and interpreted in a rich and diagnostic, as well as summative, manner.

This kind of approach involves reporting to the public on the strengths and weaknesses of schooling, quality and assessment, as perceived by the profession itself. Here we have an example of a system checking on the quality of what it is doing, rather than the system checking on an individual school or individual children. Such an approach to assessment is more a large-scale research project. As well as obtaining other kinds of data, samples can be taken of the work and progress of students from particular socio-economic groups, to gauge whether there are gaps of attainment or perceived potential between groups of children from various socio-economic backgrounds.

Such an approach allows hard questions to be answered, such as how well a child is spelling or handling various subject conventions, and so on. This is a way of taking quality assurance in measurement of educational outcomes seriously, as distinct from a more superficial type of assessment which yields some apparently hard results in a very narrow band, but in fact tells us little about the real quality of education the students have experienced. The assessment of that has to be both qualitative and quantitative. A system official stated:

> We may not be able to measure some desired outcomes in quantitative terms, but schools can feed back samples of good work and desirable

changes in attitudes, values and some beliefs to the profession and public that will exhibit the range of material being covered and the outcomes aimed at.

The criticism of the narrow type of tests used in some states and other countries is that they yield little in terms of evidence of what schools ought to do about future educational action, once they have established what evidence they have of students' current cognitive or behavioural repertoires. One commentator maintained that 'if one is really serious about quality, then one has to test in ways which lead to an improvement in the teaching and learning in our schools'. The commentator's state had brought back into the assessment of quality in the school system, not an inspectorate *per se*, but a kind of inspection team to review schools, to be both catalytic and constructive, and not a deadening force on the development of programmes of effective teaching and learning in schools. He believed:

> it was far more healthy to have a system where things are explicit and where plans are clearly stated than to leave schools in the dark. It is better that things are explicit and people get on with the work of teaching for desired, even if non-quantifiable, outcomes than simply teaching to a set of narrow test requirements. In the past, a strangle-hold was exerted over teaching and curriculum in schools by the requirements of public examinations. This seems now to be falling away. But the next move needed is to convince the universities that the world will not fall apart if assessment moves in another direction and operates according to a different set of procedures.

Another state administrator pointed to the overt agenda of many outside forces – not excluding some senior academics and admission officials in tertiary institutions – who preferred narrow types of assessment, and sought what they believed to be 'hard' objective and quantificatory mode results. As this administrator saw it, such people want to measure achievement levels and outcomes that they can put into the hard dollar terms of funding bases for their number of effective full-time student units (EFTSUs) and other clearly simplified ratings, but:

> that kind of result is not applicable to education: one cannot measure in clear-cut, concise terms the growth of the human person – their development academically, mentally, physically, intellectually or soci-ally. At the present time, one of the greatest sources of tension in education arises from the efforts of educationists trying to comply with the requirements of government and some others to measure their outcomes – a demand in which they have little professional confi-dence, and to which they have strong conceptual objections. The temptation is to get into all sorts of assessment procedures that are in themselves skewing what ought to be happening in education.

A senior state administrator pointed to one problem area caused by moves towards new systems of measurement and assessment:

The more teachers have become sophisticated and professional and have used more subtle, reliable, honest forms of assessment, involving much more than merely giving pass or fail grades, then the more deeply suspicious some parents have become of education. Faced with this public suspicion, some educators have tended to become obscurationist and to keep people at a distance by claiming that 'We know what we are doing!' The problem arises from the sophisticated, complex and difficult nature of most modern methods of evaluation: the formulae are seen to be deep and mysterious – well beyond the power of ordinary people's comprehension. By their use of such methods of assessment, teachers have in some respects, and to a certain extent, created problems for themselves in their standing in the public eye. For this reason, if for no other, there is a need for teachers and educationists to go out and 'educate' the public about the new methods of assessment, to build up trust and awareness of the subtlety and sophistication of the evaluation process and, in so doing, engender the public's understanding and support.

This is especially important when the question of those tests employed to determine admissibility to a tertiary institution arises. Some parents have criticized the ways in which tertiary entrance scores have been achieved, when students cannot get into university (due to shortage of places – 'unmet demand' – this being due, in turn, to lack of government funding). But reservations about such admission scores have long been expressed by professionals in evaluation. Indeed, expert agencies in many places want to abolish such scores and have them replaced by student profiles, portfolios and certificates (though these will most often include a centrally issued certificate). However, public attitudes to the supposed 'objective' value of the former Higher School Certificate (Year 12) scores lives on, and in future we can expect constant arguments over such scores and other similar, supposedly 'objective' measurements of student admissibility. That is perhaps one reason, among many others, why there is a need for the introduction and verification of the validity of different types of performance indicators for tertiary education potential.

A system official in one state advised that in his system a great deal of work has been done on performance indicators. There are, for instance, documents entitled 'Performance Indicators for Equity' dedicated to establishing what subjects girls choose in preference to Physics and Mathematics, or to determining retention rates among students from particular socio-economic or minority ethnic backgrounds. Such data are relatively easy to assemble and to make judgments about; much more difficult to establish are indeterminate factors that are nevertheless strongly related to quality schooling and the educational effectiveness of a particular institution, such as the atmosphere of a school or whether children like it.

Other problems with public forms of assessment spring readily to mind. For instance, system officers will have a problem if all the resources that are put in place to meet public demands give results of tests that are seen to show that an individual child (often identifiable – or even identified!) needs help in a particular area. Another danger of a 'public' approach to assessment and the publication of what purport to be 'results' is that such publications succeed only in making it possible to compare school with school on a ranking order of the outcomes attained. Such publications of 'league table' scores and standings do absolutely nothing to allow for appropriate consideration and weighting to be given to a number of unseen variables that are often directly or tangentially related to performance. These include such matters as the student's socio-economic background, the number of students from a non-English-speaking background and deficiencies in school fabric and/or resources; these need also to be taken into account at the same time as one inspects academic outcomes *per se*.

Yet if parents exercise a choice based on overt publications of such academic outcomes only, without taking such unseen variables into account, they inevitably affect, and possibly distort, the choice available to others. Furthermore, some poorer parents (as has been seen in the East End of London, for instance, or the western suburbs of Sydney and Melbourne) have, in any case, no such choice, and so their own children's schools become even further disadvantaged (especially if resources are wound down *pari passu* with the numbers of parents not choosing them) when compared with the performances of other schools, to which better-off, better-informed or better-educated parents can afford to transfer their children. Similarly, in rural areas there is often just one school to choose – regardless of the educational provisions there, or whether teachers are enthusiastic or apathetic, and also regardless of what test results might show.

One senior policy-maker in a territory system commented that, in order to provide higher-quality education as regards outcomes, one needs to restrict coverage of curriculum subjects to achieve the depth of knowledge and understanding that is almost always associated with, and widely seen as, an indispensable feature of, quality. A senior system administrator pointed out that one of the problems with determining quality outcomes in the cognitive realm at school-leaving level is that of failure in earlier years: one needs to target as far down as the lower primary levels for the beginnings of a concern for and the production of quality, and address the problems there, rather than attempting band-aid solutions later.

Some members of the community have strong hopes for the achievement of quality as demonstrated in the outcomes of schooling, particularly concerning equality. But the quality many of them have in mind here relates to one kind of 'equality' – in the sense of equality of outcomes: success at the end of formal schooling, or of a course within it, is (or should be) the complete fulfilment of each individual through the development of his or her capacities and qualities. This notion of the 'realization of every student's potential' (what we have elsewhere called the 'jug' metaphysic) has considerable force among those parent groups whose young have generally not coped so well with academic courses in the school and have not achieved the intellectual advance that some sections of the community so much prize.

There is yet another version of 'equality', however: that is, the idea that outcomes should be identical. But if one interprets *equality* as being able to get the *same* results out of everyone, then there is an obvious risk of losing quality – and compromising equity. If one is (mistakenly) looking at and hoping for an outcome that values getting every child to the same level, and sees this as equity, then one risks only the production of a lowest-common-denominator outcome, which for some students would mean mediocrity, and in this way the schools would lose quality.

A further definition of equality of outcomes says that the sorts of outcomes and benefits that might be enjoyed by boys as a group (particularly those from well-off and supportive environments) should be available to girls as a group, to various ethnic groups, or to country or urban children who hitherto have not been able to secure access to them or participate in programmes for them. This seems to us to be a reasonable version of an aspiration for 'quality' of access and educational opportunity. We should, of course, still want every student to be given the chance to develop as far as their interests and ambitions take them. But this means the provision of opportunities and appropriate teaching and learning styles to allow all students to advance and grow in domains other than the merely cognitive.

It is for this reason that a system offering a range of such opportunities, and extending the encouragement for students to grow in a range of domains other than the purely intellectual, has a responsibility to get parents on-side, to 'sell' to the wider community its programmes in schools and its wider set of aims for its students, and, in this way, to avoid criticisms. Use of a wide range of communication and dissemination techniques will make clear to the community that 'standards' – of a broad kind, that also celebrate diversity in students' outcomes – are being maintained, and that structures are in place to ensure maintenance of these standards in schools.

Within the state of one system administrator, there are achievements in this sphere: the director-general has a personal stake in the assurance of this diverse kind of quality, and expresses this by means of direct personal contact with Year 12 students. In this state, the director-general

> looks at quality students and gets their uncluttered advice on the system. They are still in the system, but they are young adults who can think clearly, more clearly than their parents, and they are the products of a fairly modern system. They give clear advice and comment, and you never cease to be completely and absolutely impressed by the standard of advice and comment coming from such youngsters within the schools. We find this right across the state. Those students are a clear indication of the quality of the teaching service and education system. They would not be at that standard if what was going on was no good.

With respect to achievements in a whole range of skills, the director-general argues, it is clear that, nowadays, very many students are better trained, more knowledgeable and performing to higher standards than their forebears. However, not all students will be given the necessary opportunities for these attainments and this is due in part to the slow rate at which the resources and facilities required in schools for that kind of quality outcome are being provided. We realize that to provide these things is very costly. Yet if we *are* to have an education that is relevant and appropriate to the needs of the students, the state and the country, together with a set of outcomes that denote quality of achievement, performance and understanding, then we must be able either to point to or to provide a range of features in a school's structure, work and organization that are going to promote quality and give students the chance to achieve it.

Identifying and Measuring School Performance

A senior policy-maker in a system observed that more stringent guidelines were being set for total school improvement in the move to assure quality. The system had instituted a strategy of school reviews, adopting more formal approaches to teacher appraisal and laying greater emphasis on performance rather than potential. She noted that the central office was beginning to make stronger interventions into schools where there were doubts about whether things were going well.

An official in another system also noted an increase in the emphasis being placed on monitoring at each level, the purpose of which was to review what was going on in schools to ensure that students received the range and quality of learning experiences and activities to which they were entitled. Furthermore, he said, the requirement to monitor school performance is now being written into the new contracts of recently appointed administrators. In yet another system, an official pointed out that his central office was moving towards being more explicit about expected student outcomes, though, interestingly, less prescriptive as to the ways in which teachers might achieve those outcomes.

A senior administrator in another state noted that a change in assessment procedures from norm-referencing to criterion-referenced testing had occurred. Moreover, in this system: 'Teachers . . . test like professionals, join with their peers in monitoring each other's work and ensuring statewide comparability in a way that does not distort meeting the needs of children.' Another administrator described how his system's stress on the production of school development plans involved the shaping and articulation of educational blueprints, aiming at and characterized by reference to development criteria. This involved cyclic review of the curriculum, incorporating a school's curriculum plan with brief and simply stated objectives. The chief concern in the system remains, however, the question of how to measure outcomes.

Despite the sophisticated processes that are being employed to assess performance, the information gained in such assessments still does not prove that schools have necessarily improved their teaching. Schools must still come back to the almost impossible task of trying to measure, both quantitatively and qualitatively, the wide range of its outcomes. In the light of the complexity and difficulty of that task, and of the diversity and heterogeneous character of the goals and ends aimed at, in a context in which accountability is of such public importance, it would not be unreasonable to conclude that the measurement of student impacts and outcomes poses the greatest challenge for system administrators in the years ahead. The professional frustration that awareness of that difficulty and complexity must engender in school-based personnel is exacerbated by the realization that, in state schools, the point has been reached where teachers and principals feel that they have to be accountable to almost everybody in the community, in order to justify continued public exchequer support for education.

CONCLUSION AND WAY FORWARD

In this chapter we have discussed the impact of restructuring and we have indicated how the school, the community and school systems have reacted to, and endeavoured to manage, the changes that have been introduced in recent times, in response to the calls for educational reforms being voiced by politicians, parents, academics and agencies of business, industry and commerce.

This is not to say, of course, that educators have not themselves had an important part to play in the reform effort. Our evidence suggests, however, that, in facing and coping with all this change and the consequences of restructuring, the part played by school-based educators has often been of a reactive kind: their response to reform has been one of managing the practicalities of introducing a series of changes, the origin of and impetus for which came largely from outside influences, embedded in wider political commitments and economic concerns, in the shaping and control of which the school-based members of the education profession have had a less important part to play.

Following our analysis of the beliefs, assumptions and values underpinning the current educational debate, and informed by it, we now move forward to the generation of our own tentative theory of quality schooling. In the final chapters of this book, we wish to suggest a way forward in education that will address some of the problems, topics and issues that we have identified as being among those that will enable a system, institution or school to identify clearly the ways and means in and by which the promotion and securing of quality schooling may best be accomplished.

We believe such ways may be found by tackling some of the key areas that have emerged from our study as important determinants of quality in teaching, learning and school management. Our attack upon this starts from this contention: we believe that schools are first and foremost institutions concerned with the preservation, dissemination and communication of valued knowledge; with the expansion of the ways in which human beings can come to know about and construct patterns of desirable life-options for themselves; and with the establishment and confirmation of widely observed and respected norms and conventions of conduct that will help our young define and structure acceptable modes of relations between themselves and others, in the home, the workplace and the wider community – everything aimed at enhancing and uplifting the quality of life for the individual and for society.

The pathways to such outcomes we see as starting and extending from the educationally prime considerations of epistemology and axiology: in order to be a person in today's world, to have a sense of one's own identity and others' worth, to function capably as a citizen in democratic societies, what does one have to be and to know? What skills and competences must one possess? What sets of values and attitudes? Of what forms of culture should one seek to develop an understanding; and to what codes of morality should one seek to conform, and why?

It may be asked why we choose these areas as the foci of our writing for the remainder of this book. The answer is simple: we believe, and our evidence suggests fairly clearly, that an inordinate degree of importance in the recent education debate has been attached to the pronouncements and views of particular sectors of society – those of business, industry and commerce – and to the programmes of politicians and political parties seeking short-term answers to economic problems of much greater magnitude and much longer-term history than can realistically be dealt with by one social institution, the school. We believe that members of the education profession have a role equal to that of politicians, businessmen, and other representatives of the community in bringing about quality schooling in the future. There is a strong sense of wanting to 'give education back to educators' expressed by many of our interlocutors; for our part, we want to make all sections of our community equal partners in determining what shall count as a quality education, apt to improve the quality of living. For us, this search starts with the question of what knowledge our community regards as of most worth, and for what purposes. For us, the contribution of every constituency is needed to provide properly informed and positively critical comment upon the hypotheses and tentative solutions by means of which our public policy-makers attempt to provide answers to these questions. We want to ensure that a whole range of perspectives and interests is brought to the fore in the examination of such hypotheses – and this means that the widest possible range of constituencies has to be educated, in order to enable them to play a full part in this process.

The importance of the contributions of educators to this wide-ranging undertaking of community education is obvious. Educators have a most important part to play: they can make a key contribution to the debate about the character and preferred direction of our community's future direction by providing leadership on questions concerning the nature of knowledge, the understanding of cultures, and the values and direction which international, regional and local communities can agree upon and employ as pointers for their longer-term development. By refocusing the education debate on such key educational, epistemological and moral issues, we would hope that all members of the education service will realize that they have a right, and indeed a special duty, to play a stronger part in ensuring that a more realistic and broad-ranging approach is taken to problems whose tentative resolutions reside in wider realms of knowledge and international mutual understanding than those of economic competition or co-operation.

In the chapters that follow, we put forward our own views about how quality schooling might be considered, conceived and achieved. These views we frame around what we see as the three key areas of enquiry in the undertaking to develop a theory of quality schooling: the development of an approach towards integrated curriculum activities; the creation and management of a democratic school; and the promotion of relationships based upon autonomy and mutuality in education and among all those constituencies in the community that have an interest in that most important resource for any nation's future – quality schooling. To the first of these matters we now turn.

Chapter 6

Redefining the Curriculum: Towards an Integration

In the foregoing three chapters we have concentrated on developing an analysis of the data collected as part of the study. In the course of this analysis, we have attempted to present the beliefs and attitudes that are brought to bear in discussions regarding quality schooling by the various actors and representatives of leading constituencies and interest groups in the field. In this analysis we have sought to elicit the background 'theories', preconceptions and values with which these actors and interest groups seem generally to be working when seeking to shape, justify or implement their policies on a range of issues having to do with the promotion and production of what they see as quality education, in quality schools, taught by quality teachers.

It behoves us now to recapitulate the stated aims of this work, articulated and developed in a preliminary way in Chapter 2, and to enmesh our findings in the previous three chapters with those intentions. It will be recalled that we stated our intentions as follows: we attempt to identify:

1 those beliefs and values that it appears proponents of activity in the field might be least willing or likely to give up when faced with challenge or pressure to produce or defend their versions of quality schooling;

2 those theories that underlie the beliefs, values and attitudes of these actors, agencies or interest groups;

3 the 'touchstone' areas on which agreement can be discerned among such groups as to the criteria, characteristics and typical features that might be distinguished and which they seek in schools to which the standard-setting appellation of 'quality school' might then be affixed.

We have covered a number of areas in which discourse on quality matters is generally and widely thought to reside – content, styles and methods of teaching, modes of learning, forms of distribution, organization and administration, and reference to a range of concerns for schooling and its outcomes by members of the community. In all of these we have endeavoured to identify common themes, areas of sameness and difference, particularly with respect to conclusions generally accepted and points of disagreement still existing.

With the benefit of the insights afforded us by examination and analysis of all these data, we wish now to articulate and elaborate upon what is emerging as our own theory on these matters, in the hope that this might offer further increments of understanding to the ongoing debate about the nature of quality and its proper modes of creation, promotion and assurance in education, and perhaps generate further proposals and agenda by means of which quality schooling may be better prepared for, planned, and secured.

Of those matters referred to in the above list, we begin by addressing what is perhaps one of the most contentious but most important subjects – that of curriculum. It is clear that quality schooling, as both an experience within and an outcome of activities in schools, will be, as much as anything else, an outgrowth of those programmes of activities and experiences that are proposed, planned, structured, delivered and assessed in such institutions, and intended to be provided and engaged in for *educational* purposes. What those purposes might be we shall discuss below.

THE CONTEXT WITHIN WHICH CURRICULUM ISSUES ARE BEING CONSIDERED

From our review on developments in the administration of schools and school systems, it has become clear that chief among those forces impacting upon education today is the awareness of economic pressures and the drive to perform well in a climate of increasing international competition and co-operation. Such pressures are driving many countries to question whether they are following the right ideals and pathways in education. From an ethical point of view, such countries are asking: are we doing the most we can to contribute to the growth and development of our people? From a competitive point of view, they are asking: how shall we be able to survive as an independent sovereign nation and an economically thriving unity, still holding to our cultural identity and the social and economic values that have been foremost parts of it in the past?

A problem here is that educational goals for curriculum implementation can realistically be set only with regard to the time and resources available for their achievement. Political time-scales, especially at ministerial level, are notoriously short; educational ones, by contrast, are long. Education, as Edward Bond (1976) remarked, 'cannot be put on like coats of paint'. Furthermore, given the lifelong duration of education, there will never be a time when we can say that the evidence as to its quality is all in. We may, of course, try to make intermediary assessments, and some of these will be directed at the formal stages of education, when one of the chief instruments of educative action will be that applied to the student by means of a structured and goal-focused curriculum.

The major question must therefore start at this point: what shall be the educational goals of a country's education system, institutions and schools; what shall be the curriculum that is held to be most conducive to those goals; and who shall decide the nature and composition of that curriculum? The answer to this last question is that the decision can only be made by a selection of judges from among a whole array of constituencies, agencies and interested parties. But the question of who makes that selection, on what basis, and how it shall be composed, is crucial to this whole endeavour.

At the present time, throughout the world, a widespread stock-taking is taking place on these and other related questions:

- Does it matter if, at the national level, legislation enacts requirements as to those subjects to be covered in the curriculum?
- How do such enactments determine delivery?
- Are there inflexibilities of institutional structure or function that inhibit change?
- If legislation sets in place the objectives and goals to be achieved in specific subjects, does this interfere with professionals' rights, not merely in respect of appropriate teaching methods and curriculum, but also in respect of their properly qualified view of what constitutes and counts as the subject itself?
- Is there any danger that the promulgation and imposition from the centre of national statements of goals and curriculum frameworks, schemes and guidelines might overtly or covertly condition and shape the nature of curriculum subjects, in such a way that the ontology of a subject can become distorted from what the professionals believe it is or should be?
- From which dominant intellectual traditions and cultural values shall the curriculum selection be made, and on what grounds?

The question of which shall be the dominant, or preferred or stipulated, cognitive categories, intellectual traditions and cultural values from which curriculum schemes are to be constructed is a crucial one. We need, however, also to include in that examination reference to the ways in which cultural values are passed on in the school as a social institution by informal or extra-curricular means, as well as formally through the child's exposure to the curriculum and to subject learning. The school is a highly effective social and socialising institution, and we need to consider how it functions and affects the learning and the development of the child, in all the various ways these occur – formal, non-formal and informal. This is particularly important in the case of the question of access to the curriculum. Should there, for example, be different curriculum goals for different groups in society? Is the curriculum we envisage for *all* students the same curriculum we have in mind when we are looking at the learning and access needs of students with disabilities?

KNOWLEDGE AND THE CURRICULUM

Our analysis suggests that significant differences can be seen to subsist between different countries and individual states in their approach to the design and implementation of educational reform conceived as appropriate to address the above questions. But no matter what the approach to the process of change, no one can doubt the overriding importance attached, in all current reform efforts, to three key matters:

- the nature and purposes of the goals of schooling;
- the body of knowledge and skills that should be constructed to help those goals be achieved;
- the quality of the teaching and learning process, their impacts and outcomes.

In planning and arranging for effective and *quality* teaching and learning, it is clear there will be some differences and difficulties over the meaning and use of such words as 'curriculum' and 'pedagogy'. It is, however, widely agreed that questions concerning the nature and number of the goals of schooling, and the curriculum appropriate to deliver them, transcend the immediate and local character, constituency and remit of the school, and that the answers to such questions as these are not to be identified merely as the sum of all the activities going on within it. There is a need for a broader account of goals and curriculum, one that takes in and involves all educational objectives, the transmission of values, attitudes and beliefs, and the educational point and purpose of all those teaching and learning activities and experiences taking place and afforded in a school – formal or informal, deliberate or casual, planned or unplanned – to which value can be attached and for which teachers and resources must be provided.

Conceptions of Knowledge and the Selection of Curriculum Content

It might be illuminating and helpful at this point to draw upon the results of our enquiry into quality schooling and to cite instances of some of the goals that have been laid down for schools' activities. We might make a start by observing that a concern of very many politicians and members of the broader community is to link education to economic advance. The function of schooling is seen as providing personnel and fuel to run the economic engine of the state – to enable a state to be, as far as possible, economically self-sufficient and, if not, to give it a leading edge of economic competitiveness in the world's economic market place.

Recent education reforms and efforts at curriculum determination in some countries make it clear that the goals of education are seen primarily in such instrumental terms: education is seen less as an activity worthwhile in its own right, and more as valuable only in so far as it leads to other ends, regarded for the time being as much more worthwhile. Of these, the chief one is, in the world today, that of economic power and self-sufficiency.

There is also, however, another current of thinking which holds that the prime function of schooling is to induct the coming generation into all those traditions, experiences and cultures that constitute both the identity and the value of being human in today's world, and that will thereby enable the graduates of educating institutions to become bearers of that culture, those traditions and values, and to cope with the demands of living in that world. Proponents of this view hold that students are therefore 'entitled' to be given access to all the great and good things 'that have been thought, said and done' in the ascent of humankind, and that form the starting-points for all future endeavours, particularly those that will stand individuals in good stead when they come to face the exigencies of daily life. These curriculum 'entitlements' can be concentrated into a number of areas of experience, culture and value, and entry into and learning in such areas will provide the building blocks for a life in society that will enable the young person to enjoy civilization and culture in all their multifarious forms, and cope with the demands and predicaments of the modern world.

Yet a third approach considers the definition of educational goals that transcend immediate economic, political or social concerns, and that stand aside from the momentary interests of particular groups or pressures. Advocates of this approach regard the central undertaking of educational endeavour as lying beyond the need for vocational training, moral development and cultural awareness. For them, what is important is the tenet that education is first and foremost about initiating and developing the life of the mind, and this is the *proprium* of 'liberal' education. A truly liberal education is one that gives a person access to and competence in all the various forms of intelligence, all the powers of rational thinking, without which any approach to other questions, whether those of vocational, moral or cultural import, or of contending with the requirements of daily life in the modern world, is impossible and unintelligible. For Hirst (1973), Gardner (1987) and others, what matters is that we direct our educational attention towards developing the powers of intelligence and the rational mind. It is in and by those modes of experience and understanding that mankind has progressively structured, developed and made meaningful, over the millennia, knowledge by which people are able to make sense of their experience and communicate about it intelligibly with others of their kind. Such modes of intelligence and rationality are of a finite, though progressively developing, number, but the number of various discrete modes of understanding constitutes the totality of the rational apparatus by means of which human beings can understand and appraise the reality they share, face the dilemmas of existence and tackle the exigencies it brings them.

These different conceptions of knowledge and goals for schooling generate different curricula whereby a student may start on the road to their achievement. Instrumental education, for example, will see it as the prime necessity that the curriculum concentrates on the transmission and acquisition of those selected bodies of content, and forms of cognitive skill, that will be causally related to vocational competence and strong economic performance. In such a curriculum, subjects such as English, mathematics, science and technology and foreign languages, and some knowledge of those aspects of history, geography and economics that can be specifically related to our national identity, social needs and economic competitiveness, will clearly be crucial. Competence in other life-skills and vocationally desirable skills, such as clear communication, team management, the organization of knowledge, research, and interpersonal relations, will also conduce to efficient and successful commercial, industrial and business production and performance.

Those who opt for an 'entitlement' curriculum will lay it down as a requirement that access to a knowledge and understanding of all the various products, artefacts and advances that have marked what Bronowski called (1973) 'the ascent of man', and to all the great human traditions of critico-creative thought (Passmore, 1967) out of which these major cultural, social and intellectual accomplishments have been wrought, will form the main content of such a curriculum. Mathematics, science, technology, the arts, religion, medicine and philosophy will be among those subjects where the store of rational excellence, culture and creativity can be discerned and concentrated, and in which human potential for future development might begin to be realized.

For the third group, what matters is that, by the skills of either cognitive psychology or epistemological and philosophical analysis, those modes of intelligence and ways of knowing that constitute the totality of human rationality, at its present stage of development, be identified and defined; and that then, in some shape or form and at some time or other, students in our educating institutions be given induction into them and practice in their application and deployment. Such ways of thinking as the mathematical, the scientific, the philosophical, the historical, the moral, the religious, the aesthetic and artistic, perhaps even that of interpersonal understanding, will all function as building blocks upon which the edifice of human intelligence and rationality can be constructed. Using these forms of intelligence and awareness, students will be able to understand and address the issues and problems arising from their situation in the world, and the needs and concerns they have; for without them no address or engagement would be possible. Initiation into *at least* these modes of awareness, experience and appraisal, such thinkers will argue, must be the prime curriculum prerequisite in any educational undertaking.

COMMON FEATURES OF EXISTING CURRICULA: A CRITICISM AND A NEW APPROACH TO PLANNING CURRICULA

At this point, it will be clear that such positions as those delineated above have some feature in common. One is that, in the quest for educational goals, there will always be some *foundations* that have to be provided, which function as basic building blocks for the construction of curricula and the articulation of appropriate teaching and learning activities and processes. The second is that those foundations will be *separable and discrete*: the central concepts, operating procedures, tests for truth claims, and criteria for evaluating success, for instance, will be different in, say, mathematics, morals and the arts, and it is these varying characteristics that require us to provide a differentiated and heterogeneous curriculum. What is agreed among proponents of such approaches is that there *are* different forms of cognition and intelligence: all that has to be done, in curriculum terms, is to differentiate them according to various categorical criteria and conceptual schemata, defend what they are and show, in educational terms, what they are for.

It should be pointed out, however, that these premises have been under considerable challenge for many years. It has been argued that their status is a function of a particular set of meta-theoretical preconceptions about the nature of philosophy and science, that is in all essentials no more than that of a dogma, to the refutation of which Quine (1951) and many others have devoted considerable logical power. By some modern curriculum theorists (Evers and Walker, 1983; Hindess, 1972; Kleinig, 1973; D. C. Phillips, 1971; Watt, 1975) such arguments have been redeployed to telling effect, and they have sought to show that the views of the curriculum foundationalists and separationists encapsulate no less an educational and epistemological dogma. There is now a substantial body of theorists who claim that the holding and promulgating of curriculum beliefs such as those described above may be seen as little more than the expression of contentious theories of intelligence and meta-cognition, or controversial and out-of-date philosophies of knowledge that, therefore, carry no particular curriculum warrant or authority.

Clearly, educational epistemologies and cognitive psychologies are key areas in the planning and formulation of appropriate curricula – but it would be a proper academic requirement that their curricular outcomes should be in accord with the most recent findings and advances in these subjects proper. And the fact is that recent work in epistemology and cognitive science suggests that the theories set out above have no more uncontested rightness, self-evidence or plausibility about them than any other set of curriculum proposals.

Post-empiricist philosophies of knowledge suggest the giving up altogether of the ideas of foundationalist epistemology and the curriculum theories deriving from them. A better way forward, it has been suggested, in any cognitive enterprise, is the working out of *ad hoc* theories to apply to the currently pressing and perplexing *issues, topics and problems* thrown up in and by such key human activities as education, medicine, social welfare, politics, government, and economics. Curriculum philosophy, seen in this light, is *not* then an activity of conceptual clarification; rather it is an activity of theory construction, correction and contention, engaged in for the purpose of providing temporary best solutions to problems, the lack of which is otherwise threatening to human well-being and social harmony.

From this perspective, those theories that have greatest power and cognitive value are those that operate to the best functional advantage. Cancer is better tackled by using and applying the medical theories of the hospital laboratory than by employing those of the folklore of traditional societies; it was modern applied physics that sent human beings to the moon and returned them safely.

So it is with this approach to curriculum construction. Curriculum building and planning, from this post-empiricist 'scientific' perspective, is devoted to the framing of answers to problems, to the examination and criticism of the hypotheses proposed as answers to those problems, and to the tentative trying out and application of those theories that have hitherto resisted falsification to the problems and difficulties that currently bedevil humankind. In this way curriculum construction becomes an activity of facing problems, planning, criticizing, and tentatively adopting as yet unfalsified hypotheses proffered as solutions to the problems at which they are directed.

Thus, it is not a priori preconceptions as to the logical structure of knowledge itself, nor a set of judgments and prescriptions relating to those desirable cognitive activities and cultural values, that determine the pattern of curriculum planning. Rather it is *problems* that provide a set of agenda for curriculum action: agenda that stand instead of much larger-scale 'aims of education'. To try to frame the latter is, we argued, a mistaken undertaking. According to Popper (1957), a total and comprehensive solution, in which large-scale and over-arching 'aims of education' might have their place, will never come. What is important is that we address the problems, topics and issues that constitute the staple of the curriculum diet for a society's schooling and educating institutions – that, in order words, we adopt pragmatic approaches to problems that press in on us today.

Curriculum Problems as a Basis for Curriculum Planning

From our research on quality schooling, we could easily construct a 'Dewey-type' curriculum comprising an intellectual attack on a range of pressing concerns and present-day perplexities. As examples of some of those problems, we might point, for instance, to such matters as the following:

- the common concern of communities to expand and enhance the literacy of their citizens;
- the need of many countries to enable their citizens to acquire the requisite skills and competences to operate in a world where the amount of available productive work is decreasing, where service industries of all kinds are increasingly likely to provide the main means of work, where advances in knowledge and the information technology revolution will mean that a worker will have to be prepared to change jobs four or five times in a working lifetime, where working life is likely to become shorter and shorter, and where – notwithstanding the increasing scarcity of salaried employment – many people will also enjoy increasing longevity;
- the problem of workplace relations in such circumstances: of how people can, in times of employment shortage, work together co-operatively so as to enhance productivity and build and enjoy a sense of workplace satisfaction and reward, instead of the industrial competitiveness and confrontation that disfigure so many of our industrial and commercial activities at the present time;
- the problem of international relations in a world with scarce resources, where the economic gulf between nations is not likely to decrease, and where commitment to various forms of extremism, political or religious, will be a continuing cause of tension and possible conflagration;
- the question of interpersonal relations, at a time when the incidence of phenomena such as substance and drug dependence, domestic violence and child abuse show no sign of decreasing, when the divorce rate is already high and climbing, and when suicide among young people is a disturbingly frequent occurrence, with all the attendant dysfunctions that these events bring about;
- the problem of constructing healthy lifestyles and a regimen of risk-avoiding behaviours, when diseases of various kinds are now continually, and in some cases increasingly, resistant to treatment;
- the problem of food supply and world hunger;
- the problem of protection of the environment;
- the problem of the increasing demand for energy at a time when the store of fossil fuels is declining;
- above all, perhaps, the problem of how to assist human beings to acquire and retain their values of *humanity*, sensitivity, sympathy and compassion, at a time when the emphasis upon what Habermas (1972) called 'technocratic rationality', upon technicization and the

dominance of particular kinds of economic interest, threaten us with the loss of a sense of individual worth and commitment to a set of values that will help define and enrich the quality of relationships between ourselves and others – what we might call the problem of the need for the *humanization* of the present-day curriculum.

There is no shortage of problems that provide a rich diet for curriculum address. What we wish to point out is that an attack upon even a few of these problems requires engagement in a number of forms of intellectual activity, imagination and creativity, so that our coming generation can not only begin to understand their difficulty, complexity and multifariousness but also start to help the present generation try to make tentative moves towards their solution. In addressing such problems, schools will be required, in a process of continuing and dynamic social and cognitive appraisal, to provide access to and instruction in those forms of cognitive operation whereby the question of understanding, dealing with and solving those problems, and a myriad others like them, can be most appropriately tackled.

Educational Purposes and the Curriculum

Mary Warnock (1978) suggested that the education of the coming generation of society is concerned with three kinds of purposes. These she terms *preparations* of various kinds: preparation for the world of work (and, we might add, for the world of non-work and leisure); preparation for the life of virtue (what we might also associate with interpersonal relations); and preparation for the life of the imagination (the ability to understand the past, to appraise all the many facets of the present, and to plan for all the potentialities of the future).

All these elements are certainly part of the operating remit of a community's educating institution, and are, for that reason, of vital curricular importance; but much more still needs to be said. Owing to the rapidly changing nature of knowledge itself, consequent upon cognitive growth and development, and the increasing refinements in the means and instruments by which knowledge is both acquired and generated (not least by the information technology revolution), and owing to the rapid increase in the range, type and complexity of the problems we daily encounter, our approach to the construction of the curriculum to prepare our students to meet their challenges must be dynamic, flexible, and responsive to rapid changes in matters of work, morals, and life and leisure choices. And those who come to it must do so on a pragmatic basis.

EDUCATION FOR DEMOCRACY: THE NECESSARY CRITERION FOR STABILITY IN CURRICULUM PLANNING?

It should be pointed out, however, that there is one element in such an approach that is still needed to provide a set of guidelines for steering current curriculum planning. What we need is a criterion of stability, consistency and coherence, so that educational institutions may guard against what could otherwise be a somewhat anarchical curriculum situation.

One way that will enable curriculum planners and developers to see the wood as well as the trees may be found in the pragmatism articulated and pronounced by Peirce (1955) and espoused so firmly for education by Dewey, Popper and their successors up to the present day (Ackerman, 1980; Mendus, 1989; Guttman, 1987; White, 1973). Such a criterion is provided by the idea of 'education for democracy'.

A modern curriculum of the flexibility and dynamism described may be constructed and continually adapted for delivery on the basis of those various foci of knowledge, skill and value that future citizens of a participative democracy will need in order for them to be able, on a fully informed and committed-for-action basis, to participate in the democratic processes of policy formulation, appraisal, criticism, application and assessment. Such participation will be required, as a matter of course, on any of the issues raised above and tackled as matters of overriding importance by the community. This could involve workplace literacy, it could be concern for the environment, it could be for the fluoridation of the water supply, or the educational imperative of inhibiting such life-threatening diseases and conditions as AIDS, drug abuse, crimes of violence and nuclear accident.

To understand and plan for dealing with any of these necessitates nothing less than the highest degree of engagement and in those intellectual forms of knowledge and criticism that enable students, as future citizens, to understand past causes, monitor and appraise the present situation, and plan, for themselves and their community, how to act in the future (an enterprise in which, incidentally, competence in harnessing the power of the personal computer will be an important aid in the quest for knowledge, the building of alternative worlds of possibility, and the running of simulations and thought experiments). This will further require that educational curricula will not be merely the setting forth of sets of facts or values that are paraded before our students for them to acquire and repeat when necessary: it will also mean an introduction to the forms of engagement in the activities of action and assessment, appraisal and planning, criticism and correction, that are called for in the very conception of an education for life as a citizen in a modern democracy.

Our claim that the construction of curricula will require not merely the setting forth of facts or values for students to acquire, but a direct engagement in forms of cognitive action, reveals that we are working here with a particular *concept of knowledge*. This is indeed so. For it follows logically from our predilection for the kind of Deweyan and Quinean cognitive pragmatism proffered above as a sound and valid basis for curriculum planning that we shall eschew those versions of knowledge that have been so much elevated by scholars such as Bloom (1956) and his followers. For such curriculum theorists, 'knowledge', it may be recalled, simply refers to those facts, or sets of propositions, that can be verified and then committed to memory for reproduction on demand. For such theorists, 'understanding' – the utilization and insightful application of knowledge – is merely a step up on some kind of ladder of cognitive operation.

We also eschew the categorization of knowledge into various 'kinds', such as the propositional, the procedural or the personal, each associated with a different form of validation. We certainly do not wish, for instance, to conform to the view that all propositional knowledge claims may be accorded credence either on the grounds of their deductive certainty (as in the axioms of mathematics or logic) or their high degree of inductive probability (as in the verisimilitudes of the natural sciences), and to see in either of them exemplars for all curriculum knowledge in the particular kinds of 'justified true beliefs' which they embody (and which would therefore privilege some 'subjects' over others, erecting a kind of curriculum hierarchy, from mathematics and the sciences at the top, to religious education, the arts and physical education at the bottom). We do not accept (*pace* Ryle 1949) that knowledge may be sharply differentiated between propositional and procedural: Edel (1973) showed convincingly that the interrelationship between them was so complex that they could not be so divided. Nor do we accept the contention that 'fact' knowledge is somehow better than 'skill' knowledge and thus stands higher on some kind of curriculum hierarchy: the complex operations involved in working a personal computer, with its highly articulated interactivity between 'knowledge-content' and 'knowledge-practice', has decisively seen the end of that myth too.

We take our beginning from the demolition of these and other similar positions so ably mounted by Hamlyn (1971). He agrees with Austin (1975) in seeing knowledge claims, at least in the propositional realm, as being 'performative' utterances, belonging in the same category of communicative interchange as 'promising', 'awarding' or 'conferring'. As against cognitive accounts based upon 'beliefs', which for Hamlyn are merely descriptions of inward states of psychological affairs, 'knowledge' claims belong in the public realm, and are candidates for what Dewey called 'warranted assertability'. In making a knowledge claim, we confer upon you the right to believe and behave as if what we tell you we know is 'true' and may be acted upon.

Knowledge, on this premise, is public, objective and testable, and what matters here is not so much the claim itself but much more the kinds of evidence and theoretical background on which we are willing to rest our future thinking and acting. Just as we are entitled to take it amiss if someone makes a promise but subsequently fails to fulfil it, so we are entitled to be deeply disappointed, even disillusioned, if someone confers a right to know upon us, which rests upon grounds that we find subsequently to have been at worst mistaken, at best uncertain, shifting or illusory. For letting someone down in that way is actually to upset the whole set of presuppositions and legitimate expectations upon which our world of cognition and shared understanding is built. When someone is discovered to have been telling a lie, the whole structure of linguistic interchange is called into question; so when someone turns out to have been less than secure in his or her claim to know something, our confidence in our own perception of reality is shaken.

So strong is the presupposition in favour of our unquestioning acceptance of our own and other people's shared experience in matters of claims upon a common framework of veridical perception, cognition and understanding that it is generally only in the presence of the possibility of uncertainty and misunderstanding that we strongly assert our claim to know something – as Wittgenstein (1953) pointed out. We know we have to objectify our knowledge claims: public communication and the claims of intelligibility require it. But we also have to make it clear that our claims are liable to error or correction; and that is why, paradoxically, when we claim to 'know' something, we are also thereby tacitly inviting our interlocutors to share *but yet to scrutinize critically and check what we say for possible error*. Knowledge is therefore public, yet also automatically open to checking, criticism, and possibly even falsification.

For that reason, knowledge, though claiming to be objective in its inter-subjectivity, is highly uncertain, highly unstable and liable to refutation. It refers *not* to facts, not to mathematical certainties, not to empirical verifiabilities; it exposes instead, and indeed draws attention to, the theoretical frameworks within which knowledge-claims are constructed and articulated, and exposes them to critical scrutiny, error elimination, and every possible attempt at disconfirmation. It is only when such claims have successfully resisted all attempts at overthrow that they may be *provisionally* accepted for the time being as having 'warranted assertability', and the theories within which they figure and from which they operate, as being, *pro tempore*, the 'best' theories for application to theoretical or practical problems that our curriculum builders face.

This is the concept of knowledge which we bring to the question of the defining of the curriculum and the elucidation of its educational purposes within today's schools aiming at quality in this, perhaps the most important, part of their mission: to communicate what presently counts as 'provisional theory', and to induct their students into all forms of procedure and all the knowledge appropriate for criticizing it and, if uncorrected, to apply it to the problems with which the constructors of their curriculum wish to face them.

From this examination, it is clear that of vital importance in the undertaking of redefining the curriculum for the future must be the debate regarding what constitutes appropriate curriculum knowledge in a modern democracy, encompassing such questions as the following:

- What counts as knowledge; how should knowledge be conceived, established and certified?
- How should knowledge be acquired and employed in a society where knowledge itself is continuing, changing and expanding?
- How can one determine, in such a case, what knowledge is of most worth for the purposes that the founders, directors and workers in public institutions have in mind, and for all the citizens of a modern democracy?
- How can the values of breadth of knowledge, depth of understanding and curriculum balance be best addressed and assured?

KNOWLEDGE, THE CURRICULUM, EDUCATION AND VALUES

This last question raises an issue of major concern in the development of our theory on quality schooling, for it raises the question of what a 'balanced' curriculum might look like, and how children's learning can be judged to be appropriately 'balanced'. What this leads to is the fundamental underlying question: what are our schools educating *for*? What are our children at school to become? What will our future citizens need in order to exercise their roles as citizens of a participative democracy – and how can the curriculum give them the necessary skills, knowledge and values? The question of values is crucial here, since this relates to the important point that values exist, and are found embodied across the whole curriculum.

Values are not definable as though they were an autonomous element in the curriculum, as being in some way a separate subject, with its own body of theory, cognitive content, typical activities, disciplinary procedures or criteria for success. As MacIntyre (1972) remarks, to speak of someone as a 'ship's captain' is to engage in a complicated activity of appraisal: the ship's captain's qualification to be described as such depends centrally upon his or her constantly exhibiting, valuing and performing certain standards for the proper performance of functions in that role. In a similar manner, Peters (1966) remarked that to be a scientist is *ipso facto* to be committed to the values implicit in the procedural principles that define the nature of the subject and prescribe its appropriate activities within it. Science is not value-free: it is shot through with value elements that help structure and define it.

Thus it is plain that questions of value in knowledge and the curriculum are not solely restricted to subjects or areas such as the humanities, the arts and religion. Questions of value also underpin, and indeed permeate, the whole syllabuses of other curriculum subjects, such as mathematics, science and technology. As a consequence, this interplay of epistemological and axiological elements and considerations, in association with reflections drawn from the psychology of learning, the sociology and anthropology of school as a social institution, and the values – both individual and social – attached to and embodied in the institution of schooling by the society in which a school is located, will obviously occupy a central place in discussions about quality education, the effective development of schools in the 1990s and into the next century, and the redefining of the curriculum.

Further Epistemological Questions and Issues for the Debate about Curricula in Quality Schools

For all the above reasons, a number of issues now come to the fore:

- the question of adjustment to epistemic change, as against the need for cognitive stability, in selecting the content of the curriculum;
- questions concerning the concept of knowledge itself that should underpin and be exhibited in curriculum development, and the related questions concerning the skills of knowledge-getting, research, and 'learning to learn';
- questions regarding the goals for education and how they will be translated into curriculum terms need to be determined;
- questions concerning the content of the curriculum and its relation-

ship to the promotion and achievement of targeted goals and ends aimed at: who will determine this and how will it be assessed?

In all this, one clear point emerges: the curriculum is no longer seen as a solid, stable and immutable organization of existing and traditional valued knowledge, but as a dynamic process involving large-scale and rapid epistemic change, planning, delivery and assessment. We have still to work out the part that co-operative relationships, including those between schools and communities, can play in the development of appropriate curricula in schools that will help each country secure its future and make the fullest possible contribution to promoting the good of countries internationally. The public character of knowledge (the *proprium* of educating institutions) and of the ends at which its dissemination is aimed will automatically involve the widest possible range of contributions in the selection and refinement of curriculum content.

We want to make it clear, however, that we are not for a moment suggesting that schools should abandon those areas of cognitive concentration and student learning activity out of which their existing curricula have been hitherto constructed. We are suggesting *two* things: *firstly*, the targeting of attention of those fields of interest and intellectual enquiry on problems of overriding human preoccupation and vital social concern – examples of which have been delineated by Bruck (1993) as including health and the human body; housing and living space; transport and mobility; energy and resources; money and wealth; love and human relations; technology and the environment; information and the media; culture and leisure. *Secondly*, and following Bruck, we believe that what schools need to encourage in the curriculum is a stress on, and the development of, an integrative perspective. This does not necessarily entail the abolition of traditional knowledge and curriculum structures; rather our proposal seeks to fuse them and focus their several contributions on a range of problems in the solution of which all have a common interest.

Our point is that the emergence and adoption of such a new integrative perspective must take our students beyond the separate and distinct subjects and disciplines upon which their school curriculum and traditional educational environments have hitherto concentrated. Some might argue that the move to such an integrative perspective requires nothing less than a quantum leap of imagination, insight and cognitive creativity, and the question is how such a Kuhnian paradigm shift in curriculum thinking is going to occur. They direct our attention to present conditions in the world which encourage them to claim that education is in a state of 'crisis', and very near the point of the kind of institutional/ psychological 'breakdown' so graphically described by Kuhn as figuring among the preconditions for paradigm shift to occur. For one thing, they say, the world is currently facing problems of survival of enormous magnitude: how, for example, are our common resources going to cope with the demands placed upon our social system by the facts of decreasing work availability, for shorter and shorter periods of working life, with wealth being concentrated in fewer and fewer hands, and such pressing health concerns as the cost of curing AIDS and sustaining an increasingly ageing population? For another, they point to the changing nature of our student population, particularly at the post-compulsory level where employment seems to be in increasingly short supply, and argue that these conditions force schools and society to adopt a radically different approach to knowledge-content, cognitive growth, and the schooling experience. All this would certainly encourage proponents of such a view to propose some kind of radical revolution in curriculum thinking and the organization of teaching and learning in schools.

For our part, however, whilst we recognize that in the development of knowledge there may well be periods of rapid cognitive advance and dynamic epistemic change such as that which underpins a more integrative approach to curriculum, we realize that in the provision and administration of schooling within a large and complex society, such proposals for radical curriculum transformation are unrealistic. Indeed, we concede that the achievement and implementation of a more integrative focus in school curriculum planning and provision of educational experiences – however desirable we think it and however much we wish to see it emerge – is not likely to be easily accomplished within the current territorial imperatives attaching to existing school departmental structures.

Moreover, it is far from clear that radical departures from existing curriculum structures would be likely to achieve the alteration in cognitive perspective for which present and future 'problematics' might seem to cry out. Instead of 'throwing the baby out with the bath-water', we would urge a more cautious approach to epistemic change: change we believe there has to be, but we believe it must *evolve* out of a realization that the framing of hypotheses to deal with the increasingly pressing, complex, protean and recalcitrant nature of community and personal problems will involve a search for, and the *development of*, expanded or altered frames of reference, patterns of thinking and focuses of concentration.

The formation of a new and integrative standpoint from which our current difficulties may be more usefully and appropriately understood, appraised and countered requires us to 'stand on the shoulders' of previous forms of intellectual enquiry, deliberation and progression. For Einstein's theories to have the intelligibility and, ultimately, the plausibility that they did, they had to be seen as successors of and reactions to their precursors in the Copernican and Newtonian traditions of astronomy, physics and dynamics. And this principle holds, we believe, in all domains of thinking and human intellectual endeavour, and in respect of all the problems that are their staple.

Perhaps, then, as a way of securing at least one step forward in the process of evolutionary curriculum change that we advocate, we might suggest that integrative studies be focused at the post-compulsory level, and may best be placed in separate 'centres', staffed by specially skilled teachers who are able to integrate the diverse areas of knowledge across departments and direct them on to these centrally compelling problems and topics of abiding human interest and the most profound personal and social concern. It is only by studying problems, topics and issues from all angles and points of view, and taking all interests and suggested treatments into account, that schools will be able to generate proposals for curriculum action which seeks to broaden students' understanding, and encourage deliberation of plans and the shaping of policies which will move students forward towards personal endeavour, community involvement, and social and political responsibility.

As Bruck (1993) points out, however, there is still one more barrier to overcome before schools can develop the integrative curriculum. The new kind of inter-subjective and integrative enquiry to which we are referring does not rely exclusively on the printed text and the purely literary mode of communication; it involves the use of all available media of communication, including computers, multimedia, television and telematics, and audiovisual and electronic technologies. Giving students access to, and the right to employ, the methods of articulation and communication with which they are increasingly most familiar, and that either transcend the territorial demarcations enforced by traditional subjects and established modes of enquiry or, indeed, create new or alternative forms of conception, categorization and the framing of 'reality', will mean that new forms of conceptualization and cognitive advance can be the more easily created; such iconoclasm will permit the emergence or deliberate fusion of the kind of integrative perspective we have in mind here.

EVALUATION AND ACCOUNTABILITY

There is perhaps one further question to be asked: whether assessment can be used as a means of reforming the curriculum. Of course assessment is vital to the curriculum: it is part of the curriculum. However, the uses one makes of the information supplied by the assessment are different from the learning involved in curriculum progress, even though such a use may be the formative one of redefining and redirecting educational progress.

Stress on assessment is educationally important during the curriculum delivery phase, when it is employed for diagnostic purposes, for this adds some rationality to learning. This use is quite different from that of the publication of final examination results, which enables the public to make what they regard as summative judgments about the supposed overall quality, effectiveness or worth of a school.

The issue at stake here relates to the philosophy of the school, the curriculum and education, and to progress in attaining the ends, of which assessment is only an indication. Assessment will determine whether or not we have a broad curriculum in operation, or whether teachers simply take up a part or even a narrow element of the curriculum, as determined by the assessors. The assessment debate in the next decade, therefore, is likely to revolve around the use made of assessment to call systems and schools to account. This is intrinsically linked to the question of what schools are about – their underlying philosophy, theories and goals.

CONCLUDING QUESTIONS

To conclude this chapter and to contribute to our stated aim of identifying agenda for future deliberation, research and educational action, we might set out some final questions and overarching curriculum issues that remain in our quest for quality schooling:

- Who should decide what in matters of curriculum construction? Should policy-makers be responsible for the formulation of the wider, higher-order goals, with education professionals overseeing the targeting of lower-level and/or more specific curriculum objectives? What part should the community play in this process and how should their contributions be weighted?

- Where does responsibility lie for defining appropriate elements of the curriculum and accountability?

- How can a curriculum be created that is easily and quickly responsive and adaptable to changes in epistemology, administration or environment, without having to have Acts and legislation changed too?

- How does one achieve an interrelationship between curriculum, student assessment and teacher education?

- How does one achieve curriculum reform as a piece of co-operative action among the different agencies and actors involved in education and its effective delivery?

- How does one best approach the relationship between assessment and concerns for equity and the socio-economic background of students? How does one ensure that the system of assessment does not dictate or dominate the educational goals? How does one develop goals that are not overly detailed, particularly in specific subject areas?

- How does one employ computers to facilitate the establishment and development of new ways of learning and discovery?

- As far as teachers and educational professionals are concerned, how does one maintain a progressive attitude towards the curriculum among teachers?

- Given the extended age group beyond the age of 16 in upper secondary schools, how might one redefine syllabuses to meet their needs and the needs of the community and economy?

- How does one redefine the curriculum in terms of the perennial questions of education's goals and objectives, and how does one relate the issue of goals to objectives, curriculum processes, implementation and evaluation?

- How does enhancing quality relate to standards of achievement? The imposition of a specific curriculum by law raises the question of fixity and ossification in curriculum knowledge and how such dysfunctional phenomena can be avoided. How can flexibility in curriculum change be ensured, so that the professionalism of teachers is not undermined?

- When considering a redefinition of the curriculum, in whose terms is that process to be framed and in response to what pressures, values and concerns?

- In what ways and for what purposes might the curriculum be most appropriately reconceptualized: according to traditional subject distinctions, or according to new conceptions and theories of knowledge?

- With what difficulties must redefinition of the curriculum contend:

adjustment as against stability in planning curriculum content; the relationship between freedom of choice, equality and equity?

- What implications might flow from redefining curricula? If one redefines curriculum in terms of its goals, what are the implications for assessment? If one redefines curriculum to respond to the needs of the changed student population, what are the implications for the traditional academic curriculum and for post-compulsory and higher education? If one redefines the curriculum in terms of new conceptions of knowledge and new ways or theories of knowing, what are the implications for teacher education and in-service educating and training?

- What articulation might be necessary between the various phases and sectors of education – primary, secondary, post-compulsory, tertiary – if both curriculum change and education for self and society are to be best achieved?

The attack on providing answers to these and other similar questions we see as the central concern of curriculum theorists at the present time, as they struggle with the working out of those programmes of knowledge, competence and value, learning in and success at which will be the strongest part of our schools' work in providing a quality education for future citizens in its community.

Chapter 7

Democratic Values and the Democratic School

EDUCATING FOR QUALITY IN THE REALM OF MORAL, POLITICAL AND PERSONAL VALUES

In the previous chapter we examined the idea of the curriculum as one of the principal means by which quality schooling can be planned, delivered and assured. We took as our *primum datum* the notion that education is centrally, though not exclusively, concerned with the transmission of knowledge and the initiation of young people into the various ways and means of constructing, confirming, testing and communicating knowledge and then getting them committed to the preparation, pursuit and practice of the cognitive enterprises valued by the community. We saw that quality could be seen to have been achieved if young people emerged at the end of their period of formal education having successfully gained a number of cognitive achievements and having become bearers of a number of valued attributes, and we tried to set out some account of those achievements and attributes, which we saw as the mainstay of quality schooling.

In that chapter, we emphasized the attributes of knowledge, understanding and a liberal viewpoint as desirable outcomes for students experiencing quality schooling. This knowledge should be broad and general, allowing 'graduates' to acquire in their schooling an awareness of the broad features of the whole domain of human knowledge, but they should also exhibit considerable depth of understanding in and extensive command of at least some of the major areas of that domain. This will involve knowledge 'from the inside' of the language and literature of certain subjects: a grasp of all the main concepts and categories of their field of knowledge, the various tests for objectivity, the purposes of the enquiry, and the considerations that make certain moves in it decisive – as well as an awareness of the range and complexity of the main writings and cognitive achievements and advances in the fields in question.

Furthermore, the successful 'graduate' should not only know what counts as evidence in a particular field of knowledge, but should also care that it should be found', investigated and evaluated according to general principles of impartiality and scholarly objectivity. The successful student will have a broad general view of where everything fits in the cognitive realm and where are the main points of purchase, relevance and applicability of the various developments in human knowledge. Importantly, the student will be concerned that value be ascribed, not only to the pursuit of such knowledge for its own sake and for the rewards intrinsic to it, but also to the use and applications that may be made of knowledge for the addressing of problems, the enlargement of human understanding and the improvement of the human condition. Knowledge, as has been remarked, will not simply lie inert but will be applied to the benefit of all humankind.

Commitment to these principles will be observable in the patterns of thinking, models of valuing and modes of behaving by which the student emerging from a quality school experience may be distinguished. To the repertoire of expert cognitive accomplishments such a student has gained through the process of schooling will be added proficiency in a wide range of skills and competences, including such important capabilities as those of oral discourse and written communication, the ability to reason logically, to seek information, to do research and know how to learn from it, the ability to take initiatives but also to work as part of a team, to be positively self-critical and constructively appraisive in one's assessments of others' abilities and contributions, and the capacity and concern for continuing intellectual and personal development. We believe all these cognitive gains and competences can be developed by means of access to and engagement in an integrated, high-class and empowering curriculum, chosen on the basis of a selection of those kinds of knowledge and modes of enquiry that will best equip students to cope with the exigencies imposed on their lives in the present, and to calculate the possibilities, take advantage of the opportunities, and plan for the demands of the future.

We sought a justification for decisions as to the subjects that should comprise a curriculum designed to introduce such knowledge to our young people, and to give them competence in all the various skills and procedures being increasingly demanded of successful 'graduates' of educational institutions these days. We also needed to provide a guarantee and a stable criterion of educational endeavour to enable all those receiving education to see the point of the curriculum decisions and choices made, either by themselves, or on their behalf and in their interest. We found such a justification in the idea of education for democracy: here, we felt, was one argument that could prove conclusive in determining all those various kinds of cognition, understanding and experience requisite for providing the information to enable our future citizens to cope with the demands of comprehending their past, monitoring the present and directing their future.

These considerations come together in the contributions citizens are called upon to make in shaping, understanding, implementing and evaluating the decisions of policy-makers working out solutions to problems of a theoretical and practical kind that have direct bearing on their lives and all their main concerns. *Democratic education* is, therefore, the culmination of a series of curriculum experiences that have, as much as anything else, to do with the idea of education not merely as induction, but, more pointedly, as preparation for the future.

This notion of education as preparation has been usefully defined by Warnock (1978) as involving at least three elements: preparation for the world of work; preparation for the life of imagination; and preparation for the life of virtue. Each of these will have its typical excellence, and each of them can be addressed within the framework of programmes for quality in schooling. This chapter will concentrate on the idea of educating for quality in the realm of moral, political and personal values – particularly those obtaining in relations between ourselves and others – that are exemplified in the social principles embodied in modern forms of democracy.

We follow Aristotle in maintaining that the two principal human excellences are those of rationality and language – in all the many ways in which these have evolved and become articulate. We argue that an understanding of values and of the language of obligation is as objective and cognitive an enterprise as any other area of human rationality and communication; that both can therefore be learnt; and that such learning can be subjected to rational and objective appraisal, criticism and amendment. We maintain, as opposed to holders of subjectivist doctrines, that it does make sense to talk of quality and excellence in these matters, without in the least countenancing the notion of infallibility or the primacy of absolute values, and that values education demands and, indeed, underlines the appropriateness of encouraging individual responsiveness, spontaneity and sensitivity – as well as imagination and creativity – in matters of culture and value.

The ideas behind democracy in and for education require it, therefore, to be explored and advocated as a proper subject for inclusion in any set of proposals to redefine and to humanize the curriculum. We argue that the objectivity and rationality of the knowledge and understanding in these matters, which we believe schools should aim for, will allow schools to become quality institutions by working out curriculum guidelines, ways of teaching and modes of organization through which they can provide an effective education in this most important realm of all human activities.

Schools will best do this by showing how value concerns, and the social and moral relations in which those concerns are embodied and characterized, are expressions of larger-scale conceptions of life and value (cf. Best, 1992). The character of the individual judgments and activities in moral relationships is determined, as Best remarks, at the level of the culture of a community – that network of language patterns, social practices and moral conventions in which human beings articulate their most cherished conceptions of the meaning and value of life. Excellence in these matters, and the work of quality schools, can contribute signally to the quality of life for all members of our community, and that is why attention to values issues and concerns in the programmes of those planning for quality in schooling is vital and indispensable.

This ethical impulse finds especial expression in the concept of democracy, since we take the fundamental presuppositions of this particular mode of government to be almost entirely moral in character. We take democracy to be that form of life, above and beyond any other, to which adult moral agents are necessarily committed in the arrangement of their social relations, the institutionalization of their political principles, and the construction of satisfying and enriching patterns of personal life choices.

Throughout this chapter we are concerned to discuss an education for democracy, and to highlight the ways in which this can provide a rationale and programme for the humanization of the curriculum and of quality schooling. We see this as a vital undertaking in times when the major thrust of curriculum activity in many countries is driven by economic imperatives, the demands of technocratic rationality, and mechanistic versions of school effectiveness; these threaten the equally important values of moral awareness, interpersonal sensitivity and cross-cultural understanding in the home, the work-place and the wider community, which have emerged so strongly in our research.

We wish to argue that the best forum for the promotion of such valued concerns is via the democratic form of life, to which, we maintain, we are all morally and culturally committed by virtue of our epistemic involvements and intellectual engagements in the pursuit of knowledge, discourse and truth, the chief stock in trade of educating institutions in the modern liberal state. We hold that this commitment necessarily issues in the induction of our young people into the various realms of public knowledge, the modes of interpersonal relations, and those ways of organizing and administering our educational systems, institutions and schools that provide the best possible preparation for members of our coming generation to take their place as mature and well-informed citizens of a participative democracy.

In the progress towards the development of our tentative theory of quality schooling, this chapter thus deals with the concept of democracy and its justification; shows up and then tries to deal with some philosophical problems; and ends by developing an account of the implications of accepting a commitment to democracy for the introduction of real democracy into the organization and administration of a democratic society's educating institutions, giving particular emphasis to the task of creating and managing the democratic school.

THE NATURE AND JUSTIFICATION OF DEMOCRACY

Political Authority, Power and Democratic Values

It may be helpful to begin our discussion of the philosophical underpinning of the idea of 'democracy in and for education' with a reference to the part democracy has played in past discussions regarding the nature of the relationship between the holding and exercise of power in social and political contexts, and the granting or vindication of the authority to do so. There is, indeed, a connection in the political realm between having authority and exercising power, for, after all, ethics is *inter alia* about the distribution and regulation of power in accordance with principles of some kind, and it is the political context that formalizes this relationship and justifies various forms of rule and the exercise of power by certain kinds of rulers and authorities.

In classical Greece, for example, there arose and were developed various conceptions and forms of the relationship between political power and authority, and these are commented upon variously in Aristotle's *Politics*:

> *Aristocracy* would be widely understood as government by the 'best' people; the rule of an elite class;
> *Oligarchy* is the rule of a few;
> *Plutocracy* connotes the rule of the wealthy;
> *Democracy* refers to the rule of the people.

These kinds of government of the different Greek city-states were, in their various ways and local forms, replacements for such odious (to the Greeks) patterns of power as were exercised by a monarch or a tyrant, and were found differently in different states. Doubtless we could all easily think of modern examples of such ancient types of ruling. Each of the types of government is commented upon variously by Plato in the later books of his dialogue on the nature of 'justice' in

The Republic (1955 edn). It is interesting, though not surprising, given the putting to death by the state of his beloved teacher Socrates, that Plato, writing from his experience of Athens, the supposed cradle of democracy, should find democracy, of all types of government in Greece at that time, to be the least attractive:

> I dare say that a democracy is the most attractive of all societies. . . .
> The diversity of its characters, like the different colours in a patterned
> dress, make it look very attractive. Indeed perhaps most people would,
> for this reason, judge it to be the best form of society, like women and
> children when they see gaily coloured things . . . in a democracy there's
> no compulsion either to exercise authority if you're capable of it, or
> to submit to authority if you don't want to; you needn't fight if there's
> a war, or you can wage a private war in peacetime if you don't like
> peace; and if there's any law that debars you from political or judicial
> office, you will none the less take either if they come your way . . .
> democracy with a grandiose gesture sweeps all this away and doesn't
> mind what the habits and background of its politicians are; provided
> they profess themselves the people's friends, they are duly honoured . . .
> it's an agreeable form of society, with plenty of variety, which treats
> all men as equal, whether they are equal or not.
>
> (Plato, *The Republic*, VIII)

We may contrast this heavy political irony with the words uttered two thousand years later by the American president Abraham Lincoln. In his 'Gettysburg Address' (Lincoln, 1907) he apotheosized those who had been willing to lay down their lives so that 'government of the people, by the people, and for the people, shall not disappear from the earth'.

Taking this as starting-point, and before we come to consider the question of what might be meant by the phrase 'education for democracy', we need to pose an important prior question. If there is anything good to be said about democracy – and it is the form of government that most societies these days seem to prefer – then we must ask whether sense can be made of the notion of the rule 'of the people'. What, if anything, is good about it? What, in other words, is its *value*? And when we talk about 'democratic values', what do we have in mind and why should we elevate them above other forms of social principle and political arrangement that are open to us, as the ones most to be preferred, the ones we should opt for? What is there of particular value in democracy and why, against other forms of government, should it be preferable for life of quality?

A Note about Values

At this point we might find it helpful to come to some agreed view about what constitutes a value, or set of values. Now the question of the existence and nature of a logical domain of 'value', and its relationship to the world of 'fact', has been the subject of considerable philosophical controversy over the past fifty years, and still provokes discussion. We doubt whether anything said in this short excursus will add substantially to the mountain of memoranda that has already been piled up on these matters. Research and enquiry into this whole topic, and developments of the principal notions attaching to statements of 'is' and 'ought' and the possible relations between them, have continued in the relatively recent past, and we do not propose to go further into those questions here. For the sake of convenience it seems to us that it might be best simply to offer a short definition of 'values' that may serve as a working tool for what follows.

For the purposes of this discussion, then, we take 'values' to refer to those ideas, conventions, principles, rules, objects, products, activities or procedures that people treasure, cherish, prefer, incline towards and place importance upon. Such things they make objects of admiration, high levels of aspiration or goals of endeavour in their lives and commend them so to others. This last comment enables us to argue, contrary to subjectivists and relativists of various persuasions, that value judgments are different logically from, and much more than, mere matters of taste and individual preference. Indeed, we see values, and the judgments deriving from them, functioning as the rules, conventions or principles implicit in certain manners of proceeding that furnish and act as a *standard of discrimination* (a criterion) against which other procedures, etc. can be measured and assessed, and ranking high in a scale of comparison among objects, etc. of the same class. Their interpersonal significance we regard as commendatory, action-guiding and generally prescriptive.

An examination of value discourse seems to suggest that there are a number of different kinds of value: moral, religious, aesthetic, social, political, educational, technical, economic, and so on, though some of these (e.g. social, political, economic, educational) are claimed (by Aristotle, among others) to be subclasses of one prime value: the moral. It is right that we raise the question of whether all these various species of value are indeed distinct and logically different (as ethical value seems to us, for instance, clearly different from the aesthetic), or whether they do not all in the final analysis come down to being species of the one genus: the moral. And there is the further question of how such judgments are to be justified – if indeed they can be.

This last question we can leave for the moment. We might, meanwhile, simply advance the view that, so far as *democratic values* are concerned, they seem to us to include a number of different elements – the social, political, economic and technical *inter alia* – but, above and beyond all these, to be primarily moral in nature. We characterize the main features of moral concepts, and their reference to discourse concerning the nature of democratic values and quality schooling, as follows.

On the Nature of Moral/Democratic Values

As a *primum datum* we tentatively advance the view that moral questions are about behaviour, but not simply about behaviour as such, for the question of morality does not arise except in a social and institutional setting. Nor, as has been argued previously (Aspin, 1975), does morality have as its principal subject matter a simple analysis of the way in which people do in fact behave in social settings. Rather, morality seems to us to be about the conduct of ourselves in regard to other people, and theirs in regard to us, and the way in which we agree to regulate ourselves in our interpersonal transactions by adherence to a set of principles. Our agreement to do so rests, we think, upon our recognition of the fact (if it is a fact) that, alone of all the creatures in the world, man is, as Bronowski (1973) remarks, the unique social–solitary, solitary–social creature, and that human interests, in both respects, are promoted and preserved within the nexus of relations and obligations that constitute our lives as human beings. Thus it is not the case that we 'accept' morality, and that this depends upon our 'acceptance' of the institutions in which it is characteristically exercised. Given our form of life, the presence, function and normative force of some set of regulative principles are part and parcel of the institutions into which we are gradually initiated – to change the metaphor, part of their whole warp and weft.

Morality, therefore, and *a fortiori* a democratic education (given that political judgments are a function of our commitments to certain moral preconceptions), are concerned with helping us to understand that human life is beset with obligations of one sort or another. One of the aims of this form of life, and of the values education that gives young people an initiation into it, will be to give us a knowledge of the rules which function in this particular life/social 'game', and to seek to develop in us a grasp of its underlying principles, together with the ability to apply these rules intelligently, and to have the settled disposition to do so. It will also, we believe, seek to help us to articulate the reasons which both satisfy us and are open to public evaluation on account of any particular moral decision or for any general moral code that we may make for ourselves or come to adopt within the institutional framework of our being human, both discernibly individual and yet members, one with another, of the whole class of persons, with their common physiological morphology and their similar, though distinct, intentions, volitions, emotions, deliberations, and the like.

Thus, we would hold an action to be moral if it is engaged in consciously and intentionally as part of a whole pattern of behaviour towards other people in accordance with principles. As such, it will be based upon certain beliefs about the rights and duties people have that are concerned, in some way, with the furtherance of the interests of people in general. These beliefs will rest upon certain core notions about what constitutes right and wrong and what one ought to do, as well as an awareness of what 'ought' language, in the realm of interpersonal conduct and social relations, commits one to.

The actions that we as democrats engage in will spring from a free choice on our part, as mature moral agents, and will be based upon our ability to give reasons for those choices that are relevant and appropriate, capable (in principle, at all events,) of being judged as such by people generally. This means that the moral actions we undertake will be such as can be judged to be *generalizable:* that is, impartial and equally binding on all those who regard such an act as intending to promote human welfare. The latter consideration will mean that the grounds for the action will not be trivial but will really count for something – will have 'a certain magnitude'. They will be held sincerely, and will be applied and exercised with consistency.

All these considerations can be reduced, of course, and if we were to hazard it as our view that morality was about adopting, justifying, analysing or applying principles, in interpersonal affairs in the world as we see it, that are *universalizable, overriding, other-regarding, action-guiding* or *action-prescribing*, and significantly related to the *promotion of human welfare* and the *avoidance* or *inhibition of harm to human beings*, we should have all got this down to manageable proportions. We should also want to argue, not only that human beings *qua* human beings are bound up in these kinds of obligations and responsibilities, but that their observance of these requirements is nowhere more called for than in their interchanges and enmeshments in, and observance of, the various rules and conventions governing all the occasions of interpersonal intercourse in which we are called upon, as *actors*, to participate. It is this last realization that has an especial bearing upon the question of how we are to characterize the relationships people have, and the institutions in which they develop them, when it comes down to ways in which, as 'the people', they institutionalize their political arrangements in that form of chosen self-governance called 'democracy' – the 'rule of the people by the people for the people'.

The Concepts of 'the People' and 'Democracy'

We now have a further and more difficult question to answer: who are 'the people'? This is particularly relevant in respect of the governance of schools. Different societies have answered this question in different ways: for classical Athens suffrage was restricted to male adults who had Attic forebears going back three generations; in Switzerland, until recently, the franchise was restricted to Swiss males above the age of 30; in the United Kingdom suffrage is extended to any adult over the age of 18, with the exception of the peerage and the nobility, criminals, and those suffering from psychotic disabilities and under restraint in mental hospitals.

If this is any example, it seems clear that, in many societies, suffrage is regarded as 'universal' only in so far as it remains within restricted categories. It is only relatively recently, for example, and within the past hundred years, that women have enjoyed full voting rights in many so-called democracies. Some countries that proclaim their systems of government to be democratic have often refused to enfranchise particular sections of the population on grounds that others regard as illegitimate or immoral, as witness Germany in the 1930s and South Africa until 1994.

The idea that the franchise can be withheld on illegitimate grounds (such as race, colour or social class) entails the idea that it can be withheld *legitimately*. Perhaps this is the reason why convicted offenders in prison or those suffering from disabling mental illnesses are considered as outside the number of those who may properly have access to political power in a democracy. In such cases, the presumption is against those who are unable for the moment to measure up to the demands of rationality, goodwill and commitment to social order that are presumptions of democratic action and freedom to vote.

A similar presumption operates in the case of children and young people. One thing upon which all the systems cited above, and many others, seem to agree is that young people below a certain age shall not count as valid persons to be included in the constituency of the electorate: that their *chronological* age below a certain number of years shall be held to count as sufficient disqualification from the extension of the suffrage to them. One supposes that the reason for this is the feeling that democracy requires some state of 'readiness' for voting and political action in the citizen. The normal presumption is that this state is reached as a result of maturation, education and the development or emergence of a political will.

It is this that must give us pause, however. Is it not odd that, in educating our children and young people as future citizens, we do so (a) by means of *compulsions* of various sorts, and (b) in institutions that are, certainly in practice and maybe also in principle, anything *but* democratic? What are we then to make of the notions of 'education as a species of democracy' or 'education *for* democracy'? Indeed, given the prime original meanings of *demos* and *kratos* ('people' and 'power'), what, definitively, can we make of the idea of *institutions*, in which the notions and values of 'democracy' and the rights of 'the people' are supposed to be embedded and embodied? Is there not some paradox in the notion of the development of a predilection for democracy that is built upon compulsion? Can we really 'force people to be free'?

Democracy: A Set of Valued Procedures and Principles

R. S. Peters (1966) puts forward one way of overcoming this problem. He maintains that:

> It would be reasonable to expect . . . that the concept [of democracy] itself would intimate what was distinctive about it. . . . Because we cannot give particular substance to the concept of 'the people' then we might think there is more to be gained by trying to give a procedural, or formal, account of 'democracy'.

The procedures delineated in Peters' account of democracy operate, he claims, as manifestations of an underlying set of *presuppositions of democracy*. Because, as Aristotle would have it, 'all political decisions are moral decisions "writ large" ', and because the acceptance of the state's authority is made rationally, then in a democratic state the citizens must, according to Peters, necessarily be committed to reasons and to the 'fundamental principles of morality' (such as fairness, liberty, consideration of other's interests, respect for persons, truthfulness and avoiding inflicting unnecessary pain on people). Such principles, he contends, are presupposed in our commitment to democratic values and the democratic form of life, in which we settle our differences on important matters of belief and behaviour by appeal to and employment of rational procedures.

We might therefore go on ourselves from Peters' suggestion and pick out what would probably be regarded as typical characteristics associated with and found in democratic institutions. We believe that the following criteria are widely rated as among the chief values (ethical, political and social) underlying and embedded in the democratic process:

- That policies and actions be based on *decisions* and not arbitrary or autocratic acts of will.
- That decisions be arrived at by *rational discourse* and on the

grounds of the objective and convincing character of the arguments advanced to support them.

- That, in general, *suffrage be universally extended* and full powers and rights made available to all people in the state, subject to limitations of age or other such qualifications as render citizens incapable of making their vote (for example, prisoners).
- That all citizens *vote, decide* and *act freely* according to their conscience, and without being subject to duress.
- That, in general, the *will of the majority* should prevail.
- That, in general, the *rights of minorities* be preserved, respected, allowed full and proper hearing and given due consideration.
- That *regular periodic review* be made of policies and practices.
- That the *principle of reversibility* should obtain.
- That all citizens be guaranteed rights of *access, equity* and *participation* (direct, wherever possible) to and in the political process and institutions.
- That those responsible for the implementation of policies be *accountable* to the whole of the body politic for their conduct.
- That *all count equally* for one, and none for more than one, in matters of voting, decision-making and accountability.
- That *powers be separated* and distributed equitably among government, executive and judiciary.
- That there be a *system of checks and balances* to ensure that no part of the system can gain pre-eminence and overriding control.
- That *arrangements be socially and politically operative* and not mere rhetoric; in other words, that social justice should obtain.

These democratic values are in turn strongly related to and underpinned by certain moral principles. In Peters' view these may be judged to be *presuppositions* of all so-claimed democratic forms of life and forms of political arrangement:

EQUALITY: There shall be no discrimination between or against one group of people and in favour of another, without good, relevant and socially operative reasons being given. All people and human beings are to be presumed to be equal until grounds are given for treating someone or some group differently.

Similarly all shall have FREEDOM until reason is given for constraints to be applied and freedom to be taken away. TOLERANCE and the CONSIDERATION OF OTHER PEOPLE'S INTERESTS ensure respect for another person's right to be different. RESPECT FOR OTHER PEOPLE reflects our regard for them as 'ends-in-themselves' equally with us and our concern to preserve and promote our own *and* other people's search for happiness together with a determination to see that they do not come to harm.

These presuppositions, we may say, imply certain social procedures and institutions which will function so as to:

- consider the interests of the governed;

- allow the free expression of public opinion;
- guarantee public accountability;
- encourage the emergence of consensus decisions;
- rely on and institutionalize the willingness of the governed to participate;
- give citizens experience in such democratic institutions.

It is Peters' contention that, in the light of these presuppositions and the requirements they generate, the justification of democracy is synonymous with the justification of morality. He claims that we can *educate for democracy* by initiating children into the world of basic moral principles, so making them necessarily democrats. This means that education as a moral term is, if properly conducted, inevitably at one and the same time an induction into the moral and the democratic form of life.

Some Problems with the 'Procedural' View

Unfortunately, there are some problems with this view. Schumpeter (1967) claims, in contradistinction to Peters' argument, that the 'concept [of democracy] itself' is of little help in this debate, since there are at least two concepts of democracy. There is, on the one hand, the ideal *classical democracy*, which Schumpeter calls 'an institutional arrangement for arriving at political decisions which realizes the common good by making the people itself decide issues through the election of individuals who are to assemble in order to carry out its will'. Some people, comments Schumpeter, have become cynical about this. They have described *modern democracy*, on the other hand, as 'an institutional arrangement for arriving at political decisions in which the individuals acquire the power to decide by means of a competitive struggle for the people's vote' (cf. Graham (1976); see also Harrison (1970), Honderich (1974) and Pennock (1974)).

Now there is also another point to be made about the meaning and value of those terms. In public discourse on matters of vital significance involving the use of such terms, there is often such contention about their meaning and applicability that the only thing about which, one *can* be certain in such arguments is that people will disagree profoundly and widely upon the question of what explicit substantive or procedural content can be packed into them. Gallie (1964) calls such terms 'essentially contested'; he maintains that there are seven conditions of 'essential contestedness' and that the term 'democracy' satisfies these conditions, making it thus an 'essentially contested' concept. Different countries have a great diversity of approaches to government while yet describing themselves as 'democratic'.

How, then, we may ask, are forms of government designated 'democratic' to be characterized, if indeed they can be unambiguously defined at all? Perhaps they cannot be; perhaps the best we can hope for is an acknowledgement of the need to seek, from usage, context, interlocutor's intentions and the general 'flavour' of the discourse in which such words have their home, an appropriate basis for our use of the term 'democratic', and an appropriate set of forms and procedures in which democratic principles and institutions are developed and deployed.

If so, it would follow that the concept admits of 'an indefinite number of possible descriptions', and this might possibly suggest that there is something strange in Peters' formal account, concentrating, as it does, solely upon procedures.

We might also reasonably ask whether, on Peters' grounds, some modes and institutions for the delivery of what are purported to be democratic forms of government are not really ruled out. Would we, for instance, see a single-party state as 'democratic' in the above sense? And, while it does not follow from the above analysis that the 'Westminster' system must be the only form which democratic government can take, does not its adoption by very many countries claiming to be democratic suggest that there is something substantial in that form of constitution that goes beyond mere forms and procedures, thereby intimating that democracy must be found in a conjunction of particular forms and contents?

Koerner (1967, 1973) asks whether Peters' view that we accept the authority of the state rationally is really so straightforward that he can simply assert it. Surely, one might argue, we need to engage in and conclude upon some further justificatory argumentation to support Peters' contention if the primacy of rational procedures and the need for reason-giving as a precondition of the democratic life are to be sustained and given a real point of purchase?

Wollheim (1972) goes further, however. He asks: is there not an inherent contradiction in Peters' account? If I am committed to reason (presupposition 1) and also to the fundamental principles of morality (presupposition 2), then by what authority, it may reasonably be demanded, does a *consensus* decision take precedence over mine? Wollheim attempts to resolve this paradox by making a distinction between what he calls Direct and Oblique principles. Others have disagreed with his proposed solution, in particular Graham (1976), who replaces it with the view that in the real world 'there is no democracy'.

We may ask, along with a number of other critics of Peters' justification of democracy (such as Kleinig, Koerner and Watt), whether Peters' transcendental arguments concerning his fundamental principles of morality are sound. It is one thing to argue that those who question the value of democracy are *ipso facto* committed to the sort of life-form that democracy is; it is quite another to claim that this thereby necessarily commits them to democracy as the *best* form of government. To argue that this is so is to commit the fallacy of thinking that, if you secure our agreement that clothes are things worth having and wearing, you have automatically thereby secured our commitment to the wearing of particular styles or fashions. Government involving reasoned discourse is one thing; it does not follow that the only form of such government is the democratic (in our sense), nor that, of all forms of government that are called 'democratic', the Western model is self-evidently the best and most fully paradigmatic version of it.

We might add that Peters' conception of educating for democracy appears to involve both a contradiction and a category shift, these being glossed over by an appeal to various psychological considerations which are put forward to resolve a *conceptual* difficulty. And we might also ask whether democracy is *really* to be identified by its form rather than its content. The fact that we can satisfy Peters' formal criteria using examples taken from states that we would not call democracies suggests that the term is an evaluative one. Instead, perhaps it might be wiser to examine the conceptions of democracy urged upon us and take Wittgenstein's advice to 'look and see' what a particular 'democratic' society approves or disapproves of in its own particular working out of the social institutions that govern it. This might then provide us with a substantive and reasonably objective account of the concept – but it would be an account requiring local adaptation and interpretation.

The Values Informing Democracy and Education: An Alternative View

Instead of all this, and as a way of avoiding the difficulties, we wish to maintain that the prime focus for democratic values in education comes from one of the central concepts in education: that of *knowledge*. We want to argue that the pursuit of truth in all its various forms – the search for evidence by which our knowledge claims may be objectified and assessed; the generation, growth, dissemination, communication about and criticism of new knowledge; the impartial and careful scrutiny and assessment of the various cognitive claims we encounter and make ourselves; and the need to establish and internalize stable and agreed criteria of meaning and intelligibility in all interpersonal discourse, not only those focusing upon knowledge and truth – involves its own ethical imperatives, and all of them are democratic. The ethical and socio-political values that come in democratic education are a function of *educating* institutions' epistemological preoccupations (other forms of upbringing, training, etc. which are not democratic, are authoritarian and based upon the desire to propagate a 'faith' system of belief; such institutions are in principle totalitarian). In educating institutions these values are functions of knowledge, knowledge-getting, and knowledge-disseminating that entail freedom of belief, equal right to criticize, tolerance of and respect for others' points of view, telling the truth and impartiality.

We also want to argue for the inherence of certain democratic principles in speech and discourse generally – to contend that the presumption of equality, toleration, generalizability and prescriptivity is implicit in every occasion of human communication. Just as Hare (1952) argues that human discourse is an activity that is the very stuff of morality, so also we claim that the very activity of learning, speaking and understanding a language is in some sense a democratic enterprise. It presupposes the same commitment to telling the truth, to treating interlocutors as equals, to allowing freedom of expression, to tolerating what people say and respecting their rights to parity of esteem.

This is a point made strongly by Ackerman (1980) in his celebration of 'conversation' and its presuppositions as being an instantiation of the moral or democratic form of life and an exemplification of liberal education at work. A liberal education does not only teach people to communicate and to converse, but teaches them *eo ipso* to be autonomous moral agents, sensitive, benevolent and considerate human beings – and good democrats.

Implications of Democratic Values for Education

Ackerman (1980) and Powell (1970) have pointed out the presumption that democracy, of all types of informal social relationship and formal institutional arrangement, requires a well-informed and liberally educated citizen body to exercise its powers and to participate in debate relating to decision-making, the outcomes of which will prove binding on all citizens. This presumption and the requirements it entails place enormous emphasis on education and the production of a curriculum for democracy. They carry with them the requirement that future citizens will not only be exposed to all the various ways and means of knowledge and understanding on which they might need them to draw to exercise their franchise, but will necessarily become immersed in, and committed to keeping abreast of, the epistemic changes and cognitive developments that the dynamic character of understanding, appraising and judging involved in participating in the democratic form of life in a rapidly changing environment will require and bring on.

More than that, however, understanding, appraising and judging will not by themselves be enough to ensure full democratic participation in the processes of policy information, implementation and assessment to which the modern citizen might be called upon to contribute. Not only must future citizens, in their schools, be given exposure to and provided with the opportunity for the acquisition of knowledge that is appropriate for the democratic form of life, but, as Powell (1970) argues, there must be the opportunity for engagement and practice in *activities* appropriate to a democratic form of life, and a set of organizational and administrative arrangements that will exemplify democracy. Adoption of these procedures and practices will then function as preparations for the life of the democrat when maturity is reached and suffrage finally conferred.

The question concerning the justification of compulsory education posed above might be answered as follows: that we take (and enforce) decisions on our young people's part that they would take for themselves had they the requisite education, information and wisdom to enable them to do so, and proof of this is that the end of compulsory schooling is not coterminous with arrival at adulthood. In this way we solve the paradox of compulsory education for democracy by compelling attendance at educational institutions that may *seem* to be autocratic but should turn out eventually (at least in principle) *not* to be so. Perhaps universities and other tertiary educating institutions are the best exemplification of this principle.

But all this brings us back to the fundamental question: What do we mean by democracy *in* education? Is democracy *in* education possible?

The Democratization of Education

No one these days would seriously disagree with the proposition that education should be *democratic*; indeed, most people are concerned to create systems, institutions and schools in which the principles of democracy, accountability, access and participation are enshrined and from which graduating students might emerge with some understanding of, experience in and preference for democracy as a way of life.

We may reasonably ask, however, what might be meant by the injunction that education should be democratic. Peters (1966) has suggested that at least three interpretations could be proffered:

That the educational system of a community should be democratically distributed and organized, whatever interpretation is given to 'democratic'. A system, for instance, which neglected the education in half the population of a community, or in the policies and organization of which 'the people' had no say, would be commonly thought to be 'undemocratic'. Alternatively . . . that the organization of schools themselves should be democratic. In other words, a plea might be made for the rights of inmates, staff and pupils alike, to have some say in the running of their institution. . . . Alternatively . . . the desirability of the content of education being democratic . . .

In regard to the third point, it might be suggested that the content of the curriculum be 'democratic', in so far as that had a bearing on the responsibility for and function of the school to train future citizens in the skills and attitudes appropriate for membership of a democratic community.

Democracy and the Fair Distribution of Education

With respect to the provision and availability of education, those who view education as a public good or service would argue that the appropriate resources for it should be provided out of the public exchequer and that access to it should be fairly distributed. The reason for this is not far to seek: for people to have any chance of coming to terms with the demands of today's complex society they must have the knowledge and competences that enable them to respond to its exigencies, and on the basis of which they can best contribute to the health and welfare of that society. This in turn presupposes a thorough grounding and training in the means of acquisition of the requisite knowledge and competences. Clearly, it is going to be through some form of educating institution that such grounding will be provided.

Further, however, if people are to have any understanding of that range of activities from among which they may construct a satisfying and life-enhancing pattern of preferred activities (J. P. White, 1973, 1982), then they will require exposure to and some practice in those activities themselves. This means that the range of possible options from among which they might ultimately make their choices must be opened up to them by someone who already has considerable comprehension, from the inside, of what it means to engage in them and what are the various satisfactions and illuminations that engaging in them makes possible. Again, this requires education – but education provided on an equitable basis for all future citizens of a democracy, which can make such choices possible for them.

However, one problem might arise from our putting forward the view that education should be fairly distributed. This could be taken to mean that education is a 'thing' rather like a commodity – though a precious one, as manifested in the fact that there is great demand for it. And in the (sometimes fierce) competition that might take place for access to or 'possession of' this commodity, it would be likely that some 'consumers' would in all probability end up with more or less of it than others. Such a conception would militate against the possibility of evenness in the distribution of and access to education. But there are many, nevertheless, who hold to the view that it is the function of schooling and tertiary study to produce an outcome, to come up with the right 'product', as though education were a production process involved in the 'turning out' of finished artefacts on some kind of conveyor belt.

There is a particularly pernicious side to this debate, as Hunt (1987) points out. This is the tendency, observable in the impulse of quite a few educational institutions today, not excluding some schools and universities, to adopt 'corporate' styles of management and the delivery of a set of 'products' or services, produced according to, or indeed exhibiting, the standards of 'best international practice', as though educational programs and qualifications were based upon offering some kind of 'merchandise' to a set of 'customers', and elevating and licensing the (quite fallacious) prescription that 'what our stakeholders want or need must be given to them'. In this way the undertakings of education are made to appear as if they are concerned first and foremost to be economically useful, 'relevant' or socially just, and thus to provide for the satisfaction of national, regional or local economic needs by developing the appropriate commodities or human resources; or to extend and promote the agenda of particular ideological, political or social programs.

One only needs to state this view to see its refutation. As philosophers and educationists from Plato to Newman to Hirst have argued, a liberal education is first and foremost about developing the life of the mind and extending the boundaries of its understanding in ways that will expand the store of human knowledge and wisdom. The chief purposes and justification of the activities of institutions making the achievement of a liberal education by their students their primary goal are centred on intrinsic, not extrinsic, values and only then about disseminating these findings so that all may share in their illuminations and possible benefits. It is only in this sense and to this extent that a school or a university's 'mission' has to do with promoting the good of the social whole, though of course such 'goods' may also accrue as outgrowths of their primary task. Therefore any account of education as an induction into the world of knowledge and understanding will need first and last to refer it back to the necessity of the institution, development and promotion of the powers of rationality and critical intelligence in the minds of all young people.

It is a prime function of the liberally educated mind to develop and deploy the appropriate intellectual resources to point out the fallaciousness of conceiving the work of *educational* institutions along the above lines. It is unfortunate that some politicians – and even academics – these days seem not to understand this fundamental point about the nature and values of educational institutions, in which the democracy of knowledge and the testing of its claims are public values whose impersonal character renders them immune to private agenda or sectional interest but open impartially to all who would want to engage in them for the insights and illuminations they offer and confer.

An appropriate rejoinder to all this is to argue that education is much less a 'commodity' and much more one of those community institutions embodying and providing certain social 'goods', like basic housing, health, welfare, and an equitable system guaranteeing the upholding of law and order. Without access to and participation in these 'goods' a person's chances of the enjoyment of all the rights and privileges of a democratic form of life would be significantly impaired.

Hence, in practical terms, fair distribution of such social 'goods' as education must mean that every student is entitled to a fair share of books, equipment, apparatus and so on; that every school will receive a fair supply of teachers; that no school will, without special reason, be treated more favourably than another; that there should, in principle, be no difference in the educational treatment of children unless there are valid grounds for it. This is the prime principle of social justice: that all will get a share of the resources available to provide them with access to and equitable participation in democracy. This does not mean that all should receive the *same* share (cf. Rawls, 1972).

Democracy and Accountability

As has been set out above, there are certain underlying presuppositions and requirements arising from them that are implicit in our predilection for the democratic way of life. One of these is the need for public accountability. It would clearly be absurd to develop an elaborate system for consulting the people on matters of public policy without also providing institutional procedures for governments to be subject to rigorous public scrutiny and review, taken to task for incompetence, or replaced if their conduct of affairs is unsatisfactory. One corollary of this is that governments can be changed without revolution. There are, of course, many methods of ensuring public accountability in the sphere of government, at least in principle.

Look now to education, however: if schools are to be democratic on the above model, we may think it reasonable to ask whether there are any similar provisions, conventions or rules of procedure at work in a school, and available to all interested parties, by which a school's community may be certain that the democratic principles of consultation, accountability and reversibility are respected, provided for and guaranteed to operate. If such procedures are not found, or such guarantees cannot be given, then the community may with some justification move swiftly to see that they are put in place. Even if this is only at a higher level of generality, and a wide degree of discretion can be given to teachers and education officials in matters of minutiae, it is nevertheless crucial that, for a school to be seen as at least minimally democratic, parents, employers and the community in general should have the right to have its policies explained and justified to them and, if they find such explanations deficient or such justifications lacking plausibility, to have the means at their disposal to have such policies changed. This will be especially important if, as is now widely the case, some form of devolution, delegation or decentralized system of school management is in operation.

Knowledge, the Curriculum, and the Teacher's Authority

At the same time as making the above requirements of the 'democratic' school, however, we must be careful not to operate with some views and versions of the nature, purposes and values of democracy at work in educational institutions, views that, as D. Z. Phillips (1973) has very powerfully warned us, may well be mistaken or fallacious. Phillips points out that the authority of a teacher or other professional person derives from her qualifications demonstrating mastery of a subject, apprenticeship on the way to acquiring it, and the way her work conforms to, exhibits and possibly even extends its defining standards, intellectual conventions, and operating procedures. It is the disciplinary procedures of a subject or field of study that establish the criteria of what is proper and improper, allowable and prohibited, intelligible and meaningless in an educating or professional setting, and these structure and define any person's admissibility to the open community of the subject, which *only* then operates on a democratic basis. We do not grant degrees or award school leaving certificates simply on the grounds that a student has merely attended the course or been around in the institution: that student must have struggled to achieve some degree of mastery in his or her subjects of study, and must have succeeded to some extent.

This caution obtains especially in the case of those who argue that the subject of study should come from the student herself, develop from her interests, etc., and who maintain that it is such preoccupations as the students' own interests, 'social relevance' or 'political correctness' that should determine what subjects should be taught and what curriculum made available in a school or university. Indeed, D'Souza (1992) has recently mounted a forceful and deeply troubling demonstration of the points to which this kind of thinking and demand can lead in tertiary institutions. Both the range of subjects and the standards of what should be taught are inherent in and generated by the concept of knowledge itself and in the nature of its development by its leading proponents, researchers and practitioners.

In evaluating the success of programmes of teaching and instruction, therefore, what is to be judged is not the student's prior interests, personal taste or individual preference, but the grasp and understanding the student has of a subject or domain, and the competence that student can show in demonstrating and working according to its canons and procedures. Most importantly, however – and this is where we believe Neill (see below) to have been mistaken – before students (particularly those at school) can make any decisions about what subjects they should study, they must by definition be given some (at least minimal) understanding of what the subjects are and what counts as valid, intelligible and competent within them. And this plainly implies prior teaching, and the ostensive activity of an exponent who is already to a considerable degree well on the inside of the subject, and who is teaching her subject, demonstrating her mastery, or educating her students *not* in accordance with the dictates of her own private agenda, sectional concerns or political preoccupations, but with all her epistemic commitment and pedagogical effort devoted to getting her students to be her equals in the open, objective and impersonal world of knowledge and its various claims to acceptance.

Democracy, Teachers and their Role as Professionals

There are other requirements for education institutions beyond being fairly distributed and accountable. One would be that the body of teachers should be professional: knowledgeable, discerning, critical and responsible. This is because, in the vital matter of gaining, communicating and evaluating knowledge and intelligence in today's complex information society, the teacher has a special interest in the preservation, dissemination and promotion of the values of knowledge. For, as has been argued above, there can be no coping in today's society, and no reflection on and choice of those things to which individuals want to devote their time and main concerns, without the activity of teachers to point to and propound the knowledge appropriate to that endeavour.

Thus teachers, as experts in various fields of knowledge and as leading proponents of the difference that knowledge can make to the improvement of community welfare, have a special right to be listened to on matters of epistemic progress and cognitive importance as fundamental conditions of individual educational development and general social benefit. To this extent, the teacher is, as Peters remarks, 'a custodian of the quality of life of a community'. Teachers for this reason have a special responsibility to do all they can, individually and collectively, to improve the survival of their democracy and the worth of individuals' lives in it, by insisting on the availability of high-quality educating institutions and a democratically empowering curriculum in them.

The role of teachers as epistemic experts in the guardianship of the quality of life in a democracy is guaranteed by the ways in which they, and other members of the education and public welfare professions, continue their studies, upgrade their qualifications, and take courses of academic, professional and personal development. Teachers, and indeed professionals of all kinds, have an overriding interest in keeping abreast of the latest developments and most recent changes and advances in their fields of knowledge and professional concern. It is only in this way that they can continue to draw sustenance from the academic and professional well-springs that first nourished them as students being trained and educated in various tertiary institutions and that are subsequently essential to the maintenance of their academic and professional authority.

It is for this reason that teachers become members of subject associations, professional bodies and trade unions. Their experience and activities in such settings enable them to shape, effect and evaluate their professionally informed decisions on vital matters of educational policy, curriculum planning, delivery, administration, monitoring and assessment. Work and progress in these bodies offer to teachers, above and far beyond the lay-person, ready access to shared epistemic resources *and* a sense of combined strength and readiness for professional engagement and action. It is this that makes an informed, responsible and committed force of knowledge professionals a prerequisite in the creation and management of a democratic school. We may now go on to try to characterize the meaning of that phrase a little more precisely.

CREATING AND MANAGING THE DEMOCRATIC SCHOOL

The School as a Democratic Institution

In attempting to characterize the notion of a 'democratic' school, we might make a beginning with a quotation from the work of A. S. Neill (1968), the late founder and principal of Summerhill, the school located in Leiston in east Suffolk, England:

> The loyalty of Summerhill pupils to their own democracy is amazing. It has no fear in it, and no resentment. I have seen a boy go through a long trial for some anti-social act, and I have seen him sentenced. Often, the boy who has been sentenced is elected chairman of the next meeting. . . . The sense of justice that children have never ceases to make me marvel. And their administrative ability is great. As education, self-government is of infinite value . . .

We might perhaps think that Neill's emphasis on trial, sentence and, presumably, some form of punishment suggests that its institution and use at Summerhill may have been rather more negative and coercive than liberating and positive. We may also wonder whether the successful operation claimed for that school might not have been possible only as a function of the enclosed environment and the very small number of students involved. Yet the contrast between what were claimed to be typical features of the Summerhill school democracy and the organizing principles of a conventional school would certainly bear some further reflection. The two models involved may be capable of characterization along the following lines:

At Summerhill:

> Students have a major say in running the school.
> There are no authority figures.
> Attendence at lessons is optional.
> There is a relaxed approach towards discipline.
> There is considerable emphasis on play.
> There is a premium on letting children develop and follow their own interests.
> Nothing is compulsory.

At a conventional School:

> Students have little say in the running of school.
> There are strong authority figures.
> Attendance at lessons is compulsory.
> There are strong attitudes towards discipline and punishment.
> There is a greater emphasis on the need to develop skills, and on the importance of hard work at mastering them.
> There is a strong emphasis on getting students to work at learning what is held by the school authorities to be in their interests to study.

> Most activities and pursuits are compulsory, such as games and
> physical education, and aesthetic, moral and religious values.
> Discipline is externally imposed, not internally chosen.

It is of course highly questionable whether government schools should seek to emulate Summerhill or other such 'alternative' schools, which in any case are almost always independent, often boarding, sometimes highly selective, and almost always decidedly expensive. Nevertheless, government schools might still learn some very useful lessons in democracy from the approaches of such schools. They would do well to remember, though, that many of the other practices found in or associated with the operation of such schools might lead only to difficulties or even disasters in the conventional sector. Such difficulties might arise not least in those matters concerned with attendance at lessons (compulsory or optional?), participation in curriculum activities (serious or non-serious?), and relations between students and staff.

Not everyone, for example, sees any sense in allowing children and young people to devote much of their time in school to 'play' and to non-serious activities and pursuits. Teaching and learning are needed if young people are to acquire personally enriching, socially necessary knowledge and community-acceptable skills; and sometimes, for reasons already given, students have to be required to work hard to acquire such knowledge and conform to such norms and conventions of conduct as are called for and appropriate in the hard work of study. Teachers may of course choose to educate by methods of teaching involving activities that are playful, create enjoyment, or are carried out with humour all round; but that does not belie the deeply serious purpose of the actual subjects of study. Furthermore, in the exercise of such requirements devoted to serious educational aims, one cannot conceive of public institutions operating without sanctions of some sort, whether praise for hard work leading to success or blame for lack of attention or effort required to achieve good learning outcomes.

This holds good, too, with respect to matters of conduct and behaviour generally. Though there is much to be said for involving all a school's students in securing and caring for good order and conditions in which the disciplines involved in learning are more likely to be effective, there is nevertheless every reason to hesitate before conceding powers of (to take Neill's example) counsel, judge and jury in disciplinary matters to those whose maturational growth does not yet enable them to think in the complex, articulate and sophisticated ways required for the assessment of claims about conduct, the evaluation of evidence, the calculation of consequences, and the matching of appropriate sanction to particular offence. It would clearly be a difficult business, and one likely to cause problems, to elevate those who have as yet made relatively little progress through the stages of the development of moral autonomy to positions in which those highly complicated and refined skills are at a premium. These are matters which even some adults find difficult and demanding, and in which principals and teachers are constantly aware of their own shortcomings. How much less, then, should we imagine that persons below the age of maturity or most students at school will be capable of exercising them.

On the mater of curriculum choices, too, though it might be reasonable to give students the option to decide between some subjects offered to them in school, it is surely reasonable to do so only when they have some minimal understanding of those things between which they are choosing. As students we might, for example, properly have some say in deciding whether we should learn Arabic or Zulu, or choosing between astronomy and zoology, but the decision that the curriculum of a school should be arranged on the basis of students *having* to do modern language studies or science is most properly one for the whole community. Schools are not apart from the community in this: they cannot, as one private religious establishment in London discovered when examined by Sir Keith Joseph's inspectors from the Department of Education and Science, teach exactly what they like, nor can the students choose whether to attend or not to attend classes, without the wider community wanting to have some further say about that. The body of mature citizens, being well aware of the kinds of knowledge, skills and values required for successfully coping with the demands of life in a modern democracy, may think it perfectly in order to ask whether children and young people are self-evidently the best judges of what they should study and work hard at acquiring. The community, having a legitimate interest in the knowledge and skills to be expected of its future citizens, values the part it plays in determining the content of their education and the factors that should be taken into account when schools are framing their curricula, and is willing these days to specify those factors in some detail.

There is also the question of the interpersonal relationships carried on in an educational establishment, both those between staff and students, and those among students. Some government schools clearly have much to learn from Summerhill in this respect: the ease of approach and ready acceptance of individual differences, the use of given (first) names and the acceptance of all as being moral equals worthy of adult address, observed and practised in relations between students and staff at Summerhill, might be looked on with envy by students in more conventional schools, where a considerable degree of distance and a sense of superior–inferior relations very often obtains. The style of Summerhill's relations set a model for, and might well be emulated by, staff in such schools, to the betterment of their students' learning. Relations between students and students are, of course, much more difficult to regulate and direct towards positive educational outcomes. But the experiences described in Neill's and others' writings on this subject suggest that, in this area too, many conventional schools have a great deal to learn from Summerhill's methods: current reports regarding the incidence of bullying, intimidation and harassment in many schools do not find any echo in the Summerhill environment, where mutual tolerance and regard seems to be a value enshrined in students' acceptance of the responsibility they have to creating an effective and mutually supportive learning environment.

Doubtless positive and negative comments might be made on other aspects of Summerhill, and the debate continues. But for us perhaps the chief value of Summerhill lies in its democratic form of life, where the students do have a considerable (though not a determinative) say in the manner in which their school is run and on the matter of what subjects and skills, within the range on offer at the school, they shall be required to learn. The idea of the 'negotiated curriculum' is a good example of this principle being put into practice.

These reflections on the lessons that can be drawn from the Summerhill model of the democratic school may then encourage us to go forward and make a positive set of suggestions as to ways in which government schools can avoid the pitfalls of a too slavish imitation of such educational innovations, while at the same time profiting from the kind of thinking that animates their establishment and operation. Working on this basis, we may now think it entirely reasonable to require of government schools, in so far as they aspire to function as agents of initiation into the democratic form of life that characterizes the adult society in which they are to operate as citizens, that they should adhere strongly to the principles, if not the letter, of the kind of school *Charter for Democracy* put forward by Tony Knight (1985) (see opposite page).

It is worthwhile comparing these prescriptions with the kinds of rules and disciplinary procedures that generally obtain in many government schools of today. It could be interesting to try to work out what kinds of places schools would be if we legislated for the enforced conformity in all our schools to the kind of requirements, set out above, that as citizens of democracies we all insist upon and take for granted in our institutionalized forms of democracy. If we were to require the acceptance of the principles implicit in Knight's charter and the setting in train of deliberate moves to implement some such system in our schools tomorrow, we should have to look, first and foremost, to the ways in which school councils, principals and teachers would react to that challenge. For it is among such constituencies that the question of creating and maintaining a democratic school gets its real point of purchase.

The Position of the Principal, School Council, Staff and Students

Any discussion on democracy in schools must inevitably involve an appraisal of the role, powers and authority of the principal. We need to consider ways in which principals exercise their authority and practise leadership, for by doing so we might begin to tackle the question of whether, and if so in what sense, their school is a democratic community.

Democratically minded principals will usually consult the whole of their staff on a wide range of important educational issues. Such principals will hold regular meetings of deputy principals, directors of studies, heads of departments and subject teachers to discuss matters that affect the academic and intellectual life of the school. In such discussions principals will also exercise leadership in making proposals regarding matters of principle, policy and delivery, and open their ideas on these matters to appraisal and further elaboration. Such principals will also constantly communicate with those whose school responsibilities lie in its organization and administration: deputy principals, house directors, year leaders, guidance and counselling staff, and so on, consulting them over matters affecting the management and running of the school.

At such meetings democratic principals will ensure that all will have a say and none will be counted as more powerful than anyone else. Where necessary, external advisers or interest groups or individuals can be brought in: social case workers, careers advisory officers, welfare agencies, health and social service

CHARTER FOR DEMOCRACY

RIGHTS AND RESPONSIBILITIES
of students and teachers in a democratic school

Expressions of Unpopular Opinion:

Rights to freedom of speech (not slander or defamation) and peaceful assembly

Responsibilities of students to listen and not obstruct the opinions of others; of schools to provide forums for assembly and student press

Protection of Privacy:

Rights to be protected from the abuse of authority; to be protected from harassment; to be protected from unlawful attacks on honour and reputation.

Responsibilities of students to protect their own and others' property; of the school to provide parents and students with access to student's personal record, test results and evaluations; of the school not to divulge student records without permission of students and/or parent.

Due Process:

Rights of access to legal protection under the law; to be presumed innocent until proven guilty; to participate in classroom and school decision-making.

Responsibilities of students to be *accountable* for personal actions; of the school to provide forums for students to negotiate grievances; of the school to issue all students annually with a list of their rights and responsibilities.

Freedom of Movement:

Rights to be free from subservience to the will of others; to be free from cruel and unusual punishment; to be treated with dignity; to maintain a social identity.

Responsibilities of the school to create choices in language communication; of students and teachers not to humiliate, harass, or physically maltreat others; of students not to infringe upon the rights of others.

department officials, and representatives of employers, trade unions, parents and religious groups. All have a valid contribution to offer in matters affecting the educational welfare of the school and the various aspects of the development and growth of its students. Principals will try to shape, direct and monitor the decision-making process; they will ensure that decisions reached are put into effect; and they will take measures to assess and evaluate the effectiveness of decisions that are made. They will report on and take responsibility for these processes to the school council, the appropriate authorities, and the wider school community. The same requirements, *mutatis mutandis*, will operate with respect to the roles and responsibilities delegated to, held by and exercised among other staff colleagues working in the school in the interests of its students and the wider learning community.

Students too can be involved in the running of their school in a number of ways. One of them is by the class, tutorial group and house system, which offers students good experience of and training in democratic procedures. Class, house and group meetings may still operate according to democratic group principles and methods in what may be the wider and more authoritarian structure of the school. Occasionally, the principal may be an autocrat, but at least if she or he allows class and house meetings then there must inevitably be some procedures – those of discussion, of respecting and tolerating others' points of view, of voting, of keeping records, of personal participation in decision-making, of being willing to carry responsibility for implementing, monitoring and amending group decisions, of being punctual and courteous, and so on – that will count as conforming to the community's expectations that its younger members have at least some training in democracy.

The institution of school captains or senior students is a classic device for involving students in the running of the school. In any secondary school they can play an important part in maintaining discipline and in the arrangement and completion of certain tasks or duties, though Peters adds the cautionary advice that 'Office-holders should be appointed on a purely functional basis for limited periods with defined spheres of competence.' Within such clearly defined guide-lines, the advantages of engaging the more mature students in taking a role in the running of their school and of helping to consolidate and enhance the quality of life and work in it are obvious. The same will be true of the opportunities opened up to students for learning the skills of leadership, democratic participation and personal responsibility offered by games, physical pursuits, outdoor activities, various forms of community service, and participating in or running school clubs and societies of all kinds.

The *school council*, where it includes student representation, is another means of offering students direct experience of democratic principles and procedures. But of course its membership will range much more broadly than merely staff and students: if a school council is to be democratic, it will seek representation from all the constituencies and communities in which the school 'lives and moves and has its being', and in the name and pursuit of whose interests it claims to operate.

This will mean that, to be democratic, a school council must have, in its composition, not only representatives of students and staff: it will need membership from parents, business, industry and commerce, trade unions and professional associations, other educational institutions in the locality, other community and local welfare agencies and organizations, the local Education Ministry or other authority, and (where necessary) minority ethnic, cultural and/or religious groups. Only then will it be able to say that it can guarantee the widest possible consultation of, communication with, and accountability to, all its community's interests. And only then will it be able fully to address its principal terms of reference: to provide access to and ensure effective participation in a high-quality and empowering programme of educational experiences, and in ways that maximize and make most efficient use of all the various resources (human, capital, material) placed by that community at its service and disposal.

There is also a great deal that can be done to promote the value of democracy in the manner of conducting the relations that subsist between a principal and the school staff. If that relationship should be marked by the characteristic features of very many bureaucratic institutions, then it is unlikely that either staff or students of such a school would feel that they had a strong sense of belonging, ownership or commitment to the values of collegiality and partnership in the excitement of the joint cognitive enterprise that, we argue, should typify communication and advance in the intellectual realm. A school where the usual pyramid structure for the organization and administration of pedagogic and professional duties and responsibilities obtains sounds to us less like the kind of participative democracy we have in mind, and rather more like the command structure of a marine barracks. Indeed, there are some who fear that the move towards local management for schools bids fair to increase the already considerable powers of the principal. This form of local management, we believe, militates directly against the achievement of a proper degree of democracy in the running of the school, and the co-operation of all its inhabitants in promoting its mission.

We can understand, then, the argument of many that the powers of the principal ought to be open to a much greater degree of public accountability. For this reason we want to suggest that one way of promoting democracy in education would be to subject to a radical reappraisal the way in which business is managed and duties are apportioned in schools. For example, since the appointment of principals and staff is now much more open and democratic than it used to be, we believe that such principles should also obtain in the appointment and distribution of responsibilities. Why is it that the more senior one becomes in a school's organization, the further away one gets from the classroom? Why should not the business side of the school operations be managed by a class of professional business and office managers employed specifically for those restricted purposes, for which they have received appropriate training and qualifications, thereby allowing the educational professionals more time to allocate to educational activities and issues?

We are not, of course, arguing for the doctrine of the separation of powers in the running of the school. But the idea of councils, committees, working parties, advisory bodies, special commissions and programme teams, with terms of reference limited to specific functions and the fulfilment of that set of obligations to which schools are subject, does not, we think, require that there be only one chief executive operating on the autocratic basis on which some principals in the past have been seen to be operating in some schools. Teachers have qualifications, professional accreditation and employees' rights; these should be taken advantage of in utilizing and directing their expertise, energy and enthusiasm to whatever places in the panoply of a school's activities their presence and working will best benefit the school and its students, and the wider community. The best place for decisions to be made on these matters might perhaps be an academic, a programme or a curriculum sub-committee of the school council, or a quality teaching and learning committee operating inside the school, where staff and students are represented and can play a full part in advising the chief executive officer of the school council.

The Curriculum, Teaching and Learning as Exemplifications of Democracy

With the foregoing in mind, then, we might now feel it possible to tease out some general requirements for the hoped-for growth in democratic understanding and practice which will emerge particularly from the work our students do in their engagement in curriculum activities. Students need to be given experience, practice and maybe even formal training in the running of democratic institutions, and they will certainly acquire such practice in some of the ways set out above. But whether students join clubs, run societies or are appointed as senior students is often a matter of luck, personal inclination or particular need. With the curriculum, however, there can be no such fortuitous element. Engaging with the curriculum is, after all, why students are there in the first place, and their greatest and most numerous opportunities for growth into the democratic mentality will arise from their being exposed to liberal democratic procedures within their classrooms, subjects and lessons.

Democratic teaching and learning will involve having recourse to such strategies as the use of hypothetico-deductive methods, discussion, debate, argument and independent research as best pedagogic practice in teaching and learning activities, rather than by the teachers' simply lecturing, instructing or employing other such didactic and more formal approaches. In all the preferred ways mentioned, it is possible for students to observe the democracy of knowledge at work, get some understanding of its operating norms and conventions, and gain experience in, and hence acquire a taste for, the manning and running of democratic institutions, of which knowledge-getting and assessing is the chief exemplar.

Given the point that in the pursuit, dissemination and gradual mastery of knowledge the principles of reason generally are implicit, student learning and discipline will need to be conducted in ways in which there is clear agreement that some means of acquiring knowledge and some kinds of behaviour – violence, bullying, bribery, intimidation, harassment, the use of belittling or demeaning language – are out of place in the realm of knowledge and the freedom of the democratic classroom, and will not be accepted. They will need to be told and shown that commitment to rational ways of doing things carries as a consequence the promotion of certain desired and valued forms of conduct: telling the truth, not stealing or copying from other people's work, not fudging the results you come up with, not manufacturing or distorting evidence, keeping promises, not causing other people unnecessary pain, treating other people equally, allowing other people their own room to have their say and make decisions and choices for themselves, not interfering with their freedom to do as they wish until their choices threaten to interfere with the choosings of others – the list goes on, and can be added to in the light of our own experience or classroom situation.

Perhaps a good place to begin, as E. R. Braithwaite (1959) so well perceived and described in *To Sir, with Love*, is with the fundamental demand for courtesy, civility and consideration for others in the classroom. In respect of the minimal demands of politeness and care about other people, as well as all the values and practices set out above, students will need first to be shown, and daily to be exposed to, all those forms of interpersonal conduct that civilized people take courtesy and politeness to consist in. Then as Braithwaite ably showed, students can be helped and encouraged to make a start on learning to act according to the canons and criteria of proper behaviour themselves, in the hope and confident expectation that in time they will come to appreciate the utility and value of doing things in those ways rather than others, and to choose some ways of arranging their political and social relations rather than others. When they reach that point we may say that they have learned the lessons intended for them in the creation and implementation of the idea of the democratic school.

The Need for Caution, Effort and Knowledge as a Safeguard of Democracy

However, students need also to come to appreciate that democracy is a way of institutionalizing our political arrangements and our social intercourse that is very *difficult to sustain*. It requires constant nourishment and the most determined efforts at preservation. Without such care and attention, it is easy to overthrow it, and when it is overthrown the cost in human misery and suffering is enormous and takes sustained effort, time and expense to recover from, as peoples of Eastern Europe, Vietnam and Cambodia are still painfully discovering.

They need also to come to realize that a community's commitment to democracy is *expensive*. It is expensive *of effort:* democracy requires work and active engagement on the part not only of those who run it but also of those for whom it is run. It is expensive *of time:* the conception, development, establishment and refinement of democratic institutions are not something that can happen overnight, nor, as we shall see below, can a sufficient number of democratically minded citizens (with the considerable repertoires of intelligence, knowledge and competence, and the reservoirs of goodwill, required for the operation or even compliance with the norms and demands generated by those institutions) be expected, like Topsy, just to grow up of their own accord. And, finally, it is expensive *of resources:* it goes without saying that the running of democratic institutions, and constant recourse to their various ways of consultation, policy determination and evaluation, require the investment of appropriate levels of finance and funding.

Students may also need to be reminded that a commitment to the democratic way of doing things provides the community with no guarantee of infallibility:

plans put forward and policies implemented are not always successful. Indeed, such is human fallibility, such the resistance to change of existing well-established community institutions and social practices, so great that phenomenon called by existentialists the 'facticity' of external circumstance, that citizens committed to democratic values in all forms of political arrangement, cultural organization and educational establishment will be only too well aware of what efforts and expenditures of time, effort and money, what increments of knowledge and critical awareness, and what measures of patience, benevolence and emotional resilience are called for on the way to achieving their goal.

Education Indispensable to Democracy

Thus only gradually, with immense expenditures of time, effort and resources, will our students begin to understand that democracy requires, on the part of its citizens, knowledge about, interest in, an active commitment to participate in, the various forms and institutions of democracy, and a widespread and generally accepted willingness to *work* those institutions: that, without continuing succour and sustenance from those springs of life, democracy is a delicate plant that may well wither and die. Its growth and flourishing depend on a number of factors, all of them deployed by those who have come or been brought to the view that it is worth all the trouble.

Citizens of a democracy do not, as Peters intimates, simply arrive at political maturity and stand ready, willing and able to run its institutions. They have to be *trained*. In a democracy, people must know their rights and be ready to exercise them – and both they and their children must value, appreciate and practise that knowledge and the commitments that go with it. It follows that one cannot achieve a good democracy without good education, and indeed education in an institutional setting of a particular sort: it will surely be reasonably clear that, if a school is run by autocrats, it will not be likely to produce democrats. Indeed, we might say that a school will hardly produce democrats if it is *not* run by people committed to and living the principles of the democratic form of life and government.

If, then, we can encourage our students to play with, and strive to achieve, some understanding of, competence at and commitment to employing open-ended approaches and principles of critical appraisal in their acquisition of knowledge and the contributions they make to the running of their schools, and if we in our turn can see democracy actually at work in our schools, then we might be reasonably confident that our students will themselves ultimately become democrats in the rest of their lives.

Democratic Principles and the Need for Engagement in Appropriate Activities

At this point, however, the question may well arise: How we can ensure that this criticism, when called for, will be caring not carping, positive not destructive, restorative not detrimental? Above all, how we can ensure that questioning and critical enquiry, while rigorously scrutinizing and assessing policies and practices even at the most fundamental level, do not deny the worth of, nor act with the ultimate aim of subverting, the whole system and its values, in which such criticism is allowed and has a constructive place?

The work of Karl Popper (1943, 1960), the Austrian philosopher, may help the educator in this context. Popper's contention is that democracy works best when faced with problems. All societies have problems to deal with: some require explanations to be found for phenomena that appear anomalous or puzzling; others require answers to be found in the form of policies for the rectification of mistakes or for solution of difficulties whose arrival or continued presence is damaging to the effective functioning of the social whole. Societies differ as to the ways in which they tackle these problems, depending on whether (we might observe) they are 'open' or 'closed'.

Now, when a theoretical explanation or policy recommendation is put forward as an answer (explanation or prescription) to a problem in an open, democratic society, the typical way in which, according to Popper, such societies approach those proposals will be to take them as hypotheses that must be openly tested and criticized. Take any policy proposal – on language teaching; on decreasing gender bias in maths, science and technology; on catering for the educational needs of disadvantaged children or students from minority ethnic groups: treat it as a tentative hypothesis and ask, simply, will it work? And this means putting it to the test: trying it out and seeing. If it will work and will resist for the time being all the attempts at criticism and refutation (a central value of open societies and the democratic form of life) that members of that open society will want to direct at it, then it may be accepted for the time being as a provisional account or as a tentative policy, one that we may cautiously proceed to address ourselves to or put in place for our problems. If it will not work, then either its failure will be manifest or time will allow scrutiny and criticism of it, through open democratic structures, that will lead to its correction and improvement.

On this basis, those committed to the increase of democracy in education need to be prepared to come up with proposals for developing democratic values, as exemplified in policies for devolution, equity, or giving students the means for enhancing their and their communities' quality of life. But they will also need to be ready to subject them to inspection, critical scrutiny and rejection or amendment, or have other people do it. If that assertion is true, then it follows that a major key to the democratization of schools is the democratization of principals and school councils. They will be the prime agents of the changes necessary to create and manage effectively the transformation of society, from the hierarchy and the patriarchy of the present to the democratic schools and the democratic society of the kind that we might all hope to see in the future.

Educating for Democracy: Contradiction, Tautology, or Impossible Ideal?

We therefore come back again to the key question for the attempt to increase quality in schooling. In what sense, if any, can we properly talk of and plan for 'education for democracy'? Is this phrase a truism, a contradiction in terms, or just simply an unrealizable ideal?

In attempting to answer this question, we should perhaps make one preliminary observation. For we should note with caution that 'education for democracy' is a *slogan*; and it is important briefly to comment on the logic and function of such slogans. Slogans are, as has been remarked, 'empty of all positive content but rich in emotional appeal'. They provide 'rallying symbols' (Scheffler, 1960) for those committed to particular causes or sets of causes: slogans are usually intended, by those who wave the banners containing them, to have the same effect as moral imperatives. But slogans can also serve as instruments for the dispersal of the uncommitted or the positively hostile to those causes. Their utility is that they can mean all things to all people; in other words, we can, like Humpty Dumpty in *Alice in Wonderland*, make the slogans 'democracy' and 'education' means almost anything we like, within reasonable limits. And that is why it behoves us to try to be particularly clear about what we have in mind when we are framing educational proposals, plans and policies predicated on the idea and value of 'education for democracy'.

So much is necessary as a prelude to the discussion of the above question. Our aim will be to argue (a) that the idea contained in the slogan cited above does not contain a contradiction; or (b) that definition of its terms will reveal it as either (i) a contradiction or (ii) a tautology.

We might begin by suggesting a couple of possible meanings for the idea of 'education for democracy'. We might, for instance, read it as meaning something along the following lines: 'one can educate for the maintenance of democracy' or (better) 'one should educate to produce democrats'. Now, *if* we take the slogan as containing a contradiction, then it will mean that either one cannot *educate* to produce good citizens for a democracy; or that one may do so but the end-product will not be *democrats*. Our view is that the first of these alternatives is the correct one. The evidence to support this contention arises from an account of 'education'.

We take 'education' to be an *activity* – deliberate, self-conscious and aimed at achieving some ends that are an improvement upon what has been accepted from the past. We say this because one cannot educate by accident. Expressions like 'the only education I received was on the streets' (which seems to suggest that a society may indeed educate accidentally) take their force from a contrast with education as provided and engaged in deliberately by people working with learners in formal and institutional settings. We should not normally apply the term 'educated' to someone who claimed that 'experiences on the streets' were all the experiences they had that they were prepared to count as 'educational'. Of course, locutions like 'formal education' suggest that there could be such a thing as 'informal education', and this is indeed so. But by the use of the latter term we should merely be implying things about the institutional, pedagogical or methodological aspects of the educational process, not that it was *unconscious*.

Further evidence that education is an activity is provided by the concepts 'teaching' and 'learning', which are also used as names for particular activities that are seen as essential parts of any process describable as 'education'. 'Learning' is an 'achievement' word (in Ryle's (1949) sense): expressions such as 'I have learnt the names of all the rivers, capes and bays of the United Kingdom, but I can't remember them' might reasonably evoke the response, 'Then you haven't really learnt them.' And one cannot *succeed at* or *achieve* something in learning without meaning to do so. In our view, then, learning is an active endeavour in the sense of being a conscious undertaking to reach a goal by means judged by the actor to be the best (all things considered) for doing so.

'Teaching' is not necessarily an achievement word ('I am teaching English literature to 4C but without much success' seems a reasonable and intelligible remark to make), but to teach is certainly also an activity, for one cannot do it accidentally: one notices and looks for success in it. Given that the main parts of formal education consist as much as anything else in teaching and learning, we might therefore reasonably claim that the major parts of education involve conscious and rational activity, aimed at the acquisition of knowledge, belief and skills of various kinds. And the achievement of these on the part of the student is a matter of value and importance to the student, the school and the community.

Education is also a *process* in that it requires at least a learner; it usually requires an educator, some information (or a notion of desired terminal behaviour), and the transmission of that information by morally reputable means, and it relates to some wider ends than the mere receipt and reproduction of information. We should not generally regard someone as 'educated' to the extent that she could simply reproduce the information which the educator organized for her consumption as part of the process of making her educated (though it does make sense to say, 'I was educated at Preston Girls' High School' or '... at Durham University'). Statements like 'He's an educated person but that's no reason to expect him to solve a problem he didn't do at school'; or 'He was educated as an historian but he can't tell you anything about the Treaty of Utrecht because that isn't his period'; or 'She was educated at a private school and hasn't ever considered voting anything but Conservative' are therefore educationally odd; indeed, on our analysis, they are (potentially, at any rate) contradictory. This is because the study of problems in mathematics, history and politics at school seen as an *educating institution* (not a spy school, a bridge school or a driving school) is usually part of an effort on the part of a teacher to (a) bring the student to recognize and solve problems of similar structure with different values for the variables, and then (b) to enable her to select as problematic certain questions which interest or puzzle her, to frame them as clear problems, to recognize what would count as evidence for their solution, to frame hypotheses as to how they might be solved, to put those hypotheses into effect, and then to evaluate their outcomes – as Dewey (1938, 1966) says, to 'undergo' their consequences.

The aim of all educational processes, on this analysis, seems to be the reaching of a kind of *autonomy* (even if limited) *in whatever field is studied*. As we see it, education involves acts like judging, questioning, considering, criticizing, doubting and making up one's mind *for oneself*. The end purpose of this is that educated individuals should come to adulthood capable of reckoning up, deciding about and acting on what they themselves see as being in their best interests. They will, on occasion, be willing to subordinate those interests to the greater good of the whole community; and able to realize, when they do not do this, that they could be guilty of putting their own interests before those of other people and in that way could be open to moral censure and blame.

Let us, therefore, now come closer to the case in point. What might one say about the process undergone by the student in the third example cited above, regarding her political affiliation's being decided by her schooling? If that schooling had indeed included political *instruction* of a conservative character, we might be inclined to say that the student had been indoctrinated rather than educated. Many authors in this field (cf. Snook, 1972) seem to hold the view that to indoctrinate is to inculcate particular kinds of value preferences. We would disagree with this position and contend rather that 'education *for* anything' (where the goal includes elements of value), which would normally tend to predispose the actor to decide how to act in one way rather than another in moral, political, social or religious matters, is indoctrination. Indeed, any attempt to present questions of value as matters of fact, or opinion as established truth, or the requiring of an unquestioning acceptance of certain sets of unexamined propositions for which no, or highly slanted, evidential support is given, is also indoctrination. So part of the definition of indoctrination has to be concerned with the content of acts or beliefs as qualifying them for that label.

Another part of this must also have to do with the means by which such instruction or education is attempted to be imparted. It is entirely possible to use indoctrinatory methods to produce an *appearance* of open-mindedness and independent thinking, as for instance when one is asked to give reasons for making particular moral judgments or advancing particular religious opinions. One may of course have been taught justifications and the ways of making appropriate answers to the various objections one will be likely to encounter in such cases, to a high degree of generality and sophistication. But this is still indoctrination: the essence here is the idea of 'doctrine'. For this reason both content and method are parts of indoctrination, though the former is perhaps more telling.

As opposed to this, however, we might say that an essential part of educating a young person to be an 'actor', a 'chooser', indeed a 'person', is helping to develop in that person the power of autonomy – of having free choice and independence in judgments or conduct, especially in moral or political matters. If one cannot decide moral or political issues *for oneself* then one cannot be held to have made a free choice, and, for that reason, one cannot be held responsible for the consequences. That would put one on a par with lunatics, animals and babies: the difference between such creatures and adult human beings is that the latter have acquired the power to make decisions and choices autonomously, with full information about, awareness of, and willing acceptance of responsibility for, their likely outcomes.

This is why 'autonomy' in moral or political matters cannot be *taught* as a series of rules or propositions or as a recipe set of skills. Even if rules are taught, the ability to operate with them in a skilful manner is 'caught'. For example, doing a succession of addition sums, one hopes, will lead to the child's being able to do addition sums she has not seen, to the point at which she can say, 'Now I know how to go on' (Wittgenstein, 1953). But this cannot be taught, only demonstrated. How much more, then, must the ability not only to operate with rules but to choose between conflicting rules be a matter of example.

Moral or political autonomy therefore depends on the learner's observing a moral or political free agent at work, and in situations calling for the exercise of independent moral or political judgment. Techniques such as brainwashing or conditioning, the use of force, lying and manipulating, and so on, which are normally associated with indoctrinatory aspirations and intentions, are ruled out, since such immoral behaviours (immoral because they treat students as less than full moral persons in their own right) would be dysfunctional in any attempt to make the student morally autonomous.

As Aristotle (1934 edn) points out, the house-builder or the harp-player becomes good at that task by being required to exercise it in appropriate circumstances. Aristotle uses the concepts of justice and temperance to put this in a framework of moral and social values, from which the appropriate implications for education and democracy flow almost self-evidently:

> Acts done in conformity with the virtues are not done justly or temperately being in themselves of a certain sort, but only if the agent himself is in a certain state of mind when he performs them: first he must act with knowledge; secondly, he must deliberately choose the act, and choose it for its own sake; and thirdly the act must spring from a fixed and permanent disposition of character ... inasmuch as virtue results from the repeated performance of just and temperate actions ... the agent is just and temperate not when he does these acts merely, but when he does them in the way in which just and temperate men do them. It is correct therefore to say that a man becomes just by doing just actions and temperate by doing temperate actions; and no one can have the remotest chance of becoming good without doing them.
> (*Nicomachean Ethics*, Book II, iv. 3–4, 1105a 29–1105b 1 and 1105b 4–12)

Thus one becomes a morally autonomous person or a good democrat by being exposed to all the practices and institutions of morality and democracy from the very earliest times and, by habituation, imitation and direct personal involvement, one actually acquires their values and grows into the state of being in which one has a settled disposition to adhere to, exemplify and practise them. This growth takes place by a kind of process of osmosis and gradually maturing appreciation of the prime value of those activities, practices and institutions in influencing behaviour, helping to determine human affairs and conducing in that way to the promotion of happiness and welfare and the diminution of harm and suffering.

We may now draw all this together. In one sense the slogan 'education for democracy' does indeed contain something of a contradiction. This is because, as we have seen, any process aiming at the student's taking a *particular* position on matters of value or opinion is indoctrinatory. Therefore, to try to 'educate' for democracy by *teaching* or *giving instruction in* 'democratic' rules and behaviour is, in a quite decided sense, to fail to educate: it is to indoctrinate. If we continue to take the view that there is a contradiction here, then it goes even deeper than that. For any attempt to *indoctrinate* for democracy is bound, practically and conceptually speaking, to fail. The citizen of a democracy is, ideally, as autonomous as it is possible to be, helping in the business of 'government' (at however low or high a level) and making decisions according to the evidence and to conscience. We have seen that autonomy (like 'criticism' or 'taste') is not so much taught as caught, in the sense that one may, after a series of ostensive definitions and guided attempts of one's own, finally 'see the point'. Therefore, to try to 'indoctrinate' our young for democracy is to make them unfit as citizens for a democratic role and, indeed, for a democratic form of life.

So, 'education for democracy', viewed as a contradiction with the emphasis on *for*, is a very deep contradiction indeed, and is an undertaking that is bound to fail. This brings us on to our final point, which is that, in quite another sense, 'education for democracy' is a *tautology* – and, as a tautology, it is bound to *succeed*. We can easily see from the foregoing account of democracy and education how this is the case. Education is concerned above all with autonomy. This is learnt by example and personal growth in practice and confidence. An autonomous person is automatically and self-evidently a democrat. That is, the definitions offered above of both 'educatedness' and 'democrat' are both based on and encapsulate similar notions about the person's mind, conduct and ability to choose.

Our last point, therefore, is this: to see 'education for democracy' as *requiring instruction in the 'rules' of being a 'democrat'*, as if these were not themselves part of the democratic debate, is to abandon 'education', to fail to understand 'democracy', and to attempt a course of action whose contradictory nature makes failure certain and leads instead to autocracy, fascism and totalitarianism. On the other hand, where 'education for democracy' means promoting mental autonomy by encouraging the predisposition to make informed and rational choices and clearly distinguishing truth (however we define that – though clearly 'objectivity' will be a presupposition of all attempts to elucidate it) from opinion, in order to facilitate the making of such choices as a settled predisposition in the adult, one sees that the slogan's two terms mean just about the same, and in that sense the slogan is tautologous. In this sense 'education for democracy' simply means 'education': the two concepts are coterminous.

One final cautionary note is needed. The point can always be made, of course, that 'education' and 'democracy' are both 'hurrah' terms (as Ayer (1971) would call them), and we are uncomfortably aware that all definitions of them – including the ones we have given above – are functions of the definer's most profound metaphysical, ideological and moral preconceptions, beliefs and commitments. To that extent, they are, as well as being highly prescriptive, also highly contentious – and completely open to appraisal, critique and the most strenuous efforts at correction and falsification. What is remarkable is that, of all forms of political ideology or arrangement, the activities of clarification, criticism and correction are perhaps the chief characteristic features of 'democracy' as a form of government that we most commonly seek to identify: its constant concern for and preoccupation with self-examination, self-criticism, self-review and self-assessment.

What is special about and saves the democrat, in our view – and this, we believe, is finally the prime justification for our preferring democracy over every other form of government and trying to choose and create a 'democratic' school over any other style of educational administration – is that she follows the Popperian path in accepting and embracing that very attempt at refutation. The democrat places a premium upon exposing even the most cherished of her beliefs, definitions, policies and plans to public scrutiny, review and possible refutation.

The very activity of democratic debate is itself a transcendental deduction of its being and value.

It is this realization that gives intelligibility and point to the remark of Sir Winston Churchill, speaking in the House of Commons in 1947 on 11 November – a significant day, as Australians will tell you, for the concepts of accountability, open government and the need for democratic education:

> Many forms of government have been tried, and will be tried in this world of sin and woe. No one pretends that democracy is perfect or all-wise. Indeed it has been said that democracy is the worst form of government – except for all those other forms that have been tried from time to time.

Chapter 8

Autonomy and Mutuality: Towards a New Conceptualization of Relationships in Quality Schooling

In this chapter we continue the development of our theory of quality schooling emanating from our analysis of data and consideration of existing bodies of literature relevant to the field. We begin the chapter by discussing the goals of schooling within the context and references of the concepts of autonomy and mutuality. These same concepts, we argue, also provide us with a useful framework for examining administrative relationships between the school, the system and the wider community. Part of that wider community consists of the tertiary education and training institutions, and in the final section of the chapter we seek to show how quality schooling becomes part of the services offered and the provision made for the education profession by such institutions as part of their duties and responsibilities of community involvement.

AUTONOMY, MUTUALITY AND THE CONCEPT OF QUALITY

As we have noted in Chapter 1, although issues of quality in education have been a matter of concern for some time in different institutions, systems and countries, getting clarity and agreement on matters to do with quality schooling has proved far more difficult. The reason for this, we argued, is that quality is an 'essentially contested' concept; the only thing one can be certain about, in our search for what some might hope to discover as the 'real', 'central' or 'essential' meaning of 'quality', is that people will be uncertain and probably in disagreement about the term.

Instead of engaging in a futile search for the real meaning of quality, we countered with the positive suggestion that the best we can do in our attempt to get something of a grip on its meaning is to follow Wittgenstein's advice (Wittgenstein, 1953) and *look at its use* in conversations employing that term and centring on that topic, and its increasing importance in institutional planning, direction and evaluation.

At the end of our research endeavour, although we cannot identify an essential meaning for the concept of quality, our observation of talk about it indicates the operation, within broad parameters, of a lodestone in such talk. In people's discussions and debates about quality we found that what clearly matters, and what helps us to begin to dimly discern some sort of 'truth', is the irregular flow and shifting interplay of a number of factors. These include: intellectual backgrounds and traditions; individual and collective intentions, the motivations and interests of participants in the debate; the contexts in which such debates take place; the outcomes aimed at and the purposes held in mind; and the consider- ations that make certain criteria important and certain moves decisive. These and other such locating devices have given us far more of the flavour, direction and sense of the particular ways in which quality has significance in such dis- cussions than any number of sophisticated definitions and conceptual analyses.

The interesting thing about the study we have conducted is that our examin- ation of the *use of the term* in the educational community appears to indicate a wide measure of agreement on certain 'core' values. These core values are widely observed to subsist in, and then looked for as characteristic features of, the 'quality', 'good', or 'effective' school, and, when found or agreed upon, are seen as ends to be aimed at or values worth promoting in the activities and undertakings of schools. These values help to structure and define the direction and aims of educational policy and practice. We have discerned a number of core values that might be said to be typical of quality schools. It appears that such schools should:

- give their students access to, and the opportunity to acquire, prac- tise and apply, those bodies and kinds of knowledge, competences, skills and attitudes that will prepare them for life in today's complex society;
- have a concern for and promote the value of excellence and high standards of individual and institutional aspiration, achievement and conduct in all aspects of its activities;
- be democratic, equitable and just;
- humanize our students and give them an introduction into, and opportunities for acquiring, the values that will be crucial in their personal and social development;
- develop in students a sense of independence and of their own worth as human beings, with confidence in their ability to contribute to the society of which they are a part in appropriate social, political and moral ways;
- prepare our future citizens to conduct their interpersonal relation- ships in ways that are not inimical to the health and stability of society or the individuals that comprise it;
- prepare students to have a concern for the cultural as well as the economic enrichment of the community in which they will ulti- mately play a part, by promoting the enjoyment of artistic and expressive experience in addition to the acquisition of knowledge and its employment;
- conjoin education for personal autonomy and education for com- munity enmeshment and social contribution, enabling each student to enrich the society of which he or she is to become a part as a giver, an enlarger and an enhancer, as well as being an inheritor and recipient.

These are cited only as illustrations of some of the values of quality schooling; no doubt there are others. But what our research does suggest is that, whatever other functions a quality school might be said to perform, it is vitally concerned with the promotion of these values at least.

As an aside, we might point out that this list constitutes a somewhat different set of criteria for quality or effective schooling from that which emerges from studies using the strictly quantitative approach emanating from the Mr Gradgrinds of the educational community. Such an approach, which has dominated American and some European models of school effectiveness, runs the risk – indeed faces the danger – of creating a situation in which the outcomes of education are articulated in such a way that the curriculum concentrates on, and becomes narrowly prescriptive of, instrumental and economic goals; indeed such an approach can, by definition, concentrate only on those goals that are readily measurable in numerical terms.

The point that emerges strongly from our enquiry into quality schooling is that central to the concept of quality schooling is an emphasis upon *values*. Further, we believe that the chief of these incorporates a dual emphasis:

- one, upon the development of autonomous individuals, with their own powers of independent judgment and the capacity to be self-motivated and self-starting in action;
- the other, that such autonomous agents must at the same time, and necessarily, be taken up into patterns and networks of mutual interrelation with other individuals and with the whole community in all its economic, social and political aspects.

Such interrelationships form and structure the set of agreements and conventions about an inner core of values (some might say, a value system) that then, in their totality and interdependence, function to provide us with the various kinds of capacities and strengths needed to deal with the difficulties, problems, tensions and controversies that so beset the field.

We found in our study, however, that the problems relating to the investigation of the concept of quality schooling are not only of a meta-philosophical kind; they also require discussion and agreement at the substantive level. The discussion about autonomy and mutuality translated into the social setting immediately involves reference to questions concerning how we wish individuals to develop, and which form of society will best facilitate this development. For example, discussion between proponents of social justice, viewed as equality of treatment or of opportunity, and advocates of individual excellence resting on and incorporating a requirement of complete personal freedom, embodies differences of value judgments of a markedly substantive kind. These differences are most obviously articulated and then transposed into a highly contentious but binding political reality when we come, for instance, to adjudicate upon the claims of political parties whose programmes are calculated best to express those differences and translate them into social operation.

The key questions in quality schooling, therefore, are ones not merely of meta-ethics but also those that concern the form and content of our systems of values, codes of ethics and standards of conduct that are to be translated into policy and become normative for both the individual and society. In our debates about the future of education, these questions should be of central concern, and should precede any discussions about restructuring involving decentralized and devolved administrative structures. Our contention is that agreement on the substance of the values and agenda that should underpin our educational norms and conventions must necessarily come before any discussion of the ways and means of their institutional realization and implementation. It is only, we maintain, when we have secured some form of agreement about substance that we can then tackle the further problem of operationalization and implementation.

THE OPERATIONALIZATION AND IMPLEMENTATION OF QUALITY SCHOOLING

Education: A Public Good or a Commodity?

In Chapter 1 we showed how proponents of quality schooling in countries such as Australia, Denmark, France and Norway traditionally supported the principle that access to intellectual challenge, and a high-quality and empowering curriculum in a caring and personally concerned environment, were among the most important features of a more just society – one in which social justice and equality of opportunity stood as achievable goals for education. In contrast, we saw that the conservative philosophy, adopted in countries such as England and Wales, was more minimalist as regards equity and social justice and the form in which they are applied to education: it embodied the view that education, as an agency, could do little to redress the major inequalities existing in society. From such a perspective, the administrative response to the promotion and provision of quality schooling left a far greater degree of responsibility for achievement to individual motivation and talent, and much more responsibility for management to the local school site and the influences of the educational market place.

We saw also how the observable differences in the political and ethical considerations between parties debating the best way to ensure quality in schooling relate to the commitments that people have to a set of beliefs regarding the nature of human beings, the most desirable form of society, and the ways in which they can best arrange and institutionalize their relationships for the various purposes they have in mind. Such differences of vision and perspective are fundamental to our conceptions of the idea of 'public service', the public provision and resourcing of goods and services, and to our response to the questions associated with restructuring education and the decentralization and devolution of decision-making to schools. In addition to these differences of political and ethical orientation, we also saw how particular preferences in economic theory are having a significant, and not always beneficial, impact and effect on education – and indeed on community agencies more widely.

The market approach, for example, puts enormous stress upon the supposed freedom of the individual client – the parent and child – and on the freedom of the provider – the individual school. This has enabled conservatives to promote the superficially beguiling policies of parental choice, but, at the same time, it has also enabled them to locate blame for low-level performance and educational under-achievement in the supposed inadequacies of individuals rather than in structural features of society or the obvious imperfections of institutions and public agencies.

The conservative emphasis upon the educational market place also enables them to restructure schools in such a way that major decision-making is relocated to the school site and major responsibility for resource provision and resource management is located at the local level. For schools operating under such terms and conditions, 'success' is determined by their success in attracting – or choosing – the right class of customer, who can thereafter attract to the school the educational dollar to ensure the school's continuing survival; schools that 'fail' in the educational market place, in these terms, like bankrupt businesses, 'go to the wall' and are simply closed, thereby avoiding for government the potentially unpopular political decisions of appearing to have discriminated against one section of society in favour of another. In this context, we have the devolution of both problems and blame to the local school site and its management: governments do not decide to close schools; it is simply 'market forces' that are alleged to do that.

If the market prevails, if education is seen as some kind of commodity to be offered for sale and 'bought' at a price, if additional enterprise is expected for schools to generate further funds on a local basis, then inequity and inequality within a system of education will almost certainly increase. The stark reality is that much-sought-after schools begin to discriminate against certain types and classes of student; that the curriculum generally becomes narrower and more responsive to the demands of economic and societal elites; and that there are increasingly many people who simply cannot afford to buy the educational goods and services that such institutions offer.

In contrast to the notion of education as a commodity stands the notion of education as *a public good*, access to which is a prerequisite for informed and effective participation by all citizens in a democratic society. The same may be said of such services as health, welfare and housing, all of which, with education, constitute the infrastructure upon which individuals may hope to construct, realize and work at achieving their own versions of a life of quality. It is upon this notion of education as as public good that education for all children was made available in many countries. And in the modern world, with so many and such complex demands and difficulties – economic, social and cultural – which our future generations will have to cope with, it is that principle, we argue, that we should be least willing to give up.

Certainly no one would suggest for a moment that education, health and welfare services are 'free' and require no resources; they have to be funded and supported financially and in a myriad other ways. But these are services that are vital and indispensable to the nature, quality and operation of the society in which we all live and share as citizens. Our point is that individuals can only develop as autonomous agents fit to participate in society if they are sufficiently informed, prepared and predisposed; if they are healthy and well fed; and if they have the minimal domestic conditions for perpetuating existence. In our view, the whole of our society has a direct interest in securing, providing and safeguarding those prerequisite conditions and services on the basis of the contributions that all of us who benefit from them see are in our interest to make to the common wealth in a common exchequer.

What must also be noted, is that our world is a complex conjunction of aggregations of individual human beings; we do not live on desert islands – indeed we could not start our existence or survive if we did. The personal freedom and individual choice that are so much prized by exponents of the market philosophy are possible only as an outgrowth of the knowledge and values that other members of society have opened up to us, and of an intimation of what choices are available, and what choosing, and the calculation of its consequences, might mean. For most of us, this has first been made available through our schooling experience.

It is a paradox of our existence that our autonomy requires the work of other people. It is given to us and increased by our education, and that requires the learning of language and the transmission of knowledge. Both of these are social activities and public enterprises in which at least two people must engage in an interaction predicated upon the assumption of the mutual tolerance and regard that is embodied only in the institutions of society. Without the one, there cannot be the other; and without that key institution called education, there can be neither. Autonomy is the flower that grows out of seeds planted and tended by heteronomous hands.

All this, at rock bottom, is what taxes are for – and those of us with differential levels of resources contribute to the exchequer differentially as a result and in proportion. It is that contribution that grants us licence to access those good things that society wishes to be available for enjoyment by all its members, and this brings out the very mutuality and interdependence of our economic arrangements for funding and running our society and providing appropriate levels and kinds of service for the benefit of all its constituents – including those who, because of history, handicap, weakness or sheer misfortune may not able to contribute much to it at the moment but still need its support. And this makes society and its various institutions, especially the school, the very place and forum in which individuals can further develop their pattern of preferred life-options and so increase their autonomy, and in which all sections of the community co-operate mutually for the benefit of the societal whole.

The Redistribution of Power and Administrative Responsibilities: A Reconceptualization of Relationships

In the drive towards increasing the quality of schooling, education authorities in many countries have been engaged in reforms which have direct implications for the redistribution of power and administrative responsibility among the various levels within the education system, including the school itself.

Although many of these reforms have been undertaken under the overt agendum of decentralization and devolution, we have observed that the situation is far more complex than this. A closer examination of data and practices has suggested that any attempt to elucidate the redistribution of power is likely to encounter, and have to deal with, a far more complex set of factors and variables

than any account based on a one-dimensional conception of changed arrangements along the centralization–decentralization continuum would intimate.

In the state system of education in Western Australia, for instance, much of
the rhetoric of school reform over the last decade has incorporated a good deal
of talk and attention devoted to the idea and importance of the devolution of
decision-making to the local school site. Like uncertain teenagers, however,
governments, policy-makers, administrators and school-based personnel are now
beginning to ask, 'How far should we go?' For, while current moves towards
increased devolution are certainly giving schools increased responsibility in certain areas of decision-making, many school-based personnel express concern
regarding the loss of the sense of security, support and safety that was previously
such a valued feature of the relationships between schools and the centre. 'Do
we', they are asking, 'want or need all that freedom? Is it good?'

Erich Fromm (1960), in his classic study of authoritarianism, illustrated how
people, in their desire to escape from freedom, often seek to avoid the pain of
responsibility. So long as we are dependent on a higher authority, he maintained,
we can indulge ourselves with the thought that we can blame the powers above
us for our condition. To move from the comfortable conditions of the past and,
in a new set of structures and arrangements, suddenly to have to recognize
and accept that we have no one to blame except ourselves, is a fearful state of
affairs. Fromm's point is that freedom has its price: with autonomy and independence come agonizing choices, responsibilities, duties and obligations – and the
angst so well described by the existentialists.

That is indeed a dreadful prospect, but it is one with which we can deal. For
we realize that independence of thought and action, mutual concern, commitment
and disciplined confrontation are possible only in the presence of others; they
are significant parts of all adult relationships, whether they be expressed in the
personal or the organizational context. R. S. Peters put this well nearly thirty
years ago:

> This consciousness of being a person reaches its zenith, perhaps, in
> the experience of entering into and sustaining a personal relationship,
> which is based on reciprocal agreement, where the bonds that bind
> people together derive from their own appraisals and choice, not from
> any status or institutional position. They create their own world by
> voluntarily sharing together and mingling their own individual perspec-
> tives on, and developments of, the public life of their society.
>
> (Peters, 1966, p. 212)

In the concept of the dutiful servant of the Education Department, promoted
in schools and school systems in Australia and embedded in the bureaucratic
mentality of nineteenth-century colonialism, it was not, unfortunately, independence of thought and action, courage, initiative, mutual sharing, reciprocity, or
disciplined confrontation that were encouraged or valued. What was looked for
instead was conformity, acceptance and unquestioning service. What was meant
to be an escape from the nepotism and favouritism with which many institutions
had been ruled and managed in England became in Australia the dry suffocating

prison of bureaucracy, in which mediocrity flourished and compliance was rewarded.

Over the last two decades policy-makers and administrators have been working steadily to get rid of these ways of thinking and doing. But it has required a considerable attitude change to recognize that problems, and the need for policies to provide their solution, are the real driving forces behind institutional change: it is now realized that neither ossifying bureaucracy nor the progression of favoured people for favoured places is a good guide on the road towards the development of organizations and the fashioning of effective working relationships within them.

What we need now, therefore, is a reconceptualization of policies relating to educational decision-making and the administrative arrangements flowing from them. We need new sets and patterns of relationship and interactions based on new concepts and categories. The old ideas are no longer useful in describing and explaining the tortuous complexities that are now involved in and operate at the different layers, levels and loci of decision-making.

The former bureaucratic notions, based on hierarchical positional power within a single 'system', are now outmoded; other alternatives, developed in recent years, have proved similarly unhelpful. For example, the idea of a school or 'education centre' as a 'community resource', with its simple presence and availability for access by voucher-users, so celebrated by Illich (1973) and his like, fails to do justice to the necessity of continuity in the early years of schooling, or to take account of the point that education requires the heteronomous activity of significant others who induct and initiate our young into the heterogeneous sets of beliefs, norms and patterns of behaviour valued by society as a whole. Likewise, the corporate vision of education, based on the analogy of networks of business franchises and making schools look like fast-food outlets, provides a wholly inappropriate model of the educational enterprise, if we are to accept education as a 'public good'.

For our part, education *is*, we believe, a public 'good', and we all have a mutual interest in securing access to it. Without admittance to such a 'good', our young people will be much less likely to progress rapidly towards those minimal degrees of personal autonomy and civic responsibility by which citizens can ensure that the preconditions and mechanisms for community continuation, social justice or indeed any sort of advanced and sophisticated personal development are in place and available to all.

At this stage we think it important to make the following crucial point. At the present time, around the world, there is a great deal of talk about devolution, local management of schools, or self-managing schools; and there is much concentration in such discourse on independence, individuality and autonomy. To an extent this is good: autonomy is perhaps the key feature in any developed and self-conscious awareness of an individual's or institution's sense of identity and worth. But it would be a great mistake to allow this debate on changed administrative structures and relationships in education to be suborned to the discourse of 'the market' and of economic rationalism, with its emphasis on the individual and complete freedom of choice, as if to imply that schools, and the individuals within them, were in some way self-contained and hermetically sealed units, absolutely separate and free from all other-regarding considerations or obligations. We want to argue instead that the concept of education as a public good provides a decisive refutation of the concept of educational partition: in a public system of education there can be no such thing as a completely autonomous or independent self-governing school. To be sure, a certain amount of school autonomy may be readily countenanced and extended in certain areas of decision-making. It is a paradox, however, that autonomy can be rendered intelligible and made to work only within the confines of a relationship with the system and the community which is based on mutual benefit and regard.

Schools conceived thus enjoy a mutual relationship with the system and the community of which they are a part. The system ensures the basic protection of rights for all students; at the same time schools enjoy a mutual relationship with the community in which parents and other significant groups are able to have their voices heard in regard to matters of fundamental value and goals. There is also a mutual relationship within the school among school-based personnel, as decision-making is shared, owned and supported. In return, the school enjoys a greater degree of autonomy in the selection of community-related goals and the fitting of resources to meet those goals; it also enjoys a greater sense of its own standing and importance in providing community leadership, in promoting the value of education among all its stakeholders and, in this way, promoting the idea of the learning community and the values of life-long education. In sum, the model of relationships between school, system and community should mirror those of the strong, robust autonomous individual in mutual relationship with the society of which he or she is a part – our very goal in the provision of quality schooling.

THE ROLE OF TEACHER EDUCATION AND UNIVERSITIES IN SCHOOL REFORM

The notions of autonomy and mutuality are also helpful in fostering the relationship between schools and universities. Jaroslav Pelikan, in his re-examination of *The Idea of a University* (1992), refers to two books by eminent Victorians which he suggests should be a part of the canon for anyone concerned about the role of the university in modern society. The first is by George Eliot, *Middlemarch*, and the second by Cardinal Newman, *The Idea of a University*.

In *Middlemarch*, George Eliot provides us with a disturbing portrait of the scholar, Edward Casaubon. Of him, it is remarked that 'such capacity of thought and feeling as had ever been stimulated in him had long shrunk to a sort of dried preparation, a lifeless embalmment of knowledge'. Now, as Pelikan points out, Newman (1976) had much to say about 'the lifeless embalmment of knowledge', of those who 'may be imprisoned or fossilised in their erudition.' For Newman, 'the university is not a convent, it is not a seminary; it is a place to fit men of the world, for the world'.

In other words, while one aspect of the nature and purpose of a university is its concern to guarantee the community of scholars its autonomy and freedom to pursue truth, in whatever direction it might take them – the pursuit of knowledge being something that is worthwhile for its own sake – another is its responsibility to turn the scholar outwards again from inside the cloistered confines of academe in order to render to the community the fruits of those learnings which its beneficence has enabled her or him to cultivate and bring to full flower (Pelikan, 1992).

But that, of course, is only one half of the relationship between the university and the community: the other is the contribution made to the agenda of university teaching, research and publication by way of the objects of study and problems for solution that the community constantly throws up. The objects of a university's attention are threefold: the physical and geographical environment in which it works – the nature of things; the interactions between that environment and its inhabitants, and their influences and effects upon each other; and the nature, activities, pursuits and dreams of those inhabitants, both in their relationships with each other and in and for themselves.

These categories generate the raw material upon which university scholars may then apply their studies. They do so for a number of purposes: for the intrinsic value of the gains to knowledge itself; for the value of the increased understanding of past and present; and for the functional utility of being better able to predict, direct and plan for the future. Every piece of evidence that comes before us from one or the other of these various realms of study material may be examined and explained from a wide number of theoretical perspectives and a variety of interpretative constructs. In this way, our theories about these things are capable of giving us greater and different kinds of account of the empirical evidence we encounter in explaining and directing enquiries into the nature of things, people and their interactions, for the purposes for which the university was founded: for the increase of knowledge; for the teaching and dissemination of that knowledge; and for personal and community development and welfare that the availability and exploitation of such knowledge permits. It is part of any university's mission to search out all such evidence and then apply to it as diverse and wide-ranging a series of theoretic instruments as possible, in order to derive the largest possible number of illuminations for the increase of human understanding and the enlargement of human benefit. The problems are given us by the community: the tentative theories for their solution are developed in the university for application back in the place where the problems arise and are still sited.

It is therefore clear that the university and the community must inevitably combine in a mutuality of benefit, epistemic advance and community welfare. For, just as there is never a time when problems will come to an end or material for study is all in, so there will never be a time when theories and interpretations run out and humankind will have the perfect answer to all its problems. As Heraclitus wisely remarked (fr. 51): 'You can never step twice into the same river, for fresh waters are forever flowing down upon you.' This mutuality is especially important when one comes to consider the relationship between the university and the community, in respect of the education and training programmes provided, with perfect epistemic propriety, by the one and required for the institutions of the other, in professional fields of such importance to the community as law, medicine and education.

On the one hand, the work of its professional faculties allows the university to take a perfectly legitimate interest in refining and expanding the knowledge base in matters relating to the regulation of interpersonal behaviour, organic pathology and the curriculum best able to prepare our future citizens; and it is right, in promoting those developments, to claim and to insist on its academic autonomy and freedom from bureaucratic interference or government regulation in defining what counts as professional knowledge and what path research and the pursuit of truth take. The community, on the other hand, has a perfectly understandable concern that those who are going to assist it in such vital matters as the upbringing of its children, the health of its citizens, and the preservation of law and order in relations between them should be fully trained and receive valid certification to permit them to practise in the community, for the community's benefit, whether as doctors, lawyers or teachers, and in the community institutions in which concern for the value of their operations is given expression, namely hospitals, courts, and schools.

There is, therefore, a direct and continuing relationship of autonomy and mutuality between university and community with respect to education, training and professional knowledge in the various institutions and organizations that continue to uphold the values and traditions of the one while serving for the public good in the other. And this knowledge, this relationship cannot lie inert: it is organic and dynamic.

As Pelikan (1992) points out, this dynamism and mutuality of knowledge and academic–community interaction was well grasped by Newman, when writing about the place of professional schools in universities and the importance of knowledge in relation to professional skill. In his ninth essay on 'The idea of a university' he made this important remark:

> A man may hear a thousand lectures and read a thousand volumes and be at the end of the process very much where he was as regards knowledge. Something more than mere admitting it in a negative way into the mind is necessary, if it is to remain there. It must not be passively received but actually and actively entered into, embraced and mastered.
>
> (Newman, quoted in Pelikan (1992), p. 55)

How then does all this relate to the place and work of a professional faculty and school of teacher education in a university, and to the part that academics should play in training and educating professionals in the field of education, promoting educational reform and contributing to positive policy construction for the educational institutions of the community concerned with improving the quality of education?

Now is a time when faculties of education and teacher education institutions across the Western world are experiencing immense turmoil and upheaval. In the recent past, in addition to having to cope with other, larger-scale systemic problems (such as those of external or internal reorganization), such institutions and departments have had to face serious financial cutbacks, government-inspired radical reappraisals of teacher education (including increasing pressure towards the reintroduction of nineteenth-century apprenticeship models of school-based initial teacher education), and considerable problems of professional renewal. As a result, many faculties of education give all the appearance of tearing themselves apart with internal discord, in some cases not excluding fierce faction-fighting, as they undergo major paradigm shifts in respect of their attempts to cope with new developments in knowledge, pedagogy and social relations, particularly those relating to gender. Many of these problems have been compounded by their need to adjust to imperatives laid on them by central government and/or funding authorities to perform better, work smarter and, above all, give the nation what it needs to equip its future citizens with the competences and capacities that will further its economic advance.

This picture of turbulence and change might encourage some to believe that everything we face is threatening and depressive. But it might also, as we believe, present us with an opportunity to reassess those academic and professional beliefs, values and attitudes that we embody and for which we stand – those core axioms, theorems and commitments that, as Lakatos (1976) noted, we should be least willing to give up, if our academic and professional research programme is to be progressive, and if we are to play a positive part in the process of educational change.

Let us make clear our position on this. Faculties of education and schools of teacher education, we believe, must stand independent of schools and school systems, but in mutual relationship with them. Among all its other duties, a university has a duty to the community, and a need to show how its guardianship and pursuit of knowledge may contribute to the welfare of the community in which it is located and for the benefit of whose members its doors stand open. Universities have a role to play in giving service and adding value to the professions and all the various services and agencies of the community; and this is no less true for education than it is for medicine, law and architecture. In addressing the task of educational reform, a university will fulfil a duty to society which no other agency is in a position to perform – but it can do this only from a position of academic autonomy and professional independence on the one hand, and through its mutual relationship with the community on the other.

A professional faculty within a university must be concerned, in a fundamental way, with the world of learning and the interaction between learning and the problems to be solved in the professional context. To qualify as a profession, an occupation or activity must involve, we suggest, some tradition of critical philosophical reflection; the existence of a body of scholarly literature in which such reflection has been developed and debated; some agreed operating norms and conventions that establish the central concepts, tests for truth, and conditions for closure that generate its professional prescriptions; and goals which all its members are willing to work to achieve, are committed to and respect.

Part of role of the professional school, such as a faculty of education in a university, is to provide the arena in which students become familiar with that scholarly literature and philosophical debate, and the cognitive criteria, methods, categories and moral norms by which its activities are animated. Thus, in any profession, students and would-be graduates need from universities, not the latest tricks of the trade, not 'ten quick tips for teaching', not a list of ingredients to guarantee effective schooling; they need rather an informed understanding of the implications of research and reflection for improved practice in the profession, the ability to put that research into practical effect, and the intelligence and skills to evaluate that practice and refine or correct it as appropriate.

For that reason, any faculty of education which bases its programmes only on the current practices and momentary concerns of the profession, is in many ways a failure. No one supposes for a moment that faculties of medicine follow after the profession rather than standing in its vanguard, and it is right that it be so. How can a profession prosper which operates only on the basis of a continued preoccupation with the conservation of past practices; how else can it prosper other than by taking a leadership position in defining and treating the problems and exploring the improvement of pathways to the future?

So it is with education: teacher training based solely on some sort of apprenticeship model in schools runs the danger of merely reinforcing timeworn and essentially uncritical methods of teaching and outmoded educational views. The lack of informed criticism, and a university-trained preparedness to engage in it and deploy it to professional purposes, will virtually guarantee the kind of stasis and lack of progress in dealing with its most challenging problems and perplexities that is the mark of a closed professional mind in a stagnating and moribund society.

In the debate regarding school-based initial teacher education, those of us in faculties of education would do well to recall the words of American teacher Jessica Siegel, cited by Pelikan (1992), who decried her early school-based experience in the profession as follows:

> Teachers seemed convinced that there were only two ways anyone learned to teach – by teaching or by watching others teach. Learning was not an academic process as much as a tribal rite, a secret passed from elder to child, atavistic as charting the stars or planting maize.

We do not believe in teacher education as being the repository of a set of traditional procedures for the passing on of arcane secrets and the crafts of some kind of masonic guild. On the contrary, we are for openness, dynamism and organic change. We believe with Pelikan (1992) that the key functions of a university department and professional school:

- the advancement of knowledge through research;
- the transmission of knowledge through teaching;
- the diffusion of knowledge through publishing

are absolutely inseparable from the concepts of a properly liberal education. These are the foundations upon which university education and the value of the university stand, and from which it may move the community and the institutions that serve it.

With these principles in mind, we move towards the end of this section of our argument by asking the key question: what, then, might the university do to assist in the reform of education and the promotion of quality schooling? We suggest the following answers:

1 Universities can provide an arena where educators are able to

address the pedagogic challenges and institutional realities that confront them. Often this will mean discarding the conceptual maps that were useful guides as they journeyed through lands that have already been traversed and explored, and then engaging in the exciting adventure of the exploration of the new. One of the chief virtues of education in a university is to help its students become leaders in such intellectual and professional journeys.

We know, of course, that, rather than try to change their conceptual map or construct a new one, some people will try to change the new reality, expending more energy on attempting to defend their own view of the world than would have been required to revise that view in the first place. Thinking and behaving differently from the way one has always behaved represents and requires an extraordinary degree of courage and a willingness to undertake personal risk – but it is just this kind of courage in the search for truth that is part of the intellectual *raison d'être* of a university, and is the principal identifying characteristic of the truly autonomous person.

2 An associated answer is that universities may provide an independent arena for thinking about education. Here, we can help educators to question and move beyond the closed system within which many of them operate. The cool and dispassionate analyses and appraisals devoted to the understanding and evaluation of educational institutions and their evaluation, in which universities can help them learn successfully to engage, can serve as objective referents to give such educators a touchstone against which to test the realities of policy and practice in their own institutions, and to help them see ways in which their quality might perhaps be found wanting and subsequently improved.

The Doctor of Education degree, now being introduced by many universities in Australia and elsewhere, has this kind of endeavour as its central aim: the knowledge and use of the latest research findings to illuminate and ameliorate policy and practice in the education profession. Graduates with such degrees will, it is hoped, be in a prime position to offer the best-informed and most significant contribution in the identification and expansion of those activities, characteristics and virtues that will conduce to the provision, assurance and development of quality in those undertakings with which their institutions and stakeholders are centrally concerned, and for which they have greatest concern – the education, training and personal and social development of their students and the communities they serve.

3 Furthermore, in the academic environment offered by universities, educators are well placed to engage in critical reflection – what Aristotle called *theoria* – to promote not only what he termed *sophia* (wisdom and understanding resulting from an enquiry about what is) but also the notion of *phronesis* (practical judgment, or

wisdom in action) which arises from deliberation about what ought to be and results in effective theory-informed practice – what some call 'praxis'. In the concept of 'phronesis' we see the life of wisdom promoted by contemplation combined with action – practical wisdom instantiated in the very act of achieving valued ends. In this regard, we can develop in our curriculum, in faculties of education, the necessary scholarly and research footings and orientations to assist in the investigation and promotion of an approach to professional problems that will start out from the problems, topics and issues with which we are daily faced, and then marshal all our resources of equipment, intelligence and creativity to work out solutions for those problems, facing the challenges and dilemmas, adapting and consolidating as we go along.

Perhaps the proper note on which to end this chapter, and this section of the book, is to extend the metaphor W. W. Quine (1953) adopted from the work of Otto Neurath (1932), to which we have already referred. Our work of theory construction, development and correction in education is rather like a voyage across a sea. We are embarked on an exciting but difficult intellectual journey: much of the sea is uncharted, and we do not have a fully clear sense of exactly in what direction we are tending, buffeted as we are by the different winds, waves and fortunes that beat upon the boat of our current best theory and force it often to change direction – sometimes in directions we would rather not go.

The bark of our theory itself suffers from the effects of the fierce external forces in the environment, and even from the depradations of attacks from without, and we have frequently to repair it as we go along, either with material we find already there in it and which has the potential for improvement, or with material derived from what the sea washes up around us, or along the lines of other boats we see going in the same direction, but seeming to do so with rather less difficulty and rather more speed. There is never a time when we can haul our theoretic craft up into some kind of intellectual dry dock, investigate it all over and decide to do a complete overhaul or to build a fresh boat from scratch: we have to be flexible, adaptable and inventive in the repair and reconstruction of our theory, criticizing, making do and mending as we go along.

Eventually our boat will look a good deal different from the one in which our intellectual journey started, and we may not end up where we thought we should, but, if we have used our theoretic resources wisely and to good effect, have co-operated as a crew in doing the various jobs calling for different but complementary skills, and have faced all the challenges with vigour and resourcefulness and in a positive frame of mind, then we shall be not only all still alive, but fitter, leaner and theoretically better prepared to meet the challenges of the future – and we shall enjoy the chances to renew our academic strength, vigour and creativity, and the excitement of the journey itself.

Chapter 9

Conclusion

In this final chapter we offer a summary of our observations and findings, resulting from our discussions with key personnel in the wider education community on the nature, aims and values of quality schooling. In doing this, we also articulate and elaborate on our own theory of quality schooling. Our intention is to offer further increments of understanding to the ongoing debate concerning the nature of quality and its proper modes of creation, promotion and assurance in education. By so doing, we hope that we might generate further proposals and agenda, by means of which quality schooling may be better prepared for, planned and secured in schools and school systems around the world.

In Chapter 1 we attempted to highlight the place and importance of the concept and value of 'quality' as it pertains to the policy, provision and practicalities of administering schools and systems. We saw how many policy and administrative concerns are connoted by and contained under the rubric of quality: the content of education, its conception, delivery and assessment; the ways in which teaching and learning are organized; and the structures and procedures by which educating institutions are controlled and directed. All of these relate in some way or other to a range of issues to do with efficiency and effectiveness, excellence, equity and social justice, democracy, devolution of responsibility and accountability.

We have shown that quality is a term that is very difficult to define precisely, and that it can function very much as a kind of 'hurrah' word, signifying all that is good, and all that the proponents of a school's typical excellences want to claim and to see achieved. It is also capable of being employed by advocates in many different guises and for a very large number of different purposes – economic, political, moral and social. It is the complexities arising from this variety of concerns and values that make investigations of quality schooling so difficult. In the investigation of the various notions that education professionals and members of the educational community hold about quality schooling, and upon which our theory is based, we attempted to address some of these difficulties and complexities.

In Chapter 2 we outlined our approach to the research effort, and we also set out our approach to theory development and assessment, particularly as it relates to theories about quality schooling. We indicated that we are operating from a post-empiricist and pragmatic view of theory construction and research. From this perspective, we seek to test the functional utility of one theory of quality schooling over another. We do this by employing the criteria of relative simplicity, conservatism, explanatory power, testability, comprehensiveness and 'fit' with existing knowledge, in our assessment of the preferability of one theory over another. Using this approach, we argue that policy-makers and administrators may go on to extract, from the adoption of one theory in preference to another, the implicative and normative practical conclusions it generates for application to a problem situation.

Such a problem arises, for instance, when policy-makers are faced with or are deciding upon providing for a quality education, according to the particular interpretation and value they put on that notion. One interpretation of quality in schooling, for example, associates it with the desirability and vital economic importance of educating, to the highest possible standard of intellectual achievement, the cognitive competences of a high-ability few. Another interpretation, and one that is often seen to run counter to the one just outlined, is that policy-makers should, in pursuit of the goal of equity and social justice, spread resources around more broadly, so as to offer education for personal development to students from all classes and ranges of ability.

We also underlined the importance of the preferred theory being able to provide and function as a kind of 'touchstone', by and in which areas of agreement on matters of common interest and concern may be discerned, negotiated and confirmed. This might operate in the case of the example cited above. It does not necessarily follow, for instance, that a policy of concentrating upon intellectual development and academic excellence excludes or militates against the interests of children from less affluent or ethnic minority backgrounds (as the success of the operation of the Harlem Central Park East public school in New York demonstrates).

In Chapters 3, 4 and 5 we proceeded with an analysis of the data gathered during our discussions with key figures in the provision, planning and delivery of education concerning their conceptions of 'quality' in the management of educational systems, institutions and schools. It was our belief that the views of such agents would provide a solid basis for the development of a theory of quality schooling, that would be reality-grounded, coherent and comprehensive. From this analysis, we formed the view that quality is not readily identifiable with one particular characteristic or key feature of a school or other educational institution: quality has to do with, and arises from or is generated by, a range of factors, some or all of which one might expect to find in schools that are widely seen to deserve the commendatory labels of 'good', 'effective' or 'quality'.

In Chapter 3 we set out what we regarded as being the main lines of the quality debate. The dimensions of quality could be discerned largely in the tensions between the various conceptions of and value laid upon a range of concerns and desirable outcomes for a school's educational endeavours by educators and members of the community. These might include such value concerns as equity, excellence, democracy and justice. Critical among these concerns was the tension between the outcomes that people believed should function as aims for quality schooling, particularly as regards the differential stress to be laid upon such goals as the enhancement of the individual and the benefit of the community.

In the course of our elaboration upon this issue, we raised questions about some conceptions of education that seemed to us to be based upon false or mistaken premises. One of these is the idea of 'intelligence'; another is that which associates the function of education with the 'realization' of an individual's 'potential'. Both of these notions we rejected as being metaphysical in character and as involving some fallacies of ontology, epistemology and argumentation. We preferred an account of education as relating to various forms of human development. This we see as a set of processes (natural and environmental) related to effecting change and positive incremental progression towards desired ends of some kind in various fields of human communication and endeavour. We believe that any human being, given positive willingness, adequate motivation, expert and committed teaching, a supportive environment and a requisite provision of resources, is capable, in principle at any rate, of making increasingly large-scale, rapid and complex learning gains. It is through the increased provision or availability of such activities and factors, we suggest, that we observe our students' aspirations and achievements to be, by and large, rising as compared with those of their forebears, even in the relatively recent past.

Yet it is unfortunate that, although the evidence suggests that these days very many students are performing better and to higher levels of attainment than their forebears, owing to such economic factors as poverty and structural unemployment not all students are getting access to the opportunities for achieving excellence that they deserve. This is due in part to the slow rate at which the provision and range of resources and facilities in schools, requisite for a wide range of quality outcomes, are being enhanced. We realize that to provide these things is very costly; yet, if we are to have an education that is relevant and appropriate to the needs of the students, the state and the country, together with a set of outcomes that denote quality of achievement, performance, and understanding – as well, of course, as offering students the chance to raise their expectations of an enhanced quality of life – then we must be able either to point to or provide a range of features in the structure, organization, work, values and goals of a school that are going to promote quality and give its students the chances to achieve that.

It is, therefore, all the more regrettable that, in some countries, education is being blamed for an alleged lack of concern for or contribution to economic advance, yet schools are being increasingly starved of the resources that will enable them directly to contribute to that particular national concern, as well, of course, as many other important ones, to do with individual life enrichment and the securing and extension of community welfare and caring.

In Chapter 4 we focused attention more sharply on the factors that members of the educational community isolate and elevate as making for 'quality'. These include such matters as the nature, range and purpose of the goals adopted in the school as target outcomes for its students; the breadth, significance and relevance of the subject matter studied; the range and depth of the learning experiences provided in the curriculum constructed and offered to cover those subjects of study; the methods employed in the teaching and the assessment of learning; the relations between staff and students; the leadership of the principal; the relations between principal and staff; the range and quality of the resources and facilities of the institution; the connection with the supportive and interested groups and constituencies in the local community; the ways in which a school's 'stakeholders' can contribute to and be involved in the pursuit and promotion of its goals and the activities that are seen as leading towards those goals; and, finally in this list, but by no means last in importance, that elusive but critical ingredient – the atmosphere and ethos of the school.

We also found that, for schools located in a larger system, quality in a school resides as much in the consonance between the plans, goals and objectives within a school setting, and the goals, objectives and processes put in place at the systemic level to achieve them, as in these other factors.

Beyond their place in a system, however, we noted that schools exist within a community. In the attempt to achieve a measure of integration between the school and the community as regards the emphasis both attach to the provision of quality schooling, we argued that one should look to one guiding principle: schools and teachers need to examine the goals the school sets for itself and attempt to ascertain whether they fit in with the expectations that the school community has for them – that is, those expectations and valued outcomes that the school community believes are practicable and attainable.

In this endeavour, one foundation, on which many school undertakings are based, needed to be restated. Schools exist primarily to promote knowledge, learning and understanding, and it is these cognitive increments in a person's development that lead to growth in all its various aspects. Quality schools, therefore, are rather less about making people happy (although a degree of satisfaction, contentment and stimulation in their knowledge-getting experiences and activities is important for students if they are to approach learning positively), and rather more about giving people knowledge and the ability to use that knowledge, thereby equipping people to take their place in society, both as involved constituents contributing to its maintenance and progress, and as individuals constructing and choosing from among a pattern of life-options those modes of being and doing that will offer them the greatest opportunities of personal welfare and enrichment.

This means that there have now to be different, more flexible ways of imparting mainstream knowledge and of helping students to acquire it and use it. There also has to be curriculum subject content to which students can respond positively, and they must be able to negotiate, not just access to the subjects that they and their advisers believe would be in their best long-term interest, but their own preferred learning styles and end-points. This is where the vitally important process of the negotiated curriculum comes in and has its main point of purchase.

In all this, we found that the quality of education depends substantially on the quality of relationships in educational institutions, and chiefly and fundamentally those between learner and teacher. Other relationships within and surrounding the school are important too: teachers to parents, principal to staff, members of the local community (particularly representatives of business, industry and commerce) to the whole school.

We may now lay it down that, so far as the needs and interests of students are concerned, quality education is where all students are empowered through their education to a realization of their own freedom to determine issues and choices for themselves and by their own action. They will, as a result of their educational experiences, have acquired the skills to do something positive about their own futures and of those with whom they share the community in a personal, social, political and moral way. As for teachers, they need to be empowered too. Above and beyond the traditional proficiencies and competences arising from their mastery of subject knowledge and classroom management skills, they need to be empowered with new educational visions, management and pedagogical strategies, and professional resources of all kinds (equipment, apparatus, technologies and the like) to take their place as partners with members of the broader educational community in the formulation and design of educational innovations and effective principles and practices for improved teaching and learning.

We found that one critical factor in obtaining the best kind of performance from teachers is to give them a supportive and professionally conducive environment in which to work. A good-quality work life is important for teachers, to enhance the quality of their performance and enable them to pass on their knowledge, values, and philosophies of learning to their students. Part of teachers' sense of the value of the contributions they are making towards helping their students achieve a good quality of life comes from a sense of their own professional value and status, within a coherent and progressively evolving career structure; and the teachers themselves must have some direction and control of the planning and development of that career structure.

In our analysis, however, we encountered one area about which many teachers expressed concern. Faced with the numerous and increasing demands and expectations being laid upon schools by governments, industry, parents and the wider community, is it not the case that schools are being asked to take on too much? We think this is an understandable and not unreasonable source of anxiety; but in response to the reservations articulated by teachers on this question, we argued that education is not only a cognitive but a moral enterprise. Schools as educating institutions, we maintain, are underpinned by and shot through with presuppositions and requirements arising from the moral basis of the concept of education. These commit them to sets of ethical imperatives, intentions and purposes that make teachers, whether they know it or not, responsible for much more than mere subject instruction and the furthering of their pupils' academic development *tout court*.

Such academic development can only take place in a context of institutional concern for students' overall equilibrium and personal development, in ways that will enable them to capitalize upon all the opportunities for individual enrichment and social progress offered them in that institution. The work of teachers in a quality education environment is, therefore and paradoxically, not far removed from that of the roles and functions taken by social workers and family case workers, or at least of being the near-standing assistants of the professionals actually employed in those positions and for those purposes. Thus the basic and indispensable virtue required of, and expected in, quality teachers, working in a school devoted to the education of coming generations of citizens, is their cognitive *and* their moral commitment.

We conclude, therefore, that generating advance towards the education and further development of well-motivated and concerned students, ready to benefit from the experiences for personal, social and intellectual growth offered by quality teaching and learning in a caring and supportive environment, requires a body of able, highly trained, knowledgeable, and morally committed teachers and professional personnel, backed up with the requisite kinds and levels of resources, advice and support from the schools and school systems in which they work.

189

In Chapter 5 we discussed the restructuring of educational systems, the better to enhance the provision of such support. Continuing with our analysis of data, we considered the effects of change and restructuring on educational institutions and the link that this might have with the production or emergence of quality in schooling, particularly where such restructuring might be expressed largely in terms of the devolution of decision-making. Devolution, school-site management and local management of schools seem to have been the main versions of administrative rearrangement found in the rhetoric and politics of proposals for systemic restructuring. Making assessments based on and drawn from our data, however, we consider it worthwhile remarking that, if it is the case that government systems really are concerned to redistribute responsibility for educational decision-making to local initiatives, on the grounds that such devolution actually enhances the quality of education, then they seem to have failed to communicate this belief and intention effectively to the educational community.

Yet, notwithstanding a certain scepticism about the motives for devolution, and the fear that the consequences of restructuring have been mainly to displace problems, particularly in respect of resource management, from the centre to the school, our data show that school-based personnel are continually attempting to ensure that quality is a part of the daily experience of schools. They work at it informally, formally, in structured and unstructured ways, through decision-making, school improvement, school reviews, staff development, and attempts to involve parents and the wider community in the life of the school and in exploring the school ethos and culture.

One of the major difficulties at the local level is that any change must be consistent with certain agreed principles and an overall philosophy, understood and owned by all parties in the process. If school-based personnel are poorly equipped to develop the philosophical underpinnings necessary to give a sense of meaning and direction for effective school operation, the potential positive benefits of educational restructuring and school change are in danger of being lost. One of the most important next steps in restructuring, our data suggest, is to empower school-based personnel, not only with the technical skills associated with and called for by effective management and implementation of policies, but also the knowledge and skills presupposed in and required for the identification and elucidation of problems and the policies meet for their resolution, the clarification of values, and the ability to provide cogent and persuasive arguments to justify the value judgments involved in effective school management. It is the professional educators who have to present rational arguments for policy innovation, change and confirmation to all the stakeholders of the school community, not least the parents of their students.

In respect of the promotion of parental involvement, what emerges from our research as a key finding is the widely held belief that one of the most effective ways to develop parent and community involvement is through a problem-solving approach, based on activities such as the formation and implementation of a school plan. The framing and shaping of school development plans, and their concomitant requirement for assessment and review, are believed by many of those we interviewed to be among the most critical factors in the whole process of school change and improvement. Indeed, some people go as far as suggesting that the relationship between schools and parents and the community is the most important relationship for the promotion of quality and the assurance of quality control. They argue that, for these purposes, this is the key relationship to work on, not the relationship of the school with the state or federal government. Building up the capacity of the families to understand what is going on with their children and to make serious inputs into the educational process, building up the capacity of teachers to cope with children and to relate to the families: that is the essence of quality control.

The principal's part in this relationship and its processes is absolutely vital. It is the principal who will be an academic and professional leader for the whole school community in the formulation, clarification and adoption of a set of basic values and desired outcomes, arising from involvement with, and programmes of activity in, certain sorts of cognitive engagements. The total vision so composed will then constitute what might be called the school's philosophy, which will provide the epistemological, ethical and pedagogical underpinnings, set the programme of cognitive activities and determine the objectives of the whole educational endeavour in the school.

Furthermore, it is the principal's task to manage and deploy resources in order to create in the school an atmosphere in which people can relate to each other and perform well in their pursuit of the institution's quality goals. In this latter respect, it seems clear that the creation of an environment or culture in which people are able to identify, formulate and commit themselves to some sort of mission, philosophy and set of objectives, and aim for similar goals, is perhaps the most significant role of the principal. As a secondary consideration in this undertaking, the principal may be better able to perform this service and create that environment as a result of having more responsibility for resource management and allocation.

Taken all round, there is a clear need to support principals, teachers and parents in their need and desire to make quality decisions in all new areas of responsibility. For this reason, deliberate attempts have to be made to provide professional educators and school personnel, not only with the knowledge and skills referred to above, but also with access to the full extent of information, correlative implications and possible outcomes to enable them to see options, canvass opinions, and calculate and evaluate a range of possible outcomes consequent upon the adoption of some particular policy for school improvement. This means being determined to provide school staff with the appropriate kinds of intelligence and training required by the skills of decision-making, policy implementation and evaluation. The sorts of decisions that can and should be made depend very heavily on the knowledge-base school personnel work from, who takes the decisions on important issues, and on the basis of what criteria. In this regard, for schools that are located in systems, the systems themselves have a direct responsibility to offer school-based personnel the appropriate information and support.

Given the above, schools must still come back to the almost impossible task of trying to measure the wide range of student outcomes, both quantitative and qualitative, achieved at the end of the formal education process. In the light of the complexity and difficulty of that task, the diversity and heterogeneous character of the goals aimed at, and in a context in which accountability is of so great a matter of public importance, it would not be unreasonable to conclude that the measurement and evaluation of student impacts and outcomes pose the greatest challenge for system administrators in the years ahead.

In Chapters 6, 7 and 8, with the benefit of the insights afforded by the examination and analysis of data in the preceding three chapters, we embarked on the task of articulating and elaborating upon our own theory of quality schooling. In Chapter 6, we began with what had emerged from the data as perhaps one of the most contentious but most important subjects, given our claim that schools are first and foremost about the transmission and induction of our young people into the knowledge valued by the community, and about increasing and elaborating the cognitive repertoires of the community's coming generation – namely, the curriculum.

Drawing upon the results of our enquiry, we were able to identify some of the goals, and the different conceptions of knowledge that were associated with such goals, that had been laid down for schools by various sections of the community. These identifications enabled us to show up some of the implications of the definition of such goals, and the concepts of knowledge associated with them, for the selection of curriculum content. From the range of goals for education currently being prescribed for systems and schools, we focused particularly upon three models: the ideas of instrumental curriculum, the 'entitlement' curriculum, and the notion of 'education for the development of rationality'. We pointed out that such positions have some features in common: first, that in the quest for educational goals there will always be some foundations that have to be provided; and, second, that these foundations will be separable and discrete, capable of being differentiated from each other according to various modes and concepts of epistemic categorization.

Informed by recent work in epistemology and cognitive science, we proposed moving away from such 'foundationalist' epistemologies and the curriculum theories presupposing and resting upon them. A better way forward, we suggested, in any cognitive enterprise, is the working out of functional theories to apply to the currently pressing and perplexing issues, topics and problems arising from and involved in such key human activities as education, social welfare, politics, government and economics. Curriculum philosophy, seen in this light, is not an activity of conceptual clarification of a priori logical consequences and requirements entailed by adherence to empiricist epistemologies; rather it is an activity of theory construction, correction and contention, engaged in for the purpose of providing tentative solutions to problems which threaten human well-being and social harmony.

The construction of a curriculum for education, from this perspective, is not determined by a priori preconceptions about the logical structure of knowledge itself, or by a set of judgments and prescriptions relating to those desirable cognitive activities and cultural values. Rather it is *problems* that provide a set of *agenda* for curriculum action, agenda that stand instead of much larger-scale aims of education. Curriculum construction and delivery become an undertaking which is constantly being adapted, reoriented, and modified as new problems and issues arise that require adjustment and fine-tuning or perhaps to face in substantially different directions, as the whole ground for cognitive commitments and learning endeavours changes from time to time.

The educational and curriculum implications of the 'republic' debate in Australia, for instance, provide but one example of such a major shift in ground. There may just be some cognitive commitments that Australians may have to give up, in pursuit of ends they deem to be more suited to the range of problems they have to face in the future, rather than continually reworking treatments for the remediation of dysfunctional social conditions which have long presented neither difficulty nor danger. Harold Benjamin's satire (1971) on the 'sabre-toothed' tiger provides us with an eloquent demonstration of the futility of the backward-looking curriculum.

We pointed out, however, that there is one element in such an approach that is still needed to provide us with a set of guidelines for steering current curriculum planning and to justify the selection of cognitive content we make and set forth before children and young people in institutions devoted to educational purposes. What is needed is a criterion of stability, consistency and coherence, so that educational institutions might guard against what could otherwise be a somewhat anarchical curriculum situation. Such a criterion is provided by the idea of 'education for democracy'. This notion we explored in more depth in Chapter 7.

The idea of education for democracy, we felt, was one justification that could prove conclusive in determining all those various kinds of cognition, understanding and experience requisite for providing the information to enable our future citizens to cope with the demands of comprehending their past, monitoring their present, and directing and controlling their future. We found this justification in the commitment of citizens to the particular norms and conventions of conduct required from citizens in a participative democracy, for it is in the various institutions of that political form of life that citizens are required and enjoined to participate, weigh issues, make decisions and set in train policies and actions appropriate to deal with matters of great moment in the present and of considerable consequence in the future. Such issues might include, for example, the provision of the necessary infrastructure – even at the level of the provision of waste disposal facilities and sources of uncontaminated water – to make life tolerable and enjoyable; the inhibition, treatment and elimination of such social pathologies as domestic violence, child abuse and teenage suicide; and the management of the environment and the uses we make of it, in a way that would increase the quality of life for all rather than threaten and diminish the life-chances of coming generations.

We thus conclude that the democratic form of life, to which we are all morally and culturally committed, is the best forum for the promotion of such valued concerns as moral awareness, interpersonal sensitivity and cross-cultural understanding in the home, the work-place and the wider community. We believe this to be the case in virtue of the ontological and epistemic commitments, intellectual engagements and communicative interchanges to which all people are necessarily bound in the pursuit of knowledge, intelligible discourse, truth, openness and objectivity. It is our contention that, in so far as people are concerned for their access to, growth in and use of knowledge in an open society, and for the critical and reformative purposes for which they wish to employ it, they are automatically committed to the value and institution of democracy as not merely the preferred but, in fact, the only possible and logically entailed allowable form of political organization and arrangement.

We hold that this democratic responsibility necessarily issues in the induction of our young people into the various realms of public knowledge, modes of interpersonal communication and relations, and those ways of organizing and administering our educational systems, institutions and schools that provide the best possible preparation for our coming generation to take its place as mature and well-informed citizens in that participative democracy. We then go on to show how all this results in particular forms of school organization, structure and administrative arrangement, the adoption of which would begin to make schools appear different and function somewhat differently from the way they do at present.

Democratic institutions, we conclude, will be characterized by concern for and preoccupation with self-examination, self-criticism, self-review, self-assessment, and what we see as a consequential drive towards self-improvement. Heeding the words of the Austrian philosopher, Karl Popper, that democracy works best when faced with problems, the democratic school will be one committed to an evolutionary problem-solving approach to policy development and procedures of decision-making. In democratic institutions, such as we envisage quality schools becoming, an essential part of being an 'actor' and agent, or indeed a human being at all, will arise from and reside in the development of autonomy, of having independence in judgment and conduct, especially in moral and political matters – judging, questioning, considering, criticizing, doubting, and making one's own decisions freely and voluntarily as a result of engaging in such cognitive operations It is in this way that educated citizens will be acting rationally to fulfil the obligations incumbent upon them as members of a democratic society.

In an institution conceived and framed upon these lines, and in such a political environment, however, educated people cannot get where they want to go, or implement their decisions, merely by relying and insisting upon the power of their autonomy. The point that emerges strongly from our enquiry into quality schooling is the value emphasis upon the twin virtues of autonomy and mutuality. This necessary dual emphasis is addressed in Chapter 8.

The concepts of autonomy and mutuality, and the ontological, moral and relational commitments presupposed and entailed by them, contributed to the development of our theory of quality schooling, in certain major respects: one is the characters and dispositions of the human beings who emerge from our quality schools; and another concerns the nature of the institutions that we call schools, and their relationships with the systems and environments of which they are a part, including other educating institutions such as universities and the whole tertiary education sector, and the business and employment sectors.

With respect to the first of these, what emerges strongly from our enquiry is that central to the concept of quality schooling is an emphasis upon *values*. Prime among these is a dual emphasis. One element relates to the desirable outcome of schooling exhibited in the emergence of individuals with a strongly developed sense of their own identity, worth and powers of independent thought and action. The other element is human connectedness: individuals, at the same time as they develop and exercise their autonomy, are necessarily, as social beings, involved in and constrained by patterns and networks of interrelation with other individuals and with the whole community in all its economic, social and political aspects.

Concerning the schools, we believe a vitally important point needs to be made. Although there is much of value in the references to independence, individuality and autonomy frequently found in current discourse about devolution and local management of schools, we argue that it would be a great mistake to allow the debate about the best form of changed administrative structures and relationships in education to be suborned to the discourse of the market and economic rationalism with its emphasis upon the individual and complete freedom of choice, as if to imply that schools and the individuals within them were in some way separate and free from all other-regarding considerations and morally overriding obligations.

Rather than seeing education as some kind of 'commodity', we conceive of it as a *public good*. This concept and value, we maintain, provide a decisive refutation of any version of the character and *modus operandi* of educational institutions and provision that regards the outcomes of education as some sort of product. We contend that in a public system of education there can be no such thing as a *completely* autonomous or independent self-governing school. Certainly, an amount of school autonomy may be readily countenanced in certain areas of decision-making. It is a paradox, however, that autonomy can be rendered intelligible and made to work only on the presupposition, and within the confines, of a correlative concept of heteronomy.

For a school, this will come from and reside in the set of relationships it has to have with the system or with the community, those relationships being based upon a mutuality of interaction, support and benefit. The successful operation of quality schools necessarily implies their enmeshment in mutual relationships with the system and/or the community of which they are a part. We believe that the model of relationships between school, system and community mirrors those of the strong, robust, autonomous individual, connected to, and in mutual relationship with, the society of which he or she is a part. This is our very goal in the conception and provision of quality schooling.

Arising from the foregoing, then, and as a result of all the conclusions drawn and the observations made, we believe we may now come to the setting out of a set of final comments, queries, suggestions and advice that will constitute a set of agenda for those whose main concern is the pursuit of the goals of quality schooling. These may then function as main elements in a progressive research programme of institutional, curriculum and professional development designed to enhance the quality of schooling.

Agenda for Reform

CONCEPTIONS OF MANAGEMENT FOR QUALITY SCHOOLING

To begin, we have come to certain conclusions about the ways and means by which quality schooling might be engendered, and decided on a set of agenda for its establishment. We wish to suggest that there is, in fact, a new set of agenda for research and development in quality schooling, based upon a new conception of management as evolutionary problem-solving and research. This view emanates from and is a reflection of our broad acceptance of the theory of knowledge-getting proposed by the philosopher Karl Popper, and this leads to the view we take of the functioning of schools as learning institutions. Policy and administration at the system level and leadership in management at the school level are, we believe, instantiations of Popperian epistemology in action.

This conception of management is consistent with our perception of schools as adaptive learning environments committed to the communication of knowledge and the exchange of views through the transmission of knowledge and the powers of rational argument. Inherent in this vision of organizations and management is the value attached to the integration of substance and process, rather than to their separation or artificial holding apart.

We contrast this view with the concept of educational management that proposes a splitting between substance and process, and gives rise to the notion of a distinction between academic work, teaching and learning on the one hand, and educational administration on the other. We also contrast it with the view of management embedded in a hierarchical organization resting on a structure of superordinate and subordinate authority relations, a model that, as Evers (1990) remarks, is claimed to promote consistency and uniformity in the implementation and transmission of centrally produced decisions, and in the communication and diffusion of directives.

We would argue that there are two things wrong with this model. First, it requires unquestioning acceptance of the cognitive authority of centrally made decisions, plans and directives. In contrast, we contend that the whole point of Popperian epistemology is to stress 'the fallibility and uncertainty of centrally dictated authority claims' (Evers, 1990). Secondly, such a notion also militates against the vital importance, in public institutions predicated upon the 'open society' of knowledge, of a sense of shared ownership of decision-making and the necessity of bringing all our cognitive resources to bear in the drive towards error elimination in our various hypotheses for dealing with intellectual, academic and organizational problems.

On these grounds, then, we argue that Popper's notion of evolutionary and critical epistemology provides the proper safeguard against the authoritarianism and hierarchism of what we maintain are conceptually and epistemologically inappropriate approaches to school and system administration. Given a significant degree of collegial agreement about the ways in which such public goods as the getting of knowledge and the growth of understanding can be provided for, managed and evaluated, along with all the additional epistemological advantages of what Evers calls the 'adaptive learning strategies' employed in the transmission and checking of knowledge, we believe that school communities will be able to make more efficient and effective decisions through the democratic processes of open, accountable and participative decision-making.

Consistent with this approach is our notion of the role of school principals and leaders generally as giving academic leadership in a joint endeavour by a commitment to management as Popperian problem-solving. But to be successful, this approach must be employed within a process of collegial collaboration and mutual assistance in the identification of problems, the formulation of trial solutions and their implementation, and the commitment to the detection and correction of errors, in the interests of improving the quality of schooling. Only in this way, we believe, can we function effectively in the leadership and management of learning institutions, in order to improve our decision-making processes and, thereby, the quality, utility and value of the decisions that we reach.

Our motive in all this is to drive forward a set of agenda towards the refinement of theory and the improvement of practice in institutional management in educational institutions, in the work of organizations at the system level, and in the enhancement of the relationship between education and the broad field of economic, social and political contexts and concerns.

TEACHER EDUCATION AND THE ROLE OF THE UNIVERSITY IN ENHANCING QUALITY SCHOOLING

At a time of considerable controversy and debate in very many countries concerning the future of teaching education, we feel that we must emphasize the important role that university faculties of education play in setting the agenda for quality schooling, both in the preparation and further training of professionals and in the conception, articulation and evaluation of plans and policies for the establishment and extension of quality in schools. It is our belief that professional faculties such as Education have to be in mutual relationship with the professions they serve, and with the needs and interests of the wider community from whom they identify their problems for study and to whom they contribute in the development of their knowledge, their commitment to research and the extension of knowledge, and the producing of graduates.

Whilst the work of such faculties is designed to equip people with the requisite knowledge, skills and capacities to enable them to operate at a high level of specificity and expertise in their professional spheres of activity in the community, the community wants far more than specific skills and compentences in its professional graduates. We know now that commercial, industrial and business concerns put a premium upon such higher-order values as citizenship, sympathy, humanity and justice. They also want, in their potential employees, many larger, broader and more generalizable cognitive competences, such as problem-solving ability, research and critical thinking skills, team-building skills and the ability to work as part of a team, together with wide-ranging but fairly specific knowledge, such as competences in mathematics, the sciences and technology, cultural awareness, language and communication skills. These lead to what have been described as the 'three Cs' of professional knowledge required today: computing, critical thinking and communication. But both employers and members of the community also stress the crucial importance of interpersonal skills of all kinds, imagination and creativity – the fourth 'C'.

All these broad competences, vital skills and this wide-ranging knowledge feature among that list of characteristics that are the chief stock-in-trade of universities, generate their agenda for teaching and research, and figure strongly in the range of educated outcomes at which they aim. Further to these desiderata, however, universities are first and foremost about the life of the mind – the preservation, discovery and dissemination of knowledge, and the pursuit of truth in all its various forms. In other words, academic activity in a professional faculty such as Education in a university has as much to do with giving students a broad and profound liberal education as with the more directly relevant work-related attitudes, competences and values that their professional commitments will require of them.

In this respect, the work of faculties of education and schools of teacher education in setting the agenda for professional preparation and training for quality schooling is vital. Faculties of education have a theory of knowledge relating to effective professional activity; an understanding of and commitment to certain procedures of operating in the education service; particular objects of interest and attention; a set of strong cognitive bases with their own typical concepts, categories and tests for the validity and reliability of their truth claims; a professional view of effective teaching, training and learning; and a commitment to particular sets of conventions, norms and sets of ethical values relevant to education. It is, we claim, in the university setting that the broad range of the disciplines constituting a liberal education – one that is composed of those wide-ranging cognitive repertoires and competences as set out in the foregoing, and upon which the community places so much emphasis – may be most effectively institutionalized and promoted, particularly for the purposes of professional education and training.

For these reasons, faculties of education within universities are an inherent part of the provision of quality teachers for quality schools: they prepare and proffer personnel with broadly educated knowledge, competences, values and attitudes, and with the necessary depth, range and sophisticated grasp of professional knowledge in all its diversity and complexity. There is far too substantial a body of knowledge necessary to professional relevance here, and it is far too complex and sophisticated, for anyone reasonably to suppose that it could be gained in any other way than by studying it and working hard to acquire it in the appropriate academic and professional environments.

For us, the appropriate academic and professional environment for the promotion of quality teachers is a university, working in partnership with a school. Any other model seems to us to reduce teaching to the kind of 'sitting next to Nellie' apprenticeship model that passed for 'professional wisdom' about teacher education and training at the time of the Education Acts of the second half of the nineteenth century, and that disfigured so many education systems for so long.

We contend that the agenda for professional education and training activity in the field of teacher education should go well beyond the communication of mere operating procedures, rules of the craft, even tricks of the trade, that past experience suggests is virtually all that is conferred in the apprenticeship model. Our notion of appropriate agenda is one based upon the wide cognitive repertoires, professional competences and elevated values conveyed by the kind of education that only faculties of education in universities can provide, when they operate in partnership with the schools and school systems located in the communities of which they are a part.

SITES WHERE QUALITY MAY BE DISCERNED

In the development of agenda for quality schooling, it is important to recall that we have argued that it is not possible to have one single criterion of quality. We make it clear that quality may be associated with a number of distinct characteristics and features. At this point, therefore, we may perhaps best proceed by giving some tentative adumbration of the sites in which we believe quality in a school may be discerned, and the characteristic features by which it might be identified. As regards setting the agenda at the school level, we suggest that a useful guide in this endeavour is provided by the Scottish Education Office in its report to the OECD on the effectiveness of schooling and of educational resource management (1991). Extrapolating from their work on effective schooling, we suggest the following:

1 Quality in education may be judged in terms of the characteristic features exhibited by its 'graduates': what do young people know and understand; what can they do; what are their values, beliefs and attitudes, brought about as a result of their education?

2 Secondly, quality in schools may be judged by features of the processes and activities of the education that is believed to take place in them. How good is the planning of teaching and learning? How well are the various 'lessons' delivered? How well are the lessons learned? What is assessed and how satisfactorily? What feedback is provided to the students and how satisfactory and appropriate is it? To what extent are parents, the wider community, business, commerce and industry involved? Are continuity and progression to the next stage assured? If not, why not – and what mechanisms are there available for continuing review and correction of those teaching deliveries and learning outcomes found to be deficient?

3 Thirdly, quality may also be judged by the range, type, excellence and appropriateness of the resources and facilities provided. Resources include trained teachers, teaching and learning materials, accommodation, amenities and facilities, and opportunities for engaging in learning by all kinds of means, formal, informal and alternative.

4   Fourthly, quality may be judged by the ways in which schools and their operations are organized, administered and managed. How are students grouped? How is teaching arranged? What are the structure, range and relevance of the curriculum? What are the school's policies, for what purposes, and how appropriate are they? Is administration sound? Have management practices been well thought out and implemented? How adaptable and responsive to change are they? How are they evaluated and held accountable to public scrutiny and inspection?

5   Finally, quality may be judged by the tone, atmosphere and ethos of the institution. Does it provide a secure, relaxed, non-threatening, supportive and purposeful atmosphere, conducive to learning and to optimizing growth and development? Are relationships based on mutual trust and respect? Is there real equality of opportunity? Are contacts with parents, industry and the wider community supported and promoted? What connections are there with external agencies that can help foster the mission of the school?

Having looked at all these diverse sites with which quality might be associated, and around which our agenda might be framed, we might reasonably suppose that even to ask – in the search for some kind of preliminary benchmark – which, in general, is likely to be the better indicator of good quality, a set of clearly articulated and agreed procedures *or* a set of output measures (even if related to input, and the notion of *added value*), is to run the risk of dangerous superficiality and oversimplification. The search for, identification of and assessment of quality is, as the above list shows, much more complex, demanding and difficult than that. We say this to underline our point that in looking for quality in schooling we cannot expect to have one single criterion by which to generalize and then apply a single benchmark of quality to the whole of a school's processes, activities, operations and resources.

Instead, we believe schools should note carefully that the identification, appreciation and assessment of quality in any education institution must be hedged about with all sorts of caveats. A report (AVCC, 1992) on quality in higher education institutions makes this point very forcibly:

- Quality cannot be monitored across whole systems, or even whole institutions, without due sensitivity to the fact that data can be used in a comparative sense only where organization units, courses, goals and missions are identical.
- Any individual judgment of quality requires very careful consideration against a range of variable factors, such as geographical location.
- Each difference introduces another variable into the quality equation, making national judgments and evaluations so difficult as to be almost impossible.

We take this last point, together with the rest, to mean that we should be extremely cautious about assuming or inferring that what makes for quality delivery or assurance in any one school or system can automatically be transferred and applied in any other school or system *without any further need for adaptation or adjustment.* Like love, quality cannot be produced according to a recipe – even though, as lovers ourselves, we do generally all know it when we see it! In the end, quality, its recognition and reward, must come from concepts and criteria adopted or elaborated upon, and operating within and valued by the particular school, system and country.

In addressing the quality delivery and assurance *agenda,* then, we have to remember some critical notes of caution:

1 It is not logically sound to aggregate schools or departments within schools, just as it is not valid to aggregate individuals and talk about their quality in the round or in any general sense. These are the fallacies of composition.

2 It is unhelpful and uninformative to base any judgments about the quality and excellence of a school, a department or an individual member of staff or student on any particular description, observation or appraisal that might be made at any one point in time. To do so ignores past history, future intentions, and the present context and environment (internal and external), and commits the fallacy of isolating the object appraisal from its context. In other words, there must be some expectation of stability and continuity in the assessment of the activities and operations of the school, staff or student whose quality we are seeking to appraise.

3 It is not helpful, in making judgments about quality, to conflate different styles or types of appraisal, assessment or evaluation. In the formation of judgments about the quality of a restaurant, for example, the evaluations made of it by inspectors of the Department of Health are obviously quite different from those made by the inspectors from the *Good Food Guide,* and we should not confuse the two. To do so commits the fallacy of making a category mistake.

4 Instead, we do well to remember that the qualities of a school or a department exhibit different kinds and styles of quality and excellence. For that reason, the judgments relating to those different kinds are domain-specific, or else operating at a very low level of generalizability. Judgments of quality in schooling involve a search for particular kinds of excellence: this is because quality assurance is a positive form of appraisal and involves the determination to ensure the *presence* of particular kinds of virtue. Quality in a school is not, as in a restaurant preparing for a visit by Health Department inspectors, assured by a desire to ensure the *absence* of dysfunctional conditions. To think it is, is to commit the fallacy of omission.

5 The judgments of quality about which schools are chiefly concerned demand peer judgments from agents of evaluation deeply, directly and centrally involved with the nature, aims and values of the school itself, and from members of the education profession who themselves exhibit those standards in their own being and work,

201

and who are concerned to discern and define the ways in which the standards set by those things can prolong, extend or even create excellence in the domain in question. It is clear that the work of such people is of crucial importance in defining excellence: their work, therefore, needs a great deal of money, devoted to programmes of research and development of and into appropriate forms of evaluation and assessment – particularly the formative ones.

6 In this enterprise, what will be important in framing initiatives for the continuation, development and extension of the quality work that we are doing now – especially in teaching, learning, curriculum and professional development and management – will be the availability and sharing of advice, assistance, monitoring, collaboration and review.

7 These considerations generate a set of principles for application:

A In making academic and professional assessments of quality schooling we have to think about evaluation and assessment in new ways. Professionals will need to face what they do in their work and to ask themselves, and be helped to ask, what kinds of evaluation and assessment will help them to appraise what they do, in ways that will enable them to engage in activities leading to improvements in their professional practice overall. What we are after here is a process of appraisal involving future planning, the utility and validity of which may best be seen in terms of its consequences for the school, its staff and its students.

B We have to keep in mind the distinction between the different types and purposes of evaluations and appraisals. This may help to remind us that it is logically impossible to see the one form of evaluation as a mere extension of the other, or as a form of appraisal that can be built on top of the other. Again the fallacy of composition/conflation is committed by those who do this.

C We must remember that no single form of evaluation is by itself sufficient to do the job of defining and monitoring quality as a whole; instead, we have to operate with a sort of aggregate of partial and insufficient forms of judgment. This will give us an appraisal of quality that will be a broad mosaic of measures which will give us some indication of the wide range of excellences in the whole domain of academic activities and practices, interests and concerns, aims and values – but they will not give us a complete picture of, or recipe for, Total Quality, and to think that they can is to commit the fallacy of essentialism.

QUALITY TEACHING AND LEARNING

Informed by our work in this enquiry, we now feel it appropriate to draw some conclusions and propose some memoranda, in particular making some suggestions about some of those things that need to be placed on the agenda of schools eager to promote quality in teaching and learning. These include:

- the effective preparation, delivery and assessment of material in ways that fit with clearly presented purposes of courses;
- a clear view of how learning occurs which is compatible with the teaching approach;
- a willingness to explain learning views and teaching and assessment approaches to students, so as to be accountable;
- a willingness to share teaching/learning views and strategies with colleagues (to provide and receive feedback);
- a readiness to reflect on teaching/learning experiences and be prepared to invest time and effort to achieve deeper understanding and improvement.

Quality in our students will be promoted by a concentration on substantive knowledge, appropriate cognitive competences and disciplinary skills, critically reflective powers, empathy and commitment to the norms and values of the school, effective interaction and collaboration with their teachers, and acceptance of the guidance and support of leaders in education systems, institutions, and schools.

To promote these ends, we might also say something about activities that might occur in departments in schools committed to the above view of quality teaching. It is important that teachers model the quality learning attributes they aspire to see in their students by setting high standards of professional delivery and assuring quality outcomes. It is also vitally important that teachers communicate their own experiences of personal engagement in learning, and reveal their skills in the styles of thinking and working in the subjects and disciplines provided by and practised in those departments, from both teaching and learning perspectives.

Curriculum, programme and course committees are among the chief fora and centres of action responsible for setting the agenda for promoting quality in teaching and learning. This responsibility might be carried out and monitored in the following ways:

- student evaluation of sessions and courses;
- opportunities for team teaching;
- external evaluation of teaching;
- formative and summative course reviews by staff involved;
- teaching exchanges involving other departments in the school and similar ones in other schools in the state, interstate or internationally.

In order to give further consideration to items on the agenda within the school, there might be established a group of staff who have quality teaching and learning as a major professional and curriculum development priority. Their work would have school- and possibly system-wide importance, and could also bring to the school national or even international recognition. This development effort might be extended by substantial collaboration and interaction with other professions and with the community.

Further, teaching excellence could be made a very strong feature of promotion applications; this should be encouraged and expanded. Teaching excellence should be recognized and widely acknowledged; and to achieve this, more attention needs to be given, in schools and school systems, to ways in which this can be celebrated and rewarded.

One aspect of teaching excellence is a commitment to enquiry and research. Research in schools by teachers should be encouraged, developed and administered, perhaps most appropriately by the school curriculum committee, and perhaps working in concert with a university faculty of education research committee. Partnerships with university faculties for these professional purposes may bring to the school additional resources, through the research budget of the university, or from competitive research grants from government bodies.

A school curriculum committee's research agenda could have a dual orientation: to support established and experienced teachers; and to encourage those commencing a teaching career to gain appropriate experience in research and development and to aim at the highest possible quality for their teaching and development activities, as well as their own professional growth and renewal.

QUALITY IN MANAGEMENT

Movement towards a fully integrated and properly co-ordinated approach to democratic management in a school might suggest the need for a thorough-going appraisal of its organization, administration and management structures, functions and relationships. This could be done via a school 'committee of management', with the brief to examine existing and future structural arrangements and efficient functioning procedures. Efficient and effective management structures and arrangements can be under continuing appraisal in the work of such a committee. Matters of the tone, atmosphere and ethos of the school and its departments; the active staff involvement in and ownership of the school's work; the ways in which all the above features in the life and activity of the school can be effectively monitored, evaluated, appraised and, if necessary, amended or added to; and the ways in which the needs and interests of students and stakeholders – the education and welfare services, school systems, community and parent groups, employer groups and industry, commerce and business in general – are addressed and safeguarded, will also be considered as ongoing agenda in such a committee.

Questions to be posed by such a committee working towards quality in a school might include (cf. Wilson, 1993):

> What are we trying to do, and why?
> How are we doing this?
> Why are we doing it in that way?
> Why is this the best way of doing it?
> How do we know it works?

What are we good at?

How do we know?

What would we like to be better at?

What is stopping us?

What can we do about that?

What quality assurance policies and practices do we have in place or
   are we developing?

How effective are these?

How do we judge the quality of our outcomes?

In what areas and in what ways are these outcomes just, equitable
   and excellent?

What are our priorities for improvement?

In framing answers to these and other questions of this kind, it will be important for schools to consider the need for *streamlined* management processes, to free teaching staff to perform better their roles of teaching, curriculum and professional development and community liaison. Further, the school should become committed to the development of a strong *ethos of service*, in which staff recognize the primacy of the needs of students as the target of their efforts, in relation to the needs of business, industry and commerce, and of the wider community.

Schools can also become expert and active in the investigation and application of all the instruments of modern *information technology* and the ways in which it can help overcome traditional barriers to good management and communication. This activity must be increased and expanded, especially with reference to interactivity and professional collaboration with colleagues in other schools, in the system, interstate and overseas.

All these agenda may be driven forward by the school's management committee in the first instance, for later elaboration with the aid of the school's council and any system committees devoted to quality teaching, learning and management.

What will be important in framing initiatives for the continuation, development and extension of quality will be the availability and sharing of advice, assistance, monitoring, collaboration and review. This will enable schools to turn out good students, who will, in turn, be well-trained and well-qualified employees; imaginative and creative providers of services to the various trades, agencies and professions; committed and highly motivated entrants to tertiary educating institutions; and productive, thoughtful and responsible members of the community generally.

Furthermore, schools need to assure their students that they are much less interested to know at what stage of intellectual development they were when they first came to a school than in how good they become later as a result of their educational experience and engagement in the processes of further development and intellectual growth in it. Thus the assessments schools make of them must be to evaluate students on their improved attainment at the end of their period of formal attendance. What schools and the wider community are these days chiefly concerned about is the *value added* to the students' perspectives and cognitive repertoires as a result of their experiences and activities in the community's educating institutions. In giving an account of those processes and

205

endeavours, school teaching staff and curriculum planners should note the determinative importance and influence of the part played by activities of collaboration and reciprocal mentoring – between staff and staff, staff and student, and student and student – in achieving and monitoring learning gains and cognitive change.

We may say the same about setting the agenda for the processes of institutional change and development. What is of vital importance here in schools that are determined to become quality institutions, is to make people partners and sharers in the process of institutional development and improvement. It is clear that unless people are directly involved, made equal partners, and given a say in the shaping and realization of a vision of the future, the less successful will be the effort at institutional change, reform and improvement.

This adumbration of the cognitive repertoire and sets of value concerns for the work of schools allows us to draw attention to the ways in which the heterogeneous character of schools and school systems allows, and indeed encourages, different kinds of excellence to exist in them. These respond to and are expressions of differences observable in the cultures of the different subject departments, the different kinds of schools, and above all the different backgrounds, interests and abilities that their students and staff bring to them.

The modern school we speak of is multidisciplinary but also now increasingly multicultural: part and parcel of its make-up and character are real lifestyle and real thought-style differences. Those differences are exhibited in the characteristic excellences of its various disciplines, subjects and goals, in which a stress on the multivariate nature of its educational mission, curriculum construction and the composition of its staff and student body can be discerned. The stress laid on excellence in all these constituent elements must include considerations of equality and equal opportunity, access and participation, and social justice. Above all, however, the emphasis must be on *promoting excellence in all its forms*. The point of equity and social justice policies and concerns is simply to ensure that the pool of excellence in which ability can be nurtured and promoted is as widely extended as possible, and that quality can be identified and developed in all a community's young people, not just half of them.

The diverse kinds of excellence found in a school, in teaching and learning, curriculum development, administration, professional development and community liaison, and among staff and students, will mean that we cannot expect to have one single version of excellence that is operative and normative across all the work of a single school or a system. Schools have to preserve and cherish the particular sets of subject content, operating procedures, teaching methods and learning styles that typify the norms and operating conventions of the various subjects, fields of knowledge and modes of enquiry in the institutions, in order to get some sense and savour of the particular kinds of excellence pursued, practised and promoted within all of them.

THE SCHOOL PRINCIPAL, ACCOUNTABILITY AND QUALITY CONTROL

In respect of institutional management of a school or a department, we need to stress the role of a school administrator as a 'bridge' or conduit in a devolved structure, and emphasize the dual accountability of that manager, both to the system and the school council on the one hand, and also to the heads of department and the members of staff located within the school on the other. Furthermore, in an educational institution, there is of course a third, and triadic, kind of accountability:

- to the cognitive imperatives incumbent upon and accepted by any member of the community of knowledge and its subjects – to advance, transmit and sustain knowledge in all its forms, and to do so in conformity with the impartial norms and conventions governing warranted assertion, intelligibility and cognitive growth within it;
- to the teaching profession and the education service, and to serving their needs and interests;
- to the community, and to securing and promoting its welfare.

As an aside, we might add that it is this accountability – to the cognitive requirements of a field of study, subject or discipline, and to the moral responsibilities arising from teachers' work in educational institutions devoted to the furtherance of young people's interests and to community welfare generally – that makes the attempts strictly to apply the approaches of business management to the management of a school something less than conceptually or morally appropriate.

Bearing all this in mind, therefore, we take the view that among the main items of agenda for the school principal or leader will be:

- to develop a *commitment* to academic excellence, intellectual rigour and the growth of the life of the mind;
- to encourage *assent* to the proposition that among a nation's greatest powers and best gifts to the world are the powers of critical and creative imagination, conceived, brought to birth, fostered, extended, promoted and allowed full expression in our institutions of learning and education;
- to *empower* and *encourage* staff colleagues and students to pursue their own excellences;
- to develop a *culture* of learning, principled action and commitment to moral values;
- to *fight* vigorously on behalf of the school for funding in the broader arenas of the system and the community;
- to *negotiate* the distribution of those funds inside the school in an open, rational, fair and equitable manner;
- to *trust* the abilities of heads of department and others charged with financial responsibility to manage effectively their own units, within the context of a shared commitment to and ownership of the strategic plan of the department and the larger mission of the

207

school – all this within the overall supervision, guidance and responsibility of the principal and the school council.

We are convinced that these are values that principals, schools and the whole learning community should hold dear and attempt to preserve and defend at all costs. This is not to say that schools should accept a stultifying adherence to past policies or practices, which can end in stasis or ossification; it is rather to accept that future growth in knowledge has to stand on the shoulders of past cognitive achievements. It is for this reason that we believe in the obvious advantages accruing to schools from adopting an *evolutionary* and *gradualist* approach to problem-solving and the management of change.

THE EVOLUTIONARY APPROACH TO CHANGE

It is, of course, a school's chief characteristic feature to be concerned with conceptual development, cognitive growth and change, both in knowledge, with its implications for teaching and learning, and in institutional organization and administration. This is its special virtue, and the atmosphere in which teachers as educators are privileged to work. We accept that, in the pursuit and extension of knowledge, there can be quantum leaps forward and radical advances in thinking, work and practice, precipitated by sudden shifts in paradigm coming about as a result of blinding flashes of insight.

This kind of cognitive occurrence, this sudden growth in knowledge, and the excitement and enthusiasm it can generate in the breast of the individual learner or the whole learning community, is well described by the philosopher Plato in the dialogue *Symposium* and the famous seventh *Epistle*:

> Finally the vision may be revealed to him of a single science, which is the Science of Beauty everywhere, but this can only come after patient instruction and much hard work of exact science when suddenly, like a blaze kindled by a leaping spark, it is generated in the soul and at once becomes self-sustaining.

This is the kind of quality learning experience we have been talking about: the need for patient attention and thorough-going commitment to effective teaching and instruction; unremitting hard work on the part of the teacher and learner; learning that 'stands on the shoulders' of previous instruction, knowledge and understanding. It is these preconditions that provide the springboard for sudden advances in understanding and revolutionary shifts or enlargements in insight, for it is these that can most help the learner discover and realize, after all, the power and excitement that the educational process can confer. It is this that makes the remark of Bruner (1977) intelligible: 'discovery, like surprise, favours the well-prepared mind'.

With respect to institutional development, leadership and management, however, we believe that institutional transformation should come about more slowly. In our view, change should be proposed and take place via rational argument that is public, objective and impartial, and by processes that are open, consultative, participative and accountable. Yet such processes, as well as being responsible and democratic, must also operate in ways that will enable the institution to articulate and deploy policies that will be sufficiently rapid, adaptive and flexible to meet the exigencies of the new conditions and problem-situations they have to deal with, whether facing the demands of providing a new course for a new target audience, addressing the challenges raised by the arrival of a new competitor on the scene, or generating a drive for greater success in external fund-raising.

Perhaps we may conclude our outlines of agenda for the generation and achievement of quality in schools and schooling by referring to a metaphor employed in another dialogue of Plato. In the myth of the Charioteer, in the *Phaedrus*, Plato provides us with a good model for the work of a school: in the whole organization there will be those, like the powerful draw-horse between the shafts, who provide the principal momentum and do the requisite hard work. There will also be those, like the side-horse, capable of extraordinary leaps of the imagination and flights of fancy, but who will need constantly to be brought back to the importance of the task in hand, who will have to be reined in on occasion when they threaten to dash off in pursuit of unsuitable or unrealistic objectives which are not in the interests of the whole organization. Working together, however, both have the potential to give power and purpose to drawing the whole unit forward under the guidance of the charioteer of rationality, who will co-ordinate and integrate the efforts of the whole apparatus and, with larger and longer powers of vision, will make sure that the combined efforts of the three elements get them all where they want and need to go.

Perhaps we might end with a reference to Spinoza, the last sentence of whose *Ethics* reminds us that 'Everything excellent is as difficult as it is rare.' Schools already contain so much that is excellent. For our part, we are sure that they continue to be animated by a concern to tackle the difficulties that face them on the road to delivering and assuring quality in all their undertakings. We know they do so in the serious and concerned endeavour to make those excellences and qualities upon which they and the whole of society set such store, and at which they are already so good, just a little less rare and a good deal more highly valued by their peers in the education service, their clients in the professions, trades and service agencies, and their friends and supporters in the wider community. In searching for, delivering and celebrating such excellences, a quality school can provide no better service to, and confer no larger benefit on, the present and future citizens of their city, their state, their country and the international community.

Appendix 1

Organizations from which Representatives were Interviewed

Australian Capital Territory Schools Authority
Association of Independent Schools of Queensland
Association of Independent Schools of Western Australia
Association of Parents and Friends of Catholic Schools of Tasmania
Australian Council of School Organizations
Australian High School Principals' Association
Australian Parents' Council
Australian Primary Principals' Association
Catholic Education Commission, Queensland
Catholic Education Commission of Western Australia
Catholic Office of Education, Adelaide
Catholic Office of Education, Brisbane
Centre for Education, University of Tasmania
Centre for Educational Leadership, Western Australia
Curriculum Development Centre (Canberra)
Department of Education, Queensland
Department of Education, South Australia
Department of Education and the Arts, Tasmania
Department of Employment, Industrial Relations and Training, Tasmania
Department of School Education, New South Wales
Department of Technical and Further Education (South Australia)
Diocesan Office of Catholic Education in New South Wales
Federation of Parents' and Citizens' Associations (New South Wales)
FOSCO (Federation of School Community Organizations) (New South Wales)
Independent Parents' and Friends' Council of Queensland
Isolated Children's Parents' Association
Leadership Centre, Brisbane, C.A.E.
Ministry of Education, Western Australia
Ministry of Education, Arts and Health, Australian Capital Territory
New South Wales Parents' Council
New South Wales Primary Principals' Council
Northern Territory Primary Principals' Association
Parents' and Friends' Association of Queensland
Parents' and Friends' Association of Western Australia
Queensland Association of Teachers in Independent Schools
Queensland Council of Parents and Citizens' Association
Queensland High School Principals' Association
Queensland Teachers' Union

Schools Council, National Board of Employment, Education and Training
Secondary College Staff Association, Tasmania
Secondary Education Authority, Western Australia
Senior Secondary Assessment Board of South Australia
South Australian High School Principals' Association
South Australian Institute of Teachers
South Australian Primary Principals' Association
Schools:
    Anglican School, Queensland
    Anglican School, Western Australia
    Catholic Parish Primary School, Brisbane
    Catholic Secondary College, Brisbane
    Catholic Secondary College, Melbourne
    Primary School, Canberra
    State High School, Brisbane
    State High School, Hobart
    State Primary School, Adelaide
    State Primary School, Darwin
    State Primary School, Melbourne
    State Primary School, Perth
    State Primary School, Sydney
    State Secondary College, Melbourne
    State Senior High School, Perth
Tasmanian Catholic Education Employees' Association
Tasmanian Education Department
Tasmanian High School Principals' Association
Tasmanian Teachers' Federation
Teachers' Federation of New South Wales
University of Tasmania, Faculty of Education
Western Australian Chamber of Commerce and Industry (Inc.)
Western Australian Council of State Schools Organizations
Western Australian Primary Principals' Association

Appendix 2

Broad Areas Addressed in Interviews

Notion of quality education
Quality of what?
Quality for whom?
In whose interests?

By what sorts of criteria can the quality of a school system (or individual school) be assessed? What goals should be aimed for? Is too much being expected of schools?

The implications for schools and school systems of tensions in the quality debate, such as:

- the tension between providing opportunities for all students to do well and encouraging a high standard of specialized knowledge and training;
- the danger that an emphasis on accountability may distort teaching and curriculum towards an emphasis on the readily identifiable at the expense of the longer term diffuse goals of education;
- the tension between respect for teacher professionalism and the perceived need for central or national guidelines in professional areas;
- the tension between developing a more efficiently regulated system and encouraging more school-based community/parental involvement and choice.

System responsibility vis-à-vis local initiatives
What has been the background to shifts in authority?
What shifts have occurred?
What shifts are likely?

Where do you believe the pressure for such changes has come from?

How do shifts between central and local authority relate to debates about quality education?

Are there responsibilities that must be retained at the centre?

What type of accountability is required for these?

What types of school organization best enhance quality in schooling?

What sorts of decisions should be taken at school level?

What sorts of professional judgments need to be developed at school level?

Has a sense of partnership between teachers and parent come about?
If so, has it been because of central direction?

Does empowerment of students to become active partners in curriculum negotiation enhance the quality of schooling?

What is the role of the principal in all of this?

Equity and quality

Can both equity and quality be sustained simultaneously?

What have been the changes in the way these have been pursued?

How do you account for these changes?
What are the pressures for them?
What do you perceive as their significance?

Emerging directions of change

In what direction is education headed?
Where have the changes or pressures for change come from?
How has this come about?
Where will it end up?

What values or shifts in values are reflected in the changes?

What reaction is likely to be produced against the new emphases?
How do these relate to past, present or emerging conflicts or debates?

How much of the change is simply rhetorical?

Who are the key players influencing emerging directions?

How do you see the current relationship between education and the economy/politics?

What are the pressures on you or your organization regarding current changes/policies?

Apart from Education Departments/Ministries, are there other powerful institutions (e.g. publishers, employers, business, education lobby) that influence educational policy, change and understandings of quality?

What makes schools responsive to external forces?
What are these forces and where do they come from?

To what extent may the centre be emerging as a policy-developing and co-ordinating unit rather than an administrative centre?

Relationship between system reorganization and classroom teaching

To what extent has system reorganization influenced classroom teaching?

Is school improvement more dependent on the skills of specific teachers?

What are the attributes of a good teacher/principal?

What sort of school environment/school culture is conducive to quality?

Are teachers effective curriculum designers?

What are the dilemmas for teachers where system-wide frameworks in curriculum are in conflict with locally determined curriculum initiatives?

Do major themes (such as participation) filter down to the school level?

What is the effect, positive or negative, of ongoing system change on teachers?

To what extent is support for teachers and principals a requirement for quality schooling?

Specific developments to address quality concerns

What have been recent developments in:

- curriculum
- professional development of teachers and administrators
- attempts to reassure community and interest groups
- teacher training
- funding
- evaluation and reporting

Appendix 3

Categories Used for the Analysis of Data by Ethnograph

1 The contested nature of quality

1.1   Equity and quality
1.2   Quantitative and qualitative concerns of schooling (fact and value)
1.3   Quality of what?
1.4   Quality for whom?
1.5   Criteria of quality
1.6   Emergence and nature of quality debate
1.7   Issues to be considered
1.8   Tensions in the quality debate

2 Government policy and the management of schools

2.1   Pressures for policy development
    2.1.1   International pressures
    2.1.2   Economic pressures
    2.1.3   Expectations of the community
    2.1.4   Intellectual/ideological pressures
    2.1.5   Others
2.2   Contributions to policy developments
    2.2.1   Unions
    2.2.2   Parents' association
    2.2.3   Single interest groups
    2.2.4   Employers' groups
    2.2.5   Media
    2.2.6   Publishers
    2.2.7   The system
    2.2.8   Others
2.3   Australian responses
    2.3.1   Shaping of government policy
    2.3.2   National/federal
    2.3.3   State/territory
    2.3.4   Tension between state and federal response
2.4   Central and school decision-making: issues
    2.4.1   Respective roles and responsibilities
    2.4.2   Tensions
        2.4.2.1   specialized/generalized knowledge
        2.4.2.2   accountability/distortion of teaching and curriculum
        2.4.2.3   teacher professionalism/central guidelines

5 Emerging directions

Appendix 4

Questions Informing the Literature Review

1 The contested nature of quality

1.1 What is the relationship between equity and quality in education?

1.2 What is meant by quality of education, and what criteria for measuring quality have emerged?

1.3 What are the main features of the quality debate? (When did this debate emerge? What tensions are seen within the debate?)

2 Government policy and the management of schools

2.1 What are the sources of pressure for policy development (e.g. international, economic, expectations of the community, intellectual/ideological pressures, other)?

2.2 What are the sources of contributions to policy development (e.g. unions, parents' associations, single interest groups, employer groups, media, publishers, system, other)?

2.3 What is the nature of government policy and the management of schools in Australia? (How is policy shaped? What tensions exist between various government education authorities?)

2.4 What are the main issues in relation to central v. school decision-making (e.g. roles and responsibilities; tensions between central guidelines/generalized knowledge, professionalism/accountability; efficiently regulated system/school-based community/parental involvement)?

2.5 How does the school survive in an environment of changing government policy?

3 Key functional areas in which the quality of debate is being played out

3.1 How is the teaching profession responding? (award structuring, teacher education, teacher morale)?

3.2 What is the nature of the curriculum debate?

3.3 How is accountability in education practice ensured (to whom, how measured)?

3.4 What part does the provision of resources play in ensuring quality education?

4 The school and quality education

4.1   What is the nature of the goals of schooling (perceived goals and expectations/tensions/notions of academic standards/social effects of schooling/relevance of schooling)?

4.2   How are the goals attained? (roles of key people such as principals, parents, teachers, students, system officials and others; what tensions are seen among these actors in terms of roles and responsibilities; what role is played by the system; how important are resources – human, material and financial; what part is played by particular system organization; how important is the school–community relationship; what role is played by particular school organization structures and approaches to management)?

4.3   How is it decided that objectives have been obtained, i.e. measurement and evaluation (e.g. outcomes, identifying and measuring school performance, testing, school-by-school comparisons)?

4.4   How does the interaction between system organization and classroom practice affect the quality of education?

5 Emerging directions

5.1   What are the emerging directions which attempt to ensure quality/effective/excellent/successful education (Australian and international directions)?

References

Abbott, J. (1989). 'Educating people for change'. *Conference and Common Room.* **26**(1), 12–15.

Access Printout (1990). *School-based Improvement and Effective Schools: A Perfect Match for Bottom-Up Reform.* Columbia: The Information Clearing House about Public Schools.

Ackerman, B. (1980). *Social Principles and the Liberal State.* New Haven, CT: Yale University Press.

Ackerman, R. (ed.) (1992). *Reflections 1992: If Not Now, When? If Not Us, Who? Visions for Better Schools in a Better World.* Harvard University, Cambridge, MA: The International Network of Principals' Centers.

Ainley, P. (1990). *Training Turns to Enterprise: Vocational Education in the Market Place.* Hillcote Group Paper 4. London: Tufnell Press.

Alberta Department of Education (1990). *Educational Quality Indicators: An Annotated Bibliography,* 2nd ed. Edmonton, Alberta: Department of Education.

Allen, G. (1987). 'The art of the possible: personal and social education and the community secondary school'. In G. Allen *et al.* (ed.), *Community Education: An Agenda for Educational Reform,* 193–213. Milton Keynes: Open University Press.

Allen, G., Bastiani, J., Martin, I. and Richards, K. (eds) (1987). *Community Education: An Agenda for Educational Reform.* Milton Keynes: Open University Press.

Amster, J. *et al.* (1990). *Investing in Our Future: The Imperative of Education Reform and the Role of Business.* Queenstown, MD: Aspen Institute.

Andersen, B. and Klein, F. (1990). 'A study of curriculum decision-making in a time of site-based management'. Annual Meeting of the American Educational Research Association, Boston, MA.

Anderson, G. L. and Herr, K. (1992). 'Voices of the Bottom: School Restructuring for Student Empowerment'. Paper presented at the Annual Meeting of the American Education Research Association, San Francisco.

Anderson, S. E. (1991). 'Principal's management style and patterns of teacher implementation across multiple innovations'. *School Effectiveness and School Improvement,* **2**(4), 286–304.

Angus, L. (1992). 'Local school management and the politics of participation'. *Unicorn, Journal of the Australian College of Education,* **18**(2), 4–11.

Angus, M. (1990). 'Making better schools: devolution the second time round'. Paper presented at the Annual Meeting of the American Educational Research Association, Boston, MA.

Apple, M. W. (1988). 'What reform talk does: creating new inequalities in education'. *Educational Administration Quarterly,* **24**(3), 272–81.

Argyris, C., Putman, R. and McLain Smith, D. (1985). *Action Science: Concepts, Methods and Skills for Research and Intervention.* San Francisco: Jossey-Bass.

Aristotle (1934). *Nicomachean Ethics,* trans. H. Rackham. London: William Heinemann (Loeb Classical Library).

Aronowitz, S. and Giroux, H. A. (1985). *Education under Siege: The Conservative, Liberal and Radical Debate over Schooling*. South Hadley, MA: Bergin & Garvey.

Aspin, D. N. (1975). 'Ethical aspects of sport and games, and physical education'. *Proceedings of the Philosophy of Education Society of Great Britain*, **9**(2), 49–71.

Austin, J. L. (1975). *How to Do Things with Words* (The William James Lectures at Harvard University) 2nd edn, eds J. O. Ursmon and M. Sbisa. Oxford: Clarendon Press.

AVCC (1992). *Report of the Committee in Response to the 'Quality Reference'*. ed. K. MacKinnon. Canberra: AVCC.

Ayer, A. J. (1971). *Language, Truth and Logic*. Harmondsworth: Penguin.

Baars, B. J. (1986). *The Cognitive Revolution in Psychology*. New York: Guilford Press.

Bacchus, M. K. (1991). 'Equity and cultural diversity'. In W. Walker, R. Farquhar and M. Hughes (eds), *Advancing Education: School Leadership in Action*. London: Falmer Press.

Badarak, G. W. (1990). *Recapturing the Policy-Making Functions of State Boards of Education: Policy Issues*. Appalachia Educational Lab., Charleston, WV: Policy and Planning Center.

Ball, S. J. (1990). 'A national curriculum for the 1990s?' *NUT Education Review*, **4**(1), 9–12.

Ball, S. J. (1990). *Markets, Morality and Equality in Education*. Hillcote Group Paper 5. London: Tufnell Press.

Ball, S. J. (ed.) (1990). *Foucault and Education: Disciplines and Knowledge*. London: Routledge.

Ballion, R. (1991). *The Importance of Opinions in Analysing How the Education System Functions*. OECD International Education Indicators Project. General Assembly of the INES Project. Lugano, Switzerland.

Bantock, G. H. (1971). 'Towards a theory of popular education'. In R. Hooper (ed.), *The Curriculum: Context, Design and Development*. Edinburgh: Oliver & Boyd.

Baptiste Jr, H. P., Waxman, H. C., Walker D. E., Felix, J. and Anderson, J. E. (eds) (1990). *Leadership, Equity and School Effectiveness*. Newbury Park, CA: Sage.

Barry, B. (1965). *Political Argument*. London: Routledge & Kegan Paul.

Barth, R. (1991). *Improving Schools from Within*. San Francisco: Jossey-Bass.

Bash, L. (1989). 'Education goes to market'. In L. Bash and D. Coulby (eds), *The Education Reform Act: Competition and Control*. London: Cassell.

Bash, L. and Coulby, D. (eds) (1989). *The Education Reform Act: Competition and Control*. London: Cassell.

Beare, H. (1989). *Educational Administration in the 1990s*. ACEA Monograph Series No. 6. Canberra: Australian Council of Educational Administration.

Beare, H. and Sturman, A. (1991). 'Centralization and decentralization in curriculum and evaluation: looking both ways at once.' In W. Walker, R. Farquhar and M. Hughes (eds) *Advancing Education: School Leadership in Action.*, London: Falmer Press.

Beare, H., Caldwell, B. J. and Millikan, R. H. (1989). *Creating an Excellent School: Some New Management Techniques*. London: Routledge.

Beck, L. and Murphy, J. (forthcoming). *Understanding the Principalship: A Metaphorical Analysis, 1920–1990*. New York: Teachers College Press.

Bell, J., Bush, T., Fox, A., Goodey, J. and Goulding, S. (eds) (1984). *Conducting Small-Scale Investigations in Educational Management*. London: Harper & Row.

Bell, L. (1988). *Appraising Teachers in Schools – A Practical Guide*. London: Routledge.

Bell, L. (1988). *Management Skills in Primary Schools*. London: Routledge.

Bellon, T. *et al.* (1992). 'Teachers' perceptions of their leadership roles in site-based decision-making'. Paper presented at the Annual Meeting of the AERA. San Francisco, CA.

Benjamin, H. (1971). 'The sabre-toothed curriculum'. In R. Hooper (ed.), *The Curriculum: Context, Design and Development*. Edinburgh: Oliver & Boyd.

Benn, S. I. and Peters, R. S. (1959). *Social Principles and the Democratic State*. London: George Allen & Unwin.

Bennett, W. J. (1989). *Our Children and Our Country*. New York: Simon & Schuster.

Bennis, W. (1989). *On Becoming a Leader*. Reading, MA: Addison-Wesley.

Berkeley, G. (1990). 'Tensions in system-wide management'. In J. D. Chapman and J. F. Dunstan (eds), *Democracy and Bureaucracy: Tensions in Public Schooling*. London: Falmer Press.

Bernstein, R. J. (1983). *Beyond Objectivism and Relativism: Science, Hermeneutics and Praxis*. Oxford: Blackwell.

Best, D. (1992). *The Rationality of Feeling*. London: Falmer Press.

Bienayme, A. (1989). 'Does company strategy have any lesson for educational planning?'. *Prospects*, **19**(2), 243–55.

Billinas, J. (ed.) (1989). *Creating Schools for the Twenty-first Century: New Horizons for Local School Leaders*. Springfield, IL: Illinois Association of School Boards.

Binkley, M. R. *et al.* (1991). *A Sway of National Assessment and Examination Practices in OECD Countries*. OECD International Indicators Project. General Assembly of the INES Project. Lugano, Switzerland.

Birch, I. and Smart, D. (1990). 'Economic rationalism and the politics of education in Australia'. In D. E. Mitchell and M. E. Goertz (eds), *Education Policies for a New Century*. London: Falmer Press.

Blackler, F. (1984). *Applying Psychology in Organizations*. London: Methuen.

Blackmore, J. (1990). 'School-based decision-making and teacher unions: the appropriation of a discourse'. In J. D. Chapman (ed.), *School-Based Decision-Making and Management*. London: Falmer Press.

Blank, R. K. (1991). *Developing and Implementing Education Indicators*. OECD International Education Indicators Project. General Assembly of the INES Project. Lugano, Switzerland.

Blase, J. (ed.) (1991). *The Politics of Life in Schools*. Newbury Park, CA: Sage.

Blong, J. T. and Friedel, J. N. (1991). *2020 Vision: The EICCD (Eastern Iowa Community College District) Moves into the Twenty-first Century*. Davenport: EICCD.

Bloom, A. (1987). *The Closing of the American Mind*. New York: Simon & Schuster.

Bloom, B. S. (ed.) (1956). *Taxonomy of Educational Objectives: The Classification of Educational Goals: Handbook I: The Cognitive Domain*. New York: Longman.

Bolam, R. *et al.* (1992). 'Teachers' and headteachers' perceptions of effective management in British primary schools'. Paper prepared for Division A of the AERA Annual Meeting. San Francisco.

Bond, E. (1976). 'An introduction to "The Fool" '. *Theatre Quarterly*. Spring.

Boomer, G. (1990). 'Democracy, bureaucracy and the classroom'. In J. D. Chapman and J. F. Dunstan (eds), *Democracy and Bureaucracy: Tensions in Public Schooling*. London: Falmer Press.

Boomer, G. (1991). *Education and the Media: Makers or Mirrors? Dilemmas in the Development of Australian Culture*. Evolving Partnerships in Education. Australian College of Education, Fyshwick: National Capital Printing.

Bottery, M. (1989). 'The education of business management'. *Oxford Review of Education*, **15**(2), 129–46.

Bowers, B. (1990). 'Initiating change in schools'. *Research Roundup*, **6**(3), 1–5.

Boyd, W. L. (1990). 'Balancing competing policies in school reform: international efforts in re-structuring education'. In J. D. Chapman and J. F. Dunstan (eds), *Democracy and Bureaucracy: Tensions in Public Schooling*. London: Falmer Press.

Boyd, W. L. and Hartman, N. T. (1988). 'The politics of educational productivity'. In D. H. Monk and J. Underwood (eds), *Microlevel School Finance*. Cambridge, MA: Ballinger.

Boyd-Barrett, O., Bush, T., Goody, J. McNay, I. and Preedy, M. (eds) (1983). *Approaches to Post-school Management*. London: Paul Chapman Publishing.

Boyer, E. L. (1983). *High School: A Report on Secondary Education in America*. New York: Harper.

Boyer, E. L. (1985). *High School*. New York: Harper & Row.

Braithwaite, E. R. (1959). *To Sir, with Love*. London: Bodley Head.

Brennan, M. (1992). 'Improving schools – again: a tale worth retelling'. *Unicorn Journal of the Australian College of Education*, **18**(2), 25–9.

Brighouse, T. and Tomlinson, J. (1991). *Successful Schools*. Education and Training Paper No. 4. London: Institute for Public Policy Research.

Broadfoot, P. (1991). *International Education Indicators: Conceptual and Theoretical Aspects. Achievements of Learning*. OECD International Indicators Project. INES Project, General Assembly. Lugano, Switzerland.

Brodsky, J. and Masciandaro, P. (1992). 'School beatings as a change process: Buffalo and Jericho 1976–1981'. Paper prepared for the Annual Meeting of the AERA. San Francisco.

Bronowski, J. (1973). *The Ascent of Man*. London: BBC Publishing.

Brown, D. (1991). *Decentralization – The Administrators' Guidebook to School District Change*. Newbury Park, CA: Corwin Press.

Bruck, J. (1993). 'Break the disciplinary barriers'. *The Australian Higher Education Supplement*, 10 November.

Bruner, J. S. (1966). *Studies in Cognitive Growth*. New York: Wiley.

Bruner, J. S. (1972). *Study of Thinking*. Huntingdon, NY: R. E. Krieger.

Bruner, J. S. (1977). *The Process of Education*. Cambridge, MA: Harvard University Press.

Burdin, J. L. (ed.) (1989). *School Leadership: A Contemporary Reader*. Newbury Park, CA: Sage.

Burrage. H. (1991). 'Gender, curriculum and assessment issues to 16+'. *Gender and Education*, **3**(1), 31–43.

Burt, C. (1933). *How the Mind Works*. London: Allen & Unwin.

Burt, C. (1975). *The Gifted Child*. London: Hodder & Stoughton. (See also C. Burt, 'The mental differences between children'. In C. B. Cox, *The Black Papers on Education*. For a rebuttal of Burt's theories see L. Kamin (1974). *The Science and Politics of IQ*. Potomac, Maryland: Erlbaum.)

Bush, T. (ed.) (1959). *Managing Education: Theory and Practice*. Milton Keynes: Open University Press.

Bush, T., Glatter, R., Goodey, J. and Riches, C. (eds) (1980). *Approaches to School Management*. London: Harper & Row.

Business Council of Australia (1991). *Managing Public Education Systems for Improved Performance*. Business Council Bulletin, November.

Caldwell, B. (1990). 'School-based decision-making and management: international developments'. In J. Chapman (ed.), *School-Based Decision-Making and Management*. London: Falmer Press.

Caldwell, B. J. (1989). 'Paradox and uncertainty in the governance of education'. Paper presented at the Annual Meeting of the American Educational Researcher Association. San Francisco.

Caldwell, B. J. and Spinks, J. M. (1990). *The Self-Managing School*. London: Falmer Press.

Capper, C. A. and Jamison, M. T. (1992). *Outcome-Based Education Re-examined: From Structural Functionalism to Poststructuralism*. University of Wisconsin–Madison: Department of Educational Administration.

Cave, E. (1990). 'The changing managerial arena'. In E. Cave and C. Wilkinson (eds), *Local Management of Schools: Some Practical Issues*. London: Routledge.

Cave, E. and Wilkinson, C. (eds) (1990). *Local Management of Schools*. London: Routledge.

Chan, C. and Stevenson, H. W. (1989). 'Homework: a cross-cultural examination'. *Child Development*, **60**, 551–61.

Chance, E. N. (1989). 'Developing administrative union. Education and the changing rural community: anticipating the 21st century'. Proceedings of the 1989 ACRES/NRSSC Symposium.

Chapman, J. D. (ed.) (1990). *School-Based Decision-Making and Management*. London: Falmer Press.

Chapman, J. D. and Dunstan, J. F. (eds) (1990). *Democracy and Bureaucracy: Tensions in Public Schooling*. London: Falmer Press.

Christie, P. (1992). 'From crisis to transformation: education in post-apartheid South Africa'. *Australian Journal of Education*, **6**(1), 38–52.

Chubb, J. E. and Moe, T. (1990). *Politics, Markets and America's Schools*, Washington, DC: Brookings Institution.

Churchill, W. L. S. (1947). In *Hansard*. British House of Commons, November 11.

Clark, D. L. and Astuto, T. A. (1990). 'The disjunction of federal education policy and educational needs in the 1990s'. In D. E. Mitchell and M. E. Goertz (eds), *Education Politics for the New Century*. London: Falmer Press.

Clark, D. L., Lotto, L. S. and Astuto, T. A. (1989). 'Effective schools and school improvement: a comparative analysis of two lines of inquiry'. In J. L. Burdin (ed.), *School Leadership: A Contemporary Reader*. Newbury Park, CA: Sage.

Clayton, G. (1989). 'LMS and employment issues'. In B. Fidler and G. Bowles (eds), *Effective Local Management of Schools*. Harlow: Longman.

Clayton Felt, M. (1985). *Improving Our Schools*. Newton, MA: Educational Development Centre.

Clemens, T. K. and Mayer, D. F. (1987). *The Classic Touch*. Homewood, IL: Dow Jones–Irwin.

Click, P. M. and Click, D. W. (1990). *Administration of Schools for Young Children*. New York: Delman Publishers.

Clinchy, E. (1991). 'Reform, revolution, or just more smoke and heroes'. *Phi Delta Kappan*, November, 210–18.

Codd, J. A. (1992). 'The knowledge base in educational administration and the restructuring of education in New Zealand'. Paper presented at the Annual Meeting of the AERA. San Francisco.

Coffield, F. (1989). 'The year 2000: inventing the future'. *Scottish Educational Review*, **21**(2), 77–86.

Cohen, D. K. and Spillane, J. P. (1991). *National Education Indicators and Traditions of Accountability*. OECD International Education Indicators Project. General Assembly of the INES Project. Lugano, Switzerland.

Cohen, D. K. and Spillane, J. P. (1992). 'Policy and practice: the relations between governance and instruction'. In G. Grant (ed.), *Review of Research in Education*. Washington: American Educational Research Association.

Coldron, J. and Boulton, P. (1991). ' "Happiness" as a criterion of parents' choice of school'. *Journal of Education Policy*, **6**(2), 169–78.

Coleman, P. and Collinge, J. (1991). 'In the web: internal and external influences affecting school improvement'. *School Effectiveness and School Improvement*, **4**(2), 262–85.

Coleman, P. and Tabin, Y. (1992). 'The good teacher: a parent perspective'. Paper presented at the Annual Meeting of the AERA. San Francisco.

Comer, J. P. (1988). 'Educating poor mentality children'. *Scientific American*, **259**(5), 42–8.

Commission on the Future of the North Carolina Community College System (1989). *Gaining the Competitive Edge: The Challenge to North Carolina's Community Colleges.*

Conley, D. T. (1991). *Restructuring Schools: Educators Adapt to a Changing World.* Trends and Issues Series, 6. Eugene, OR: ERIC Clearinghouse on Educational Management.

Connors, L. G. and McMorrow, J. F. (1990). 'Governing Australia's public schools: community participation, bureaucracy and devolution'. In J. D. Chapman and J. F. Dunstan (eds), *Democracy and Bureaucracy: Tensions in Public Schooling.* London: Falmer Press.

Consortium on Chicago School Research (1991). 'Charting reform: the teachers' turn'. *Report No. 1 on a Survey of CPS Elementary School Teachers.*

Cooper, B. S. (1989). 'Bottom-up authority in school organization: implications for the administrator'. *Education and Urban Society*, **21**(4), 380–92.

Cooper, B. S. (1990). 'Local school reform in Great Britain and the United States: points of comparison – points of departure'. *Educational Review*, **42**(2), 133–49.

Coulby, D. (1989a). 'From educational partnership to central control'. In L. Bash and D. Coulby (eds), *The Education Reform Act: Competition and Control.* London: Cassell.

Coulby, D. (1989b). 'The ideological contradiction and educational reform'. In L. Bash and D. Coulby (eds), *The Education Reform Act: Competition and Control.* London: Cassell.

Coulby, D. (1989c). 'The national curriculum'. In L. Bash and D. Coulby (eds), *The Education Reform Act: Competition and Control.* London: Cassell.

Cox, C. B. and Boyson, R. (1975). *Black Paper 1975: The Fight for Education.* London: J. M. Dent.

Cox, C. B. and Boyson, R. (1977). *The Black Paper 1977.* London: Temple Smith.

Cox, C. B. and Dyson, A. E. (1971). *The Black Papers on Education.* London: Davis Poynter.

Crandall, D. P. *et al.* (1986). 'Strategic planning issues that bear on the success of school improvement efforts'. *Educational Administrative Quarterly*, **22**(3), 21–53.

Cremin, L. A. (1976). *Public Education.* New York: Basic Books.

Crowson, R. L. and Boyd, W. L. (1992). *Co-ordinated Services for Children: Designing Arks for Storms and Seas Unknown. A Report Prepared for the National Centre for Education in the Inner Cities.* Temple University Centers for Research in Human Development and Education.

Crowson, R. L. and Morris, V. C. (1991). 'The superintendency and school effectiveness: an organizational hierarchy perspective'. *School Effectiveness and School Improvement*, **3**(1), 69–88.

Crump, S. J. (1992). 'National reform, touchstone and policy analysis'. Paper presented to the Annual Meeting of the American Educational Research Association. San Francisco.

Cupitt, D. (1985). *The Sea of Faith.* London: BBC Publishing Company.

Cuttance, P. (1991). 'Monitoring educational quality through performance indicators for school practice'. Paper prepared for the Annual Meeting of the AERA. Chicago.

Dale, R. (1992). 'National reform, economic critics and "new" right theory. A New Zealand perspective'. Paper presented at the Annual Meeting of the AERA. San Francisco.

Darling-Hammond, L. (1991). *Policy Uses and Indicators.* OECD International Education Indicator Project. General Assembly of the INES Project. Lugano, Switzerland.

Daveney, T. F. (1973). 'Education – a moral concept'. In G. Langford and D. J. O'Connor (eds), *New Essays in Philosophy of Education.* London: Routledge & Kegan Paul.

Davies, A. M., Holland, J. and Minkas, R. (1990). *Equal Opportunities in the New Era.* Hillcote Group Paper 2. London: Tufnell Press.

Davies, B. (1992). 'School finance in the 1990s: the pivotal role of school finance in the reform of the English educational system'. Paper presented at the Annual Meeting of the AERA, San Francisco.

Davies, B. and Ellison, L. (1992). 'Delegated school finance in the English education system: an end of radical change'. *Journal of Educational Administration*, **30**(1), 70–80.

Davies, B., Ellison, L., Osborne, A. and West-Burnham, J. (1990). *Education Management for the 1990s*. Harlow: Longmans.

De Young, A. J. (1989). 'Excellence in education: the opportunity for school superintendent to become ambitious?' In J. L. Burdin (ed.), *School Leadership: A Contemporary Reader*. Newbury Park, CA: Sage.

Deal, T. and Peterson, K. D. (1991). 'Instrumental and expressive aspects of school improvement'. Draft paper presented at the Annual Meeting of the International Congress for School Effectiveness and Improvement. Cardiff, Wales.

Dean, J. (1987). *Managing the Primary School*. London: Routledge.

Deem, R. and Brehony, K. J. (1992). 'Consumers and education professionals in the organization and administration of schools: partnership or conflict'. Paper presented at the Annual Meeting of the AERA. San Francisco.

Deer, C. (1990). 'Democracy and bureaucracy: curriculum issues'. In J. D. Chapman and J. F. Dunstan (eds), *Democracy and Bureaucracy: Tensions in Public Schooling*. London: Falmer Press.

Department of Education and Science (1990). *Developing School Management: A Report by the School Management Task Force*. London: HMSO.

Designs for Change: Staff and Consultants (1990). 'Chicago principals: changing of the guard'. *Closer Look, Research and Policy Analysis Series*, 3, March.

Dewey, J. (1907). 'The control of ideas by facts'. *Journal of Philosophy*, **4**(12), 111.

Dewey, J. (1938). *Experience and Education*. New York: Macmillan.

Dewey, J. (1966). *Democracy and Education*. New York: Free Press (originally published New York: Macmillan, 1916.).

Dickson Corbett, H. and Wilson, B. L. (1992). 'The central office role in instructional improvement'. *School Effectiveness and School Improvement*, **3**(1), 45–68.

Dickson, G. S. and Lim, S. (1991). 'The development and use of indicators of performance in educational leadership'. Paper submitted to the International Congress for School Effectiveness and Improvement. Cardiff, Wales.

Donaldson, L. (1988). *In Defence of Organization Theory: A Reply to the Critics*. Cambridge: Cambridge University Press.

Drucker, P. F. (1988). 'Why service institutions do not perform'. In C. Riches and C. Morgan (eds), *Resource Management in Education*. Philadelphia: Open University Press.

D'Souza, D. (1992). *Illiberal Education*. New York: Random House (Vintage Books).

Duhem, P. (1914). *The Aim and Structure of Physical Theory*, trans. P. P. Weiner, 1954. Princeton, NJ: Princeton University Press.

Duke, D. L. (1987). *School Leadership and Instructional Improvement*. New York: Random House.

Duttweiler, P. C. and Gottesman, B. (1992). 'Assessing associate school success'. Paper presented at the Annual Meeting of the AERA. San Francisco.

Edel, J. (1973). 'Analytic philosophy of education at the crossroads'. In J. F. Doyle (ed.), *Educational Judgments*. London: Routledge & Kegan Paul.

Education Department of South Australia (1991). *Guidelines for Internal Review of School Development*. Education Review Unit.

Education Department of South Australia (1992). *School Reviews: Information for School Communities*. Education Review Unit.

Edwards, D. and Mendus, S. (eds) (1987). *On Toleration*. Oxford: Clarendon Press.

Edwards, W. L. (1991). 'Accountability and autonomy: dual strands for the administrator.

In W. Walker, R. Farquhar and M. Hughes (eds), *Advancing Education: School Leadership in Action*. London: Falmer Press.

Eisner, E. W. (1992). 'The federal reform of schools: looking for the silver bullet'. *Phi Delta Kappan*, 722–3.

Eliot, G. (1977). *Middlemarch 1871–1872*. New York: Ed. Hornback BG.

Elliott, J., Bridges, D., Ebbutt, D., Gibson, R. and Nias, J. (eds) (1981). *School Accountability*. London: Grant McIntyre.

Elmore, R. F. (1980). 'Backward mapping: implementation research and policy decisions'. *Political Science Quarterly*, **94**(4), 601–616.

Elmore, R. F. (1993). 'Choice and markets in schooling'. Paper presented at a Special Conference of the Australian College of Education on Choice and Markets in Schooling. Canberra, ACT, August 17, 1993. (Compare with paper on same theme by I. Snook. Paper to be published in *Unicorn: Journal of the Australian College of Education*, February 1994.)

Eltis, K., Braithwaite, J., Deer, C. and Kensell, H. (1984). 'Assistant schools to develop school-focused action programmes'. In D. Hopkins and M. Wideen (eds), *Alternative Perspectives on School Improvement*, Lewes: Falmer Press.

Epstein, J. L. and Dauber, S. L. (1989). *Teacher Attitudes and Practices of Parent Involvement in Inner-city Elementary and Middle Schools*. Baltimore, MD: Centre for Research on Elementary and Middle Schools.

Eraut, M. (1991). *Indicators and Accountability at the School and Classroom Level*. OECD International Education Indicators. INES Project, General Assembly. Lugano, Switzerland.

Evers, C. W. and Walker, J. C. (1983). 'Knowledge, partitioned sets and extensionality: a refutation of the forms of knowledge thesis'. *Journal of Philosophy of Education*, **17**(2), 55–70.

Evers, C. W. (1990). 'Organizational learning and efficiency in the growth of knowledge'. In J. D. Chapman (1990), *School-Based Decision-Making and Management*. London: Falmer Press.

Evers, C. and Lakomski, G. (1991). *Knowing Educational Administration*. Oxford: Pergamon Press.

Evers, C. W. *et al.* (1992). 'Ethics and ethical theory in educative leadership: a pragmatic and holistic approach'. In P. A. Duignan and R. J. S. Macpherson (eds), *Educative Leadership*. London: Falmer Press.

Evertson, C. M. and Murphy, J. (1992). 'Respondees' comments: responses from the viewpoint of administration and school organization. AERA symposium: 'Restructuring schools for learning: extending the dialogue'. Annual Meeting of the AERA. San Francisco.

Faber, C. F. (1990). *Local Control of School: Is Local Governance a Viable Option?* Charleston, NV: Appalachia Education Laboratory.

Fasano, C. (1991). *Knowledge, Ignorance and Epistemic Utility: Issues in Constructing and Organizing Indicator Systems*. OECD International Education Indicators. General Assembly of the INES Project. Lugano, Switzerland.

Fidler, B. (1989). 'Strategic management in schools'. In B. Fidler and G. Bowles (eds), *Effective Management of Schools*. Harlow: Longman.

Fidler, B. and Bowles, G. (eds) (1989). *Effective Local Management of Schools*. Harlow: Longman.

Fielding, M. (1990). 'Democratic schools for the 1990s.' *NUT Education Review*, **4**(1), 46–50.

Finn, C. Jr and Clements, S. K. (1992). 'Chicago public schools: reform or revolution?' *Chicago Watch*, 34–40.

First, P. (1992). *Educational Policy for School Administrators*. Needham Heights, MA: Allyn & Bacon.

Flude, M. and Hammer, M. (1990). *The Education Reform Act 1988: Its Origins and Implications*. Lewes: Falmer Press.

Fowler, W. J. Jr (1992). 'What do we know about school size? What should we know?' Paper presented at the Annual Meeting of the AERA. San Francisco.

Fromm, E. (1960). *Fear of Freedom*. London: Routledge & Kegan Paul. (First published as *Escape from Freedom*, 1941.)

Fullan, M. G. (1991). *New Meanings of Educational Change*. New York: Teachers College Press.

Fullan, M. G. (1984), 'The principal as an agent of knowledge utilization for school improvement.' In D. Hopkins and M. Wideen (eds), *Alternative Perspectives on School Improvement*. Lewes: Falmer Press.

Fullan, M. G. (1988). *What's Worth Fighting For in the Principalship: Strategies for Taking Charge in the Elementary School Principalship*. Toronto: Ontario Public Schools Teachers Federation.

Fuller, A. (1990). 'Compacts: the emerging issues'. *Eduction and Training*, **32**(4), 13–16.

Gallie, W. B. (1956). 'Essentially contested concepts'. *Proceedings of the Aristotelian Society*, 56. (Compare also with Chapter 8 of his *Philosophy and the Historical Understanding*. London: Chatto & Windus, 1964).

Gallie, W. B. (1964). *Philosophy and the Historical Understanding*. London: Chatto & Windus.

Gamoran, A. (1990). 'Instructional practices that affect equity'. In H. R. Baptiste, Jr *et al.* *Leadership, Equity and School Effectiveness*. Newbury Park, CA: Sage.

Gardner, H. (1987). *The Mind's New Science: A History of the Cognitive Revolution*. New York: Basic Books.

Gilbert, C. (ed) (1990). *Local Management of Schools*. London: Kogan Page.

Giroux, H. A. (1988). *Teachers as Intellectuals: Towards a Critical Pedagogy of Learning*. New York. Deigh & Garvey.

Glaser, W. (1990). *Quality School: Managing Students without Coercion*. New York: Harper Perennial.

Glickman, C. D. *et al.* (1992). 'Facilitation of internal change: the league of professional schools'. Paper presented at the Annual Meeting of the AERA. San Francisco.

Goertz, M. E. (1990). 'Education politics for the new century: introduction and overview'. In D. E. Mitchell and M. E. Goertz (eds), *Education Politics for the New Century: The Twentieth Anniversary Yearbook of the Politics of Education Association*. London: Falmer Press.

Goldman, P. and Dunlap, D. (1990). 'Reform, restructuring, site-based management and the new face of power in schools'. Paper presented at the Annual Meeting of the University Council for Educational Administration. Pittsburgh.

Goldring, E. B. (1986). 'The school community: its effects on principals' perceptions of parents'. *Educational Administration Quarterly*, **22**(2), 115–32.

Goldring, E. B. (1988). 'Evaluating principals using parental reactions: an incentive for principal–parent engagement?' *Administrator's Notebook*, **32**(3), University of Chicago.

Goldring, E. B. (1990). 'Elementary school principals as boundary spanners: their engagement with parents'. *Journal of Educational Administration*, **28**(1), 53–62.

Goldring, E. B. (1991). 'Parents' motives for choosing a privatized public school system: an Israeli example'. *Educational Policy*, **5**(4), December, 412–26.

Goldring, E. D. (1991). 'Parents: participants in an organizational framework'. *International Journal of Educational Research*, **15**, 215–28.

Goldring, E. B. (1992). 'System-wide diversity in Israel: principals as transformational and environmental leaders'. *Journal of Educational Administration*, **30**(3), 49–62.

Goldring, E. B. (1990). 'The district context and principals' sentiments towards parents'. *Urban Education*, **24**(4), 391–403.

Goldring, E. B. and Hallinger, P. (1992). 'District control contexts and school organizational processes'. Paper presented at the Annual Meeting of the AERA. San Francisco.

Goodlad, J. I. (1984). *A Place Called School: Prospects for the Future*. New York: McGraw-Hill.

Goodlad, J. I. (1992). 'National goals/national testing: the moral dimensions'. Paper presented at the Annual Meeting of the AERA. San Francisco.

Gordon, T. (1986). *Democracy in One School? Progressive Education and Restructuring*. Barcombe: Falmer Press.

Graham, K. (1976). 'Democracy, paradox and the real world'. *Proceedings of the Aristotelian Society*, **76**, 227–45.

Greenfield, T. B. and Ribbins, P. (1993). *Greenfield on Educational Administration: Towards a More Humane Science*. London: Routledge.

Griesemer, L. J. and Butler, C. (1985). 'The national reports on education: a comparative analysis'. In B. Gross and R. Gross (eds) *The Great School Debate*. New York: Simon & Schuster.

Gross, B. and Gross, R. (1985). *The Great School Debate: Which Way for American Education?* New York: Simon & Schuster.

Guthrie, J. W. (1991). 'National education goals: can we afford them?' Paper presented at the Nova University Summer Institute. Fort Lauderdale, FL.

Guttman, A. (1987). *Democratic Education*. Princeton, NJ: Princeton University Press.

Habermas, J. (1972). *Knowledge and Human Interests*. London: Heinemann.

Hall, V. and Wallace, M. (1992). 'Shared leadership through teamwork: a cultural and political perspective'. Paper presented at the Annual Meeting of the AERA. San Francisco.

Hallinger, P. and McCary, C. E. (1990). 'Developing the strategic thinking of instructional leaders'. *Elementary School Journal*, **91**(2), 89–108.

Hallinger, P. *et al.* (1992). 'Conceptualizing school restructuring: principals' and teachers' perceptions'. Paper presented at the Annual Meeting of the AERA. San Francisco.

Hamlyn, D. W. (1971). *The Theory of Knowledge*. London: Macmillan.

Handy, C. and Aitken, R. (1986). *Understanding Schools as Organizations*. Harmondsworth: Penguin.

Hanson, E. M. (1992). 'Educational marketing and public schools: policies, practices and problems'. *Educational Policy*, **6**(1), 19–34.

Hare, R. M. (1952). *The Language of Morals*. London: Oxford University Press.

Hare, R. M. (1964). *The Language of Morals*, 2nd edn. Oxford: Clarendon Press.

Hare, R. M. (1981). *Moral Thinking: Its Levels, Methods and Point*. Oxford: Clarendon Press.

Hargreaves, D. H. (1990). 'Accountability and school improvement in the work of LEA inspectors: the rhetoric and beyond'. *Journal of Education Policy*, **5**(3), 230–7.

Harman, G. (1990). 'Democracy, bureaucracy and the politics of education'. In J. D. Chapman and J. F. Dunstan (eds), *Democracy and Bureaucracy: Tensions in Public Schooling*, London: Falmer Press.

Harman, G., Beare, H. and Berkeley, G. F. (1991). *Restructuring School Management*, Canberra, ACT: Australian College of Education.

Harrison, R. (1970). 'No paradox in democracy'. *Political Studies*, **18**(4), 515–17.

Harrold, R. (1990). 'Financial issues in the tension between democracy and bureaucracy'.

In J. D. Chapman and J. F. Dunstan (eds), *Democracy and Bureaucracy: Tensions in Public Schooling*. London: Falmer Press.

Hattie, J. (1990). 'The quality of education and accountability'. In J. Chapman (ed.), *School-Based Decision-Making and Management*. London: Falmer Press.

Hattie, J. (1992). 'Measuring the effects of schooling'. *Australian Journal of Education*, **36**(1), 5–13.

Hawley, W. D. (1984). *Good Schools: What Research Says About Improving Student Achievement*. Peabody College, Vanderbilt University, Education Analysis Center for Quality and Equality.

Henderson, A. T., Marburger, C. L. and Ooms, T. (1986). *Beyond the Bake Sale: An Educator's Guide to Working with Parents*. Columbia: The National Committee for Citizens in Education.

Hess, G. A. Jr (1992). 'Popular coverage of policy relevant research'. Paper presented at the Annual Meeting of the AERA. San Francisco.

Highett, N. (1992). 'School development: an overview of the Queensland process'. *Unicorn, Journal of the Australian College of Education*, **18**(2), 17–24.

Hill, B. V. (1989). 'Shall we wind down state schools?' *Spectrum*, **21**(2), 131–43.

Hill, D. (1990). *Something Old, Something New, Something Borrowed, Something Blue: Schooling, Teacher Education and the Radical Right in Britain and the USA*. Hillcote Group Paper 3. London: Tufnell Press.

Hill, L. (1992). *Becoming a Manager: Mastery of a New Identity*. Boston, MA: Harvard University Business School Press.

Hindess, E. F. (1972). 'Forms of knowledge'. *Proceedings of the Philosophy of Education Society of Great Britain*, **6**(2), 164–75.

Hirst, P. H. (1973). *Knowledge and the Curriculum*. London: Routledge & Kegan Paul.

Hodgkinson, C. (1991). *Educational Leadership – The Moral Art*. Albany, NY: State University of New York Press.

Holmes, B. (1985). 'Policy formulation, adoption and implementation in democratic society', in J. Lavolo and M. McLean (eds), *The Control of Education*. London: Heinemann.

Holmes, M. and Wynne, E. A. (1989). *Making the School an Effective Community: Belief, Practice and Theory in School Administration*. New York: Falmer Press.

Holt, M. (1986). *Judgement, Planning and Educational Change*. London: Harper.

Holt, M. (1990). 'Case study: managing curriculum change in a comprehensive school: conflict, compromise and deliberation'. *Journal of Curriculum Studies*, **22**(2), 137–148.

Honderich, T. (1974). 'A difficulty with democracy'. *Philosophy and Public Affairs*, **3**(2), 221–6.

Hopkins, D. (1991). 'Process indicators for school improvement'. OECD International Education Indicators Project. General Assembly of the INES Project. Lugano, Switzerland.

Hopkins, D. and Wideen, M. (1984). *Alternative Perspectives on School Improvement*. Lewes: Falmer Press.

Horton, J. P. and Mendus, S. (eds) (1985). *Aspects of Toleration: Philosophical Studies*. London and New York: Methuen.

Hoy, W. K. and Ferguson, J. (1989). 'A theoretical framework and explanation of organizational effectiveness of schools'. In J. L. Burdin (ed.), *School Leadership: A Contemporary Reader*. Newbury Park, CA.: Sage.

Hoy, W. K. and Miskel, C. G. (1978). *Educational Administration: Theory, Research and Practice*. New York: Random House.

Hoy, W. K., Tarter, C. J. and Kottkamp, R. B. (1991). *Open Schools/Healthy Schools: Measuring Organizational Climate*. Newbury Park, CA: Sage.

Hoyle, E. (1986). *The Politics of School Management*. London: Hodder & Stoughton.

Hunt, F. J. (1987). *The Incorporation of Education*. London: Routledge & Kegan Paul.

Hurst, P. (1985). 'Decentralization: panacea or red herring?' In J. Lavolo and M. McLean (eds), *The Control of Education*. London: Heinemann.

Husen, T. (1989). 'Schools for the 1990s'. *Scandinavian Journal of Educational Research*, **33**(1), 3–13.

Illich, I. (1973). *De-schooling Society*. Harmondsworth: Penguin.

Isaac, J. (1981). 'Amalgamation of schools – effects on quality of work'. *Educational Administration*, **9**(2), 92–8.

Ivic, I. (1991). *Theories of Mental Development and the Problem of Education Outcomes*. OECD International Education Indicators Project. General Assembly of the INES Project. Lugano, Switzerland.

Jacullo-Noto, J. (1986). 'Interactive research and development – partners in craft'. In A. Lieberman (ed.), *Rethinking School Improvement*. New York: Teachers College Press.

Jones, A. (1985). 'Studying school effectiveness: a postscript'. In D. Reynolds (ed.), *Studying School Effectiveness*. Barcombe: Falmer Press.

Jones, K. (1989). *Right Turn: The Conservative Revolution in Education*. London: Hutchinson.

Joyce, B. R., Hersh, R. H. and McKibbin, M. (eds) (1983). *The Structure of School Improvement*. New York: Longman.

Kirk, G. S. (1954). *Heraclitus: The Cosmic Fragments*. Cambridge: Cambridge University Press.

Kirst, M. W. (1990). *Accountability: Implications for State and Local Policy-Makers*. Policy Perspective Series. Washington, DC: Office of Educational Research and Improvement.

Klein, L. and Eason, K. (1991). *Putting Social Science to Work: The Ground between Theory and Use Explored through Case Studies in Organizations*. Cambridge: Cambridge University Press.

Kleinig, J. (1973). 'R. S. Peters' use of transcendental arguments'. *Proceedings of the Philosophy of Education Society of Great Britain* (PESGB), **7**, July.

Knight, J., Lingard, R. and Porter, P. (1991). 'Reforming the education industry through award restructuring and the new federation'. *Unicorn: Journal of the Australian College of Education*, **17**(3), 133–8.

Knight, T. (1985). 'An apprenticeship in democracy'. *Australian Teacher*, **11**, 5–7.

Koerner, S. (1967). 'The impossibility of transcendental deductions'. *The Monist*, **51**(3).

Koerner, S. (1973). 'Rational Choice'. *Proceedings of the Aristotelian Society*, **47** (Supplementary Volume).

Kogan, M. (ed.) (1984). *School Governing Bodies*. London: Heinemann.

Koppich, J. E., Brown, P. and Amsler, M. (1990). *Redefining Teacher Work Roles: Prospects and Possibilities*. Policy Briefs, Number 13. San Francisco: Far West Laboratory for Educational Research and Development.

Kovesi, J. (1967). *Moral Notions*. London: Routledge & Kegan Paul.

Kuhn, T. S. (1970). *The Structure of Scientific Revolutions* (2nd edn, enlarged). Chicago: University of Chicago Press.

Kuhn, T. S. (1973). *The Structure of Scientific Revolutions*. Chicago: University of Chicago Press.

Kyriacou, C. (1987). 'Teacher stress and burnout: an international review'. In C. Riches, and C. Morgan (eds), *Resource Management in Education*. Philadelphia: Open University Press.

Labov, W. (1972). *Language in the Inner City: Studies in the Black English Vernacular*. Philadelphia: University of Pennsylvania Press.

Lakatos, I. (1976). 'Falsification and the methodology of scientific research programs'. In

I. Lakatos and A. W. Musgrave (eds), *Criticism and the Growth of Knowledge*. Cambridge: Cambridge University Press.

Lavolo, J. and McLean, M. (eds) (1985). *The Control of Education*. London: Heinemann.

Lawn, M. (1990). 'From responsibility to competency: a new context for curriculum studies in England and Wales'. *Journal of Curriculum Studies*, **22**(4), 388–92.

Lawton, D. and Chitty, C. (1988). *The National Curriculum*. London: Institute of Education.

Le Guen, M. (1991). *Measuring to Succeed: National Evaluation in France*. OECD International Education Indicators Project. General Assembly of the INES Project. Lugano, Switzerland.

Leedy, P. (1980). *Practical Research: Planning and Design*. New York: Macmillan.

Levin, H. (1991). 'The economics of educational choice'. *Economics of Education Review*, **10**(2), 137–58.

Lewis, J. H. and Taylor, D. G. (1990). *Options without Knowledge: Implementing Open Enrolment under the 1988 Chicago School Reform Act*. Chicago Urban League Department of Research and Planning.

Lieberman, A. (ed.) (1986). *Rethinking School Improvement: Research, Craft and Concept*. New York: Teachers College Press.

Lieberman, M. (1989). *Privatization and Public Choice*. New York: St Martins Press.

Lightfoot, S. L. (1983). *The Good High School: Portrait of Character and Culture*. New York: Basic Books.

Lincoln, A. (1907). *Speeches and Letters*. London: Dent.

Lipsky, M. (1980). *Street-Level Bureaucracy: The Dilemmas of the Individual in Public Services*. New York: Sage.

Lycan, W. G. (1988). *Judgement and Justification*. Cambridge: Cambridge University Press.

Lyons, R. (1985). 'Decentralized educational planning: is it a contradiction?' In J. Lavolo and M. McLean (eds), *The Control of Education*. London: Heinemann.

MacIntyre, A. (1972). *Against the Self-Images of the Age*. London: Duckworth. (Part 2, Chapters 13, 15 and 16, 'Hume on "is" and "ought" '; ' "Ought" '; 'Some More about "Ought" '.)

Marsden, C. (1989). 'Why business should work with education'. *British Journal of Education and Work*, **2**(3), 79–89.

Marsh, C. (1988). *Spotlight on School Improvement*. Sydney: Allen & Unwin.

Marsh, C. J. (1990). 'Managing for total school improvement'. In J. Chapman (ed.), *School-Based Decision-Making and Management*. London: Falmer Press.

Marshall, J. and Peters, M. (1990). 'The induction of "new right" thinking into education: an example from New Zealand'. *Journal of Education Policy*, **5**(2), 143–56.

Martin, J. A. and McGee, M. L. (1990). *Quality Circle/Site-Based Management Implementation in Public School Districts*. US Department of Education, Office of Educational Research and Improvement (OERI).

McCarthy, M. M. and Webb, L. D. (1990). 'Equity and excellence in educational leadership: a necessary nexus'. In H. P. Baptiste, Jr *et al.* (eds), *Leadership, Equity and School Effectiveness*. Newbury Park, CA: Sage.

McDonnell, L. M. and Elmore, R. F. (1987). 'Getting the job done: alternative policy instruments'. *Educational Evaluation and Policy Analysis*, **9**(2), 133–52.

McGregor Burns, J. (1978). *Leadership*. New York: Harper & Row.

McGuire, K. (1990). 'Business involvement in the 1990s'. In D. E. Mitchell and M. E. Goertz (eds), *Education Politics for a New Century*. London: Falmer Press.

McHenry, E. (1990). *What Research Says about School Reform, School Management and Teacher Involvement*. US Department of Education, Office of Educational Research and Improvement (OERI).

McPherson, A. (1989). 'Social and political aspects of the devalued management of Scottish secondary schools'. *Scottish Educational Review*, **21**(2), 87–100.

Mealyea, R. J. (1990). 'Teaching vocationalism in secondary technical schools in Victoria, Australia: the winds of change'. *Journal of Industrial Teacher Education*, **27**(4), 5–17.

Mendus, S. (ed.) (1988). *Justifying Toleration: Conceptual and Historical Perspectives*. Cambridge: Cambridge University Press.

Mendus, S. (1989). *Toleration and the Limits of Liberalism*. Atlantic Highlands, NJ: Humanities Press International.

Metz, M. H. (1990). 'Real school: a universal drama mid desperate experiences'. In D. E. Mitchell and M. E. Goertz (eds), *Education Politics for the New Century*. London: Falmer Press.

Miles, M. B. (1992). 'Forty-six years of change in schools: some personal reflections'. Invited address to Decision A (Administration), AERA Meeting. San Francisco.

Millman, J. and Darling-Hammond, L. (1990). *The New Handbook of Teacher Evaluation: Assessing Elementary and Secondary School Teachers*. Newbury Park, CA: Sage.

Mischler, E. G. (1986). *Research Interviewing: Context and Narrative*. Cambridge, MA: Harvard University Press.

Mitchell, D. E. (1990). 'Education politics for the new century: past issues and future directions'. In D. E. Mitchell and M. E. Goertz (eds), *Education Politics for a New Century*. London: Falmer Press.

Mitchell, D. E. and Goertz, M. E. (eds) (1990). *Education Politics for the New Century: The Twentieth Anniversary Yearbook of the Politics of Education Association*. London: Falmer Press.

Mitchell, G. (1987). 'Community education and school: a commentary'. In G. Allen *et al.* (eds), *Community Education: An Agenda for Educational Reform*. Milton Keynes: Open University Press.

Moll, N. P. and Kaiser, F. (1991). *Interpretation and Analysis of Cost per Pupil Indicators in (International) Comparisons of Education Systems*. OECD International Education Indicators Project. General Assembly of the INES Project. Lugano, Switzerland.

Moore Johnson, S (1990). *Teachers at Work: Achieving Success in Our Schools*. New York: Basic Books.

Moore, D. R. (1989). 'Voice and choice in Chicago: the aim of Chicago school reform'. *Closer Look: Research and Policy Analysis Series*, No. 1, March.

Morgan, G. (1988). 'Sharing the vision'. In C. Riches and C. Morgan (eds), *Management in Education*. Philadelphia: Open University Press.

Mulkeen, T. A. and Cooper, B. S. (1992). 'Implications of preparing school administrations for knowledge work organizations: a case study'. *Journal of Educational Administration*, **30**(1), 17–25.

Murphy, J. (1990). *Education Reform in the 1980s: Explaining Some Surprising Success*. Occasional Paper No. 5. National Center for Educational Leadership.

Murphy, J. (1990). *Preparing School Administrators for the Twenty-first Century: The Reform Agenda*. Occasional Paper No. 2. National Center for Educational Leadership.

Murphy, J. (1990). *Restructuring America's Schools: Policy Issues*. Appalachia Educational Laboratory, Charleston, WV and Nashville, TN: Policy and Planning Center and National Center for Educational Leadership.

Murphy, J. (1991). *The Effects of the Educational Reform Movement on Departments of Educational Leadership*. Occasional Paper No. 10. National Centre for Educational Leadership.

Murphy, J. (1992). 'School effectiveness and school restructuring: contributions to educational improvement'. Plenary address for the Annual Meeting of the International

Congress for School Effectiveness and School Improvement. Victoria, British Columbia.

Murphy, J. *et al.* (1991). 'Restructuring schools: fourteen elementary and secondary teachers' perspectives on reform'. *Elementary School Journal*, **92**(2), 135–48.

Mutchler, S. E. and Duttweiller, P. C. (1990). 'Implementing shared decision-making in school-based management: barriers to changing traditional behavior'. Paper presented at the Annual Meeting of the American Educational Research Association. Boston, MA.

Myers, C. and Bounds, B. (1991). 'Evaluation of the class categorical service delivery model: is the regular education initiative working?' Paper presented at the 69th Annual Conference of the Council for Exceptional Children. Atlanta, GA.

National Coalition of Advocates for Students (1991). *The Good Common School: Making the Vision Work for All Children*. Boston: Easey Press.

Neill, A. S. (1968). *Summerhill*. Harmondsworth: Penguin.

Neurath, O. (1932). 'Protokollsätze'. *Erkenntnis*, **3**, 204–14.

Newman, J. H. (1976). *The Idea of a University Defined and Illustrated*. Oxford: Clarendon. (First published 1852.)

Nias, J. (1980). 'Leadership styles and job-satisfaction in primary schools'. In T. Bush, *et al.* (eds), *Approaches to School Management*. London: Harper & Row.

Nicholson, R. (1989). *School Management: The Role of the Secondary Headteacher*. London: Kogan Page.

North, R. (1990). 'Computers in school management'. In E. Cave and C. Wilkinson (eds), *Local Management of Schools: Some Practical Issues*. London: Routledge.

Nucci, L. P. and Smylie, M. A. (1991). 'University–community partnerships: addressing problems of children and youth through institutional collaboration'. *Metropolitan Universities*, **2**(1), 83–91.

OECD (1988). *Decentralization and School Improvement*. Paris: OECD.

Orea Report (1990). *Toward School-Based Management/Shared Decision-Making: A Research Perspective*. Brooklyn, NY: New York City Board of Education.

Orfield, G. and Peskin, L. (1990). 'Metropolitan high schools: income, race inequality'. In D. E. Mitchell and M. E. Goertz (eds), *Education Politics for the New Century*. London: Falmer Press.

Osborne, D. and Gaebler, T. (1992). *Reinventing Government: How the Entrepreneurial Spirit Is Transforming the Public Sector*. Reading. MA: Addison-Wesley.

Ouston, J. and Maugham, B. (1985). 'Issues in the assessment of school outcomes'. In D. Reynolds (ed.), *Studying School Effectiveness*. Barcombe: Falmer Press.

Owens, R. G. (1991). *Organizational Behaviour in Education*. London: Prentice-Hall.

Parkay, F. W. and Gall, G. (1992). *Becoming a Principal: The Challenges of Beginning Leadership*. Needham Heights, MA: Allyn & Bacon.

Parker, F. (1988). 'Behind school reform, USA–England. Economics and equity'. *CORE*, **12**(3), 1–19.

Parry, G. (1990). 'The legal context'. In E. Cave and C. Wilkinson (eds), *Local Management of Schools: Some Practical Issues*. London: Routledge.

Passmore, J. P. (1967). 'On teaching to be critical'. In R. S. Peters (ed.) (1967). *The Concept of Education*. London: Routledge & Kegan Paul.

Peirce, C. S. (1955). *The Philosophical Writings of Peirce*, ed. J. Buchler. New York: Dover Publications.

Peirce, C. S. (1982–86). *Writings of Charles S. Peirce: A Chronological Edition*, ed. M. H. Fish. Bloomington: Indiana University Press.

Pelikan, J. (1992). *The Idea of a University: A Re-examination*. New Haven, CN: Yale University Press.

Pennock, R. (1974). 'Democracy is *not* paradoxical'. *Political Theory*, **2**(1), 88–93.

Peters, R. S. (1966). *Ethics and Education*. London: Allen & Unwin.

Phillips, D. C. (1971). 'The distinguishing features of forms of knowledge'. *Educational Philosophy and Theory*, **3**(2), 27–35.

Phillips, D. Z. (1973). 'Democratization: some themes in unexamined talk'. *British Journal of Educational Studies*, **21**(2), 133–48.

Piele, P. K. (1990). 'The politics of technology utilization'. In D. E. Mitchell and M. E. Goertz (eds), *Education Politics for a New Century*. London: Falmer Press.

Pirsig, R. M. (1974). *Zen and the Art of Motorcycle Maintenance*. New York: Morrow.

Plato (1955). *The Republic*, trans. H. D. P. Lee. Harmondsworth: Penguin.

Popper, K. R. (1943). *The Open Society and Its Enemies*. (Volume 1: *Plato*; Volume 2: *Hegel and Marx*). London: Routledge & Kegan Paul.

Popper, K. R. (1949). *Logic of Scientific Discovery*. London: Hutchinson.

Popper, K. R. (1957). *The Poverty of Historicism*. London: Routledge & Kegan Paul. 2nd edn (1960).

Popper, K. R. (1972). *Objective Knowledge*. Oxford: Clarendon Press.

Powell, A., Farrar, E. and Cohen, D. (1985). *The Shopping Mall High School: Winners and Losers in the Educational Market Place*. Boston: Houghton Mifflin.

Powell, J. P. (1970). 'On justifying a broad educational curriculum'. *Educational Philosophy and Theory*, **2**(1), March.

Pratt, K. J. and Stemming, R. (1989). *Managing Staff Appraisal in Schools*. London: Van Nostrand Reinhold.

Price, H. B. (1990). 'The bottom line for school reform'. *Phi Delta Kappan*. Nov, 242–4.

Quine, W. V. O. (1951). 'Two dogmas of empiricism'. *Philosophical Review*, **60**, 20–43.

Quine, W. V. O. (1953). *From a Logical Point of View*, Cambridge, MA: Harvard University Press.

Quine, W. V. (1974). *The Roots of Reference*. La Salle, IL: Open Court.

Quine, W. V. and Ullian, J. S. (1970). *The Web of Belief*. New York: Random House.

Radnor, H. (1991). 'Complexities and compromises: the new era at Parkview School'. *Urban Review*, **23**(2), 59–82.

Ramsay, W. and Clark, E. (1990). *New Ideas for Effective School Improvement: Vision, Social Capital, Evaluation*. London: Falmer Press.

Raths, J. (1989). 'Reformers' visions and tomorrow's teachers'. *Childhood Education: Annual Theme*, 263–7.

Rawls, J. (1972). *A Theory of Justice*. Oxford: Oxford University Press.

Ray, C. A. and Mickelson, R. A. (1990). 'Business leaders and the politics of school reform'. In D. E. Mitchell and M. E. Goertz (eds), *Education Politics for a New Century*. London: Falmer Press.

Reyes, P. (ed.) (1990). *Teachers and Their Workplace: Commitment, Performance and Productivity*. London: Sage.

Reynolds, D. (ed.) (1985). *Studying School Effectiveness*. Barcombe: Falmer Press.

Reynolds, D. (1990). *School Effectiveness and School Improvement in the 1990s*. A Keynote Address. International Congress of Effective Schools, Jerusalem.

Riches, C. and Morgan, C. (eds) (1989). *Human Resource Management in Education*. Philadelphia: Open University Press.

Rizvi, F. (1990). 'Horizontal accountability'. In J. Chapman (ed.), *School-Based Decision-Making and Management*. London: Falmer Press.

Rossman, G. B., Corbett, H. D. and Firestone, W. A. (1988). *Change and Effectiveness in Schools: A Cultural Perspective*. Albany: State University of New York Press.

Rumberger, R. W. (1991). *Labour Market Outcomes as Indicators of Educational Perform-*

ance. OECD International Education Indicators Project. General Assembly of the INES Project. Lugano, Switzerland.

Russell, P. and Evans, R. (1992). *The Creative Manager: Finding Inner Vision and Wisdom in Uncertain Times*. San Francisco: Jossey-Bass.

Rust, V. D. and Blakemore, K. (1990). 'Educational reform in Norway and in England and Wales: a corporatist interpretation'. *Comparative Education Review*, **34**(4), 500–22.

Ryle, G. (1949). *The Concept of Mind*. London: Hutchinson.

Sadler, R. (1992). 'Scaled school assessments: the effect of measurement errors in the scaling test'. *Australian Journal of Education*, **36**(1), 30–7.

Sallis, J. (1988). *Schools, Parents and Governors: A New Approach to Accountability*. London: Routledge.

Sarros, J. C. and Sarros, A. M. (1992). 'Social support and teacher burnout'. *Journal of Educational Administration*, **30**(1), 55–69.

Sayer, J. (1989). *Managing Schools*. London: Hodder & Stoughton.

Scheffler, I. (1960). *The Language of Education*. Springfield, IL: Charles C. Thomas.

Schiller, M. (1969). 'On the logic of being a democrat'. *Philosophy*, **44**, 46–56.

Schon, D. A. (1987). *Educating the Reflective Practitioner*. San Francisco: Jossey-Bass.

Schon, D. A. (1991). *The Reflective Turn: Case Studies in and on Educational Practice*. New York: Teachers College Press.

Schumpeter, J. (1967). 'Two concepts of democracy'. In A. Quinton (ed.), *Political Philosophy*. Oxford: Oxford University Press.

Scottish Education Office (1991). *The Effectiveness of Schooling and of Educational Resource Management*. Report to the OECD. Paris: OECD.

Senge, P. (1990). *The Fifth Discipline: The Art and Practice of the Learning Organization*. New York: Doubleday.

Shor, I. (1986). *Culture Wars: School and Society in the Conservative Restoration 1969–84*. London: Routledge & Kegan Paul.

Simon, B. (1988). *Bending the Rules: The Baker 'Reform' of Education*. London: Lawrence & Wishart.

Simon, H. (1983). *Reason in Human Affairs*. Stanford, CA: Stanford University Press.

Simons, H. (1984). 'Ethical principles in school self-evaluation'. In J. Bell *et al.* (eds), *Conducting Small-Scale Investigations in Educational Management*. London: Harper & Row.

Sizemore, B. A. (1990). 'Equity and the educational practitioner: a leadership model'. In H. P. Baptiste, Jr *et al.* (eds), *Leadership, Equity and School Effectiveness*. Newbury Park, CA: Sage.

Sizer, T. (1985). *Horace's Compromise: The Dilemma of the American High School*. Boston: Houghton Mifflin.

Skilbeck, M. (1990). *Curriculum Reform: An Overview of Trends*. Washington: OECD Publications and Information Centre.

Slater, R. O. and Tashakkori, A. (1991). *The American School Teacher: Agent of Change or Keeper of Tradition?* Department of Administrative and Foundational Services, College of Education, Louisiana State University.

Smith, R. and Macindoe, M. (1991). 'Education and interactive multimedia technologies: the remote area teacher education project (RATEP)'. *Unicorn, Journal of the Australian College of Education*, **17**(3), August, 139–45.

Smylie, M. A. and Brownlee-Conyers, J. (1992). 'Teacher leaders and their principals: exploring the development of new working relationships'. *Educational Administration Quarterly*, **28**(2), May, 150–84.

Snook, I. A. (ed.) (1972). *Concepts of Indoctrination: Philosophical Essays*. London: Routledge & Kegan Paul.

Spencer, H. (1966). 'What knowledge is of most worth?' in Part I of his *Essays on Education and Kindred Subjects*. London: J. M. Dent.

Stallings, J. A. and McCarthy, J. (1990). 'Teacher effectiveness research and equity issues'. In H. R. Baptiste, Jr *et al.* (eds), *Leadership, Equity and School Effectiveness*. Newbury Park, CA: Sage.

Sternberg, R. and Kolligian Jr, J. (1990). *Competence Considered*. New Haven, CT: Yale University Press.

Stoll, L. and Fink, D. (1992). 'Effecting school change: the Halton approach'. *School Effectiveness and School Improvement*, **3**(1), 19–41.

Teddlie, C. and Stringfield, S. (1992). 'Case histories from a longitudinal study of school effects'. Paper presented at the Annual Meeting of the AERA. San Francisco.

Tomlinson, S. (1991). *Teachers and Parents: Education and Training Paper No. 7*. London: Institute for Public Policy Research.

Troman, G. (1989). 'Testing tensions: the politics of educational assessment'. *British Educational Research Journal*, **15**(3), 279–95.

Ubben, G. and Hughes, L. (1992). *The Principal: Creating Leadership for Effective Schools*. Needham Heights, MA: Allyn & Bacon.

Van Der Vegt, R. and Knip, H. (1990). 'Implementing mandated change: the school as change contractor'. *Curriculum Inquiry*, **20**(2), 183–203.

Van Der Vegt, R. and Vandenberghe, R. (1992). 'Schools implementing a central reform policy: findings from two national educational contexts'. Symposium paper presented at the Annual Meeting of the AERA. San Francisco.

Vickery, R., Williams, I. and Stanley, G. (1993). *Review of Education and Training*. Perth: Western Australia Ministry of Education.

Walker de Felix, J. (1990). 'Introduction: research on equity in learning environments'. In H. R. Baptiste, Jr *et al.* (eds), *Leadership, Equity and School Effectiveness*. Newbury Park: Sage.

Walker, W., Farquhar, R. and Hughes, M. (eds) (1991), *Advancing Education: School Leadership in Action*. London: Falmer Press.

Walker, W. G. (1989). 'Leadership in an age of ambiguity and risk'. *Journal of Educational Administration*, **27**(1), 7–18.

Warnock, M. (1978). *Schools of Thought*. London: Faber & Faber.

Watt, A. J. (1975). 'Transcendental arguments and moral principles'. *Philosophical Quarterly*, **25**, 40–57.

Weiler, H. N. (1990). 'Comparative perspectives on educational decentralization: an exercise in contradiction'. *Educational Evaluation and Policy Analysis*, **12**(4), 433–48.

Weisbord, M. R. (1991). *Productive Workplaces: Organizing and Managing for Dignity, Meaning and Community*. San Francisco, CA: Jossey-Bass.

Weiss, C. H. (1991). *Trouble in Paradise: Teacher Conflicts in Shared Decision Making*. Occasional Paper No. 8. National Center for Educational Leadership, Harvard Graduate School of Education.

White, J. P. (1973). *Towards a Compulsory Curriculum*. London: Routledge & Kegan Paul.

White, J. P. (1982). *The Aims of Education Re-stated*. London: Routledge & Kegan Paul.

White, P. (1989). 'An overview of school-based management: what does the research say?' *NASSP Bulletin*, December, 1–7.

White, P. A. (1983). *Beyond Domination*. London: Routledge & Kegan Paul.

Whitty, G. and Edwards, T. (1992). 'School choice policies in Britain and the USA: their origins and significance'. Paper presented at the Annual Meeting of AERA. San Francisco.

Wideen, M. F. and Hopkins, D. (1989). 'School-based review: stressing the developmental side of accreditation'. *Education Canada*. Winter, 16–22.

Wilden, A. (1980). *System and Structure*. London: Tavistock Publications.

Wilson, B. G. (1993). *Committee for Quality Assurance in Higher Education: Guidelines for the Preparation of Institutional Portfolios*. Canberra: Department of Employment, Education and Training (Higher Education Division).

Winch, P. G. (1958). *The Idea of a Social Science*. London: Routledge & Kegan Paul.

Wirt, F. M. (1991). 'Role change in Britain's chief education officer.' Paper presented at the Annual Meeting of the AERA. Chicago.

Wittgenstein, L. (1922). *Tractatus Logico-Philosophicus*, trans. C. K. Ogden, London: Routledge & Kegan Paul.

Wittgenstein, L. (1953). *Philosophical Investigations*, trans. G. E. M. Anscombe, Oxford: Blackwell.

Wittgenstein, L. (1958). *The Blue and Brown Books*. (p. 87; cf. pp. 17, 20, 125) Oxford: Blackwell.

Wollheim, R. A. (1972). 'A paradox in the theory of democracy'. In P. Laslett, W. C. Runciman and Q. Skinner (eds), *Philosophy, Politics and Society: A Collection*, 4th series. Oxford: Blackwell.

Woods, P. (1986). *Inside Schools: Ethnography in Educational Research*, London: Routledge & Kegan Paul.

Wragg, E. C. (1989). 'The teaching profession of the future – nineteenth or twenty-first century model?' *Education Today*, **39**(1), 4–10.

Wragg, E. C. and Partington, J. A. (1980). *A Handbook for School Governors*, 2nd edn. London: Methuen.

Wringe, C. (1984). *Democracy, Schooling and Political Education*. London: George Allen & Unwin.

Yates Jr, D. (1985). *The Politics of Management*. San Francisco: Jossey-Bass.

Young, P. (1985). 'Schools make a difference: implications for management in education'. In D. Reynolds (ed.), *Studying School Effectiveness*. Barcombe: Falmer Press.

Zaleznek, A. (1989). *The Managerial Mystique*. San Francisco: Harper & Row,

Name Index

Subject Index